CW01272292

Lollipop Lounge

MEMOIRS OF A ROCK AND ROLL REFUGEE

Lollipop Lounge

MEMOIRS OF A ROCK AND ROLL REFUGEE

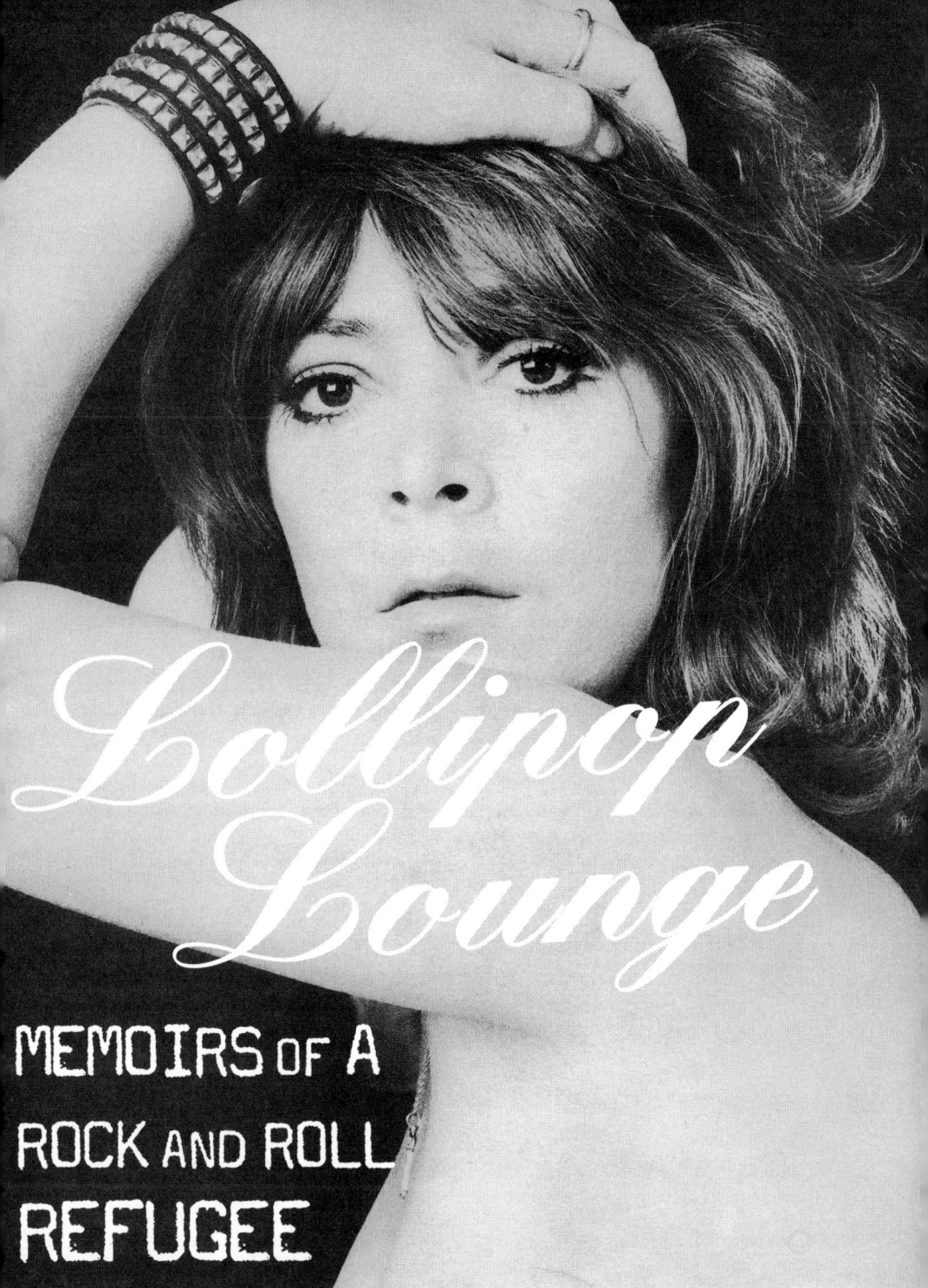

Genya Ravan

Executive Editor: Bob Nirkind
Editor: Elizabeth Wright
Design (cover and interior): Sivan Earnest
Graphic production by Hector Campbell

Copyright © 2004 Genya Ravan

Photo credits. Pages 34, 36, 44, 46: Harvey Kirson. Pages 117, 197, 202, 211, 217, 218 (top), 221, 240: Stu Chernoff (Studio Stu). Pages 218 (bottom) and 277: Chuck Pulin/Star File. All other images are from the personal archives of Genya Ravan and are used with her permission.

All rights reserved. No part of this publication may be reproduced or used in any form or by any means—graphic, electronic, or mechanical, including photocopying, recording, taping, or information storage-and-retrieval systems—without the written permission of the publisher.

First published in 2004 by Billboard Books, an imprint of Watson-Guptill Publications,
a division of VNU Business Media, Inc.
770 Broadway, New York, NY 10003
www.wgpub.com

Library of Congress Cataloging-in-Publication Data is on file with the Library of Congress.

ISBN: 0-8230-8362-4

Every effort has been made to trace the ownership of and to obtain permission to reproduce the images in this book. The author, editors, and publisher sincerely apologize for any inadvertent errors or omissions and will be happy to correct them in future editions.

*This book is dedicated to
my sister, Helen.
Also to my mother, Yadja,
and father, Natan,
(may they rest in peace).*

Acknowledgments

I would like to thank:

Bob Nirkind (for believing in the project)
Sue Lange (for turning me on to the best editor)
Paul Barnett (for being the best manuscript advisor, just like Susan said)
Terry Donnelly (for law and friendship)
Helen and Harvey (Doc) Kirson (for unconditional love)
Dr. Michael Burt (for saving my life)
Katherine Pisters (for prolonging my life)
Nancy Houlihan (still in my life)
Carole Kramer (for being there in my darkest hour)
Dr. Mark Kris (still the best)
The Award Group
The Dryfus Family—Cherie, Donnie, Bryan and Danny (for giving me some feeling of family)
Bobby Chen (a true friend and my drummer)
Irene Andersen (for getting me started on this book)
Valerie MacEwan (for your help)
and all the wonderful musicians who've graced and rocked my voice.

Contents

PROLOGUE		7
1	Coming to America	8
2	Getting In—To Get Out	26
3	Music Music Music	40
4	Goldie and the Gingerbreads Get Started	52
5	Back in the U.S.A.	68
6	Goldie and the Gingerbreads Take Europe by Storm	92
7	Goldie Solo	116
8	Ten Wheel Drive	132
9	Solo, Then So Low	160
10	Hollyweird	168
11	Productions from Hell	186
12	On the Bowery	196
13	Original Punk	208
14	"Polish" as in Shine	228
15	Rhythm and Booze	244
16	Don't Let Me Die	256
17	Doing it the Right Way	268
Epilogue		276
Discography and Production Credits		278
Index		293

Prologue

IT WAS THE SUMMER OF 1968.

A man has a gun to my head. He's shoving me up a narrow staircase; I trip and fall, but he just keeps pushing me. I get up and fall again, but he just keeps pushing me. He yells at me to shut up, all the while touching me and shoving me to the top of the stairs.

We reach the top of the stairs.

"Open that door!" He shouts the command.

"No! Please, please no!" I cry. "Don't lock me in!"

But I open the door and he starts forcing me through it into the musty, cobwebbed attic.

"I have to go home!" I implore him. "I have to go home! People will be looking for me!"

He just pushes harder. I half turn, and I can see his face is even uglier now. And then I'm in the attic. It's filled with blackness. I can see nothing.

"Please don't leave me here!"

I hear the key turn in the lock. There's just me, alone in the darkness and so terribly afraid. And then, from the corner of my eye, I see a pale glimmer of light.

"Oh, please," I whisper, "please make it a window."

I begin to run towards the light. It's a long, long way away, and it doesn't seem to come any closer. Cobwebs claw at my face, at my hair. I trip over boxes filled to bursting with forgotten memories, over broken chairs that have grown too small.

And at last I can see something. There's an old lady, flimsy as a wraith, her gray hair like the spiderwebs that still cling to me. She's sitting there under the window, rocking back and forth, alongside a dust-covered trunk.

I stumble towards her. "Oh, thank God, thank God, help me, please help me, I got to get out of here, please, I can't stay here, help me, please, please help me . . ."

She looks up at me. Her eyes are hard.

"Change the script!"

I shake my head, confused. "What?"

Louder this time. "CHANGE THE SCRIPT!"

It takes a moment for what she's said to sink in, but then I realize, Yes! Yes, I can do that! I can change this script—I'll change it right now.

On her lap she's holding a notepad. I haven't noticed it until now. I grab a sheet of paper from it and then start looking around in desperation.

"I need something to write with," I wail. "Give me a pen or a pencil!"

She speaks to me with a sort of soothing malice. "Well, my dear, that's the problem. I don't have a pen or a pencil. That's why I'm still here . . ."

I can remember waking up from this nightmare, soaking wet. The glass on my bedside table was still half full of vodka. The ice cubes had melted, making it watery, but I gulped it down anyway.

I was in a hotel room in Chicago.

And it was almost show time.

. . . Years later, I found my pen and paper. This is my script.

CHAPTER ONE
Coming to America

PEOPLE CROWDED the deck of the ship, pushing and shoving for their first look at something. What? I didn't know. I couldn't see over the railing. At seven years old, I was too small. The sounds of laughter, screaming, and crying rose up from the ship like a cloud of insects. The pandemonium scared me. I tried to figure out whether people were happy or sad. I knew, even though young and scared, that this was a different kind of hysteria from the type I'd grown used to. I'd become familiar with the sounds of sorrow and loss: the noises one hears in a prison camp.

I had, after all, survived the Holocaust.

As we rocked back and forth on the deck, I shivered from more than fear of the crowd. That day, January 4, 1947, was one of the coldest in New York City's history.

My mother stuck a white handkerchief in my hand and began pulling my arm from one side to the other, screaming as she waved the handkerchief. Then, suddenly, everyone around me began to point out over the water. We were passing something important, something that made the crowd roar again. I looked up, and this time saw what they were all yelling about: a big stone woman with one hand reaching up to the sky. It looked like she had a drink in her hand. I soon learned it was the Statue of Liberty, but at that moment what I thought was that I had seen my first American.

Welcome to Ellis Island and to the United States of America! We would start over, be a family again. That's what my parents told me and, despite the sorrow in my mother's eyes, I could sense hope.

It wouldn't last, that feeling of hope. Right from the start it seemed to me that I had the capacity to ruin everything, and generally did. Before our journey across the Atlantic, my parents had sewn money into the lining of my coat for safekeeping. In Poland, where family members were interrogated separately, I was asked, "Is there something in your pocket?"

"No," I said. Then I pointed to the inside lining of my coat and added, "But there's something in here."

The officials took the money. I didn't understand why they did, but it had been the only money we had with which to start over in America and now it was gone—and it was all my fault. "Nine months I carried you! A stone I should have had!" my mother told me over and over again in her broken English.

She would spend the remainder of my childhood making me sorry for having lost that money. If it weren't for me, she would say, the Zelkowitzes would have ridden into New York City in style in a limousine. All the rest of their lives my parents would lament, "Oy vey, we could have been so rich if Goldie had kept her big mouth shut."

My family entered the eastern United States the same way most people did during the years from 1892 to 1954, through Ellis Island. We were Displaced Persons, or D.P.'s. Only four members of my family survived World War II to travel across the Atlantic Ocean on that ship: my father, Natan Zelkowitz, my mother, Yadja, my sister, Helenka, and me, little Genyusha. Later, my mother would change my name to Goldie because she thought it sounded "more American." She didn't know that "Genyusha" translates to "Genevieve."

What I remember most vividly about Ellis Island are the inoculations. There were many shots and, like most children, I had a terrible fear of needles. My mother would trick me into going to doctors' offices there by telling me we just had to fill out more papers. "That's all we have to do," she'd say. "Just the papers and some talking. They want to ask us some more questions." Then she would grab me and hold me in place on her lap while a man in a white lab coat would come at me with a syringe. I would cry and try to break free from her grip. She'd just hold me tighter and yell at me in Polish: "Be a good girl! No crying! You must do this!"

Looking back, I realize that Ellis Island was the place where I first truly understood that my mother had an image of the perfect little girl she wanted, and that I could not be that girl—the girl who agreed with everything, smiled and was polite, who wore frilly bows in her hair and lace on her clothes.

In the prison camps of Eastern Europe, I had already learned how to hide my feelings. I knew that to cry or show emotion meant you would be singled out and punished. The same, I soon discovered, was true in the U.S.A. The way to keep my parents happy was to be quiet when I felt fear or sorrow. Eventually, as I grew older, I learned another effective technique of dealing with my emotions: I found strength in a bottle, usually at 98 proof. But that was a long time in the future.

So how did it come about that we journeyed to the United States, this strange place full of needles, hysterical people, and tall buildings? These are very painful memories for me still, and are clouded by terrible thoughts.

I was born a Jew in Poland at the onset of World War II. When I was a very small child, my family was sent to a prison camp. Thereafter, we were moved to many different camps throughout Europe. My parents suffered greatly as they struggled to keep what was left of our little family together. They had to live through unspeakable hardships, barely surviving. My own recollections, though, are of what happened to a small child. I could never ask my parents about our past. My mother would become hysterical for days if she heard any mention of our life before we came to the U.S.A. My father would speak only of life before the camps, before the horrors.

I know one of the camps we were in was a Polish forced labor camp called Skarzysko Kamiena Laga ("*Laga*" is German for camp). Located between two towns, Radom and Kielce, it was run by the district S.S. and local police chiefs, and housed Jewish men and women whose tasks were to make rifle bullets, construct railroads, and work at an electrical power plant. Most prison camps separated men from women, but this particular one kept them together. Many Jews were killed at Kielce; documents show that of the 25,000 or so Jews who passed through that Skarzysko camp, most did not live to see its liberation. We were among the lucky ones.

After we had been at the Skarzysko camp for a while, the Russians took over, and we were transferred to a Russian camp. The main thing I remember about our life there is waiting in long lines for food. When trucks pulled in, a mad rush of people surged towards them. My mother would grab me and we'd run along with everyone else. Clothes and shoes would be piled in the open backs of the trucks, and we would take what we could get. At the time, I never questioned where the stuff came from. Now it haunts me: were these clothes donations, or did they come from dead people?

And so we were shuffled from one camp to another, living in barracks and sleeping on cots. At some point we managed to escape, my parents running with my sister and me, holding our hands and dragging us for a while, then carrying us. We hid in the tall grass of what must have been a field. My mother held her hand over my mouth, almost smothering me in an effort to keep me quiet.

Sometime during our flight we went through the Black Forest on a train. We had to hang onto the outside steps of the moving train because it was so packed with people there was no room inside for us. I believe at least some of our fellow-travelers must have been gypsies; they wore bright clothing, the women with colorful bandannas on their heads and wearing long skirts layered one on top of another. I remember thinking they looked as if they were wearing their whole wardrobe at once.

As we flew across the countryside, clinging to the outside of that speeding train, we had to form a solid human knot if we weren't to fall off. Closest to the train was my mother. Then came my sister, holding onto my mother's back. Outside them was my father, who held the handles on the sides of the railway car with my mother and sister inside his arms. I was on the very outside, hanging for dear life onto my father's back.

At one point during the ordeal, my father, my beloved Ta Ta, began to scream. "Yadja! I can't hold on much longer! I'm going to have to let go!" We were crossing a river, and I looked down helplessly at the water swirling ominously below us.

"No! No! You must hold on! You must!" my mother shrieked back at him.

My memory of our bolt for freedom ends there. It is visions like this that return to haunt my dreams.

The next thing I recall is being at a displaced persons camp in New Freiman, Germany. This camp guaranteed freedom. The list of names of those waiting to be liberated was very long, but our number came up quickly thanks to my father's ties—which I was dimly aware of but didn't know much about—to the Polish underground. Only two ships were available for all the refugees out of Germany at that time. One ship would take people to Israel, and the other would go to the United States. Whichever ship came in first would be the one the Zelkowitz family would have to take. As chance would have it, the next ship to arrive was the U.S.S. *Marlene Marlin*, the one destined for the United States.

We left Hell behind us, but not the scars and memories of it. We were on the way to the land of opportunity—a country we thought had streets paved with gold and where, if you worked hard enough, you could not only survive, but prosper. We traveled to our new homeland carrying hope instead of luggage.

My family stayed at Ellis Island for about three weeks. The authorities there had to process all the new arrivals' papers. As immigrants, we were also quarantined during that time: examined, probed, immunized, inoculated, and psychologically evaluated. We were checked and rechecked by many people. After our papers were processed, we left Ellis Island and were housed in a single room at the Hotel Marseilles on West 103rd Street for two weeks. A couple called the Solomons paid for that.

Our relocation to the U.S.A. had been sponsored by a humanitarian aid organization called Joint, the Joint Distribution Committee or J.D.C., whose mission was to help rebuild the lives of Jewish Holocaust survivors from Germany and Russia. By the end of 1947, 700,000 Jews were relying on the J.D.C. for aid, our family among them. We needed to have U.S. citizens as sponsors before we could enter the country. Like posting bail, these people would have to vouch for us and be responsible should anything happen to us.

Many people came forward to help the refugees out. The list of those willing to sponsor Jewish refugee families in the United States was a long one. Sponsors first learned about the different families needing help, then chose one of them. For some reason Harry and Sheila Solomon took a fancy for Yadja, Natan, Helenka, and Genyusha Zelkowitz, and sponsored us. The Solomons were very good to the Zelkowitz family and helped us in every way they could, giving us clothes and so on. Much later, once we were established, they even lent my parents some money to buy a little candy store.

• • • • • •

Right off Ellis Island.

From the Hotel Marseilles we moved to a cold-water flat on the Lower East Side of Manhattan, on Grand Street. My memories of that first American apartment aren't filled with happiness or the promise of a better life, though. They are grim and dark.

My mother obsessively cleaned the apartment. While she mopped the floors on an almost daily basis, I would have to go upstairs to a neighbor's place. The man who lived there had children of his own, two boys, and I was supposed to play with them while my mother mopped and cleaned. Sometimes, though, he would put me on his lap and place a newspaper in front of us as if he were reading to me, then put his hands between my legs and try to get his fingers into me—and it hurt. When this began to occur more frequently, I suddenly realized I had nowhere to turn. I knew I couldn't make waves for my family, especially my mother.

Once, to avoid going upstairs, I hid under my parents' bed. I stayed there for at least two hours, most of the time just watching Mom's mop swish by. She never knew I was under there, and I never told anyone about the man. I felt that, if I told my mother, she would somehow blame me. This was one of the first of the secrets I started to keep buried inside me.

Eventually we rented another flat on the Lower East Side, this one at 202 Rivington Street. The rent was thirty-five dollars a month. I remember that moving there filled me with hope: anything must be better than the Grand Street apartment.

Rivington Street was a small, homey block, a mixed Puerto Rican and Jewish neighborhood full of life and different cultures. Many refugees had settled there. Its streets were filled with one small store after another, with apartments on the upper floors. Our building, in the middle of the block, had a concrete stoop and stairs. There was always garbage on the sidewalk in front of the building, like a welcome mat.

The apartment, a typical walk-up, was a three-room cold-water flat. We lived on the fourth floor, in apartment 4D. The entrance opened into the kitchen, and to the right there was a small bathroom with just enough room for a toilet and a small tub. The large kitchen sink was the only sink in the apartment. The bathtub usually had cockroaches in it. The door to the bathroom had so many layers of paint that it couldn't be closed, so there was absolutely no privacy. I remember the sound of my father's peeing waking me up at night.

The change of address affected my mother's mopping habits not at all: she still mopped incessantly. She used to put newspapers down on a wet floor after she'd done; I suppose she thought that would stop the rest of us dirtying her floors. I still wonder what she thought when she saw the headlines transferred in mirror-language to her linoleum.

On the corner of our block was the candy store my father would eventually buy with the Solomons' help. Then there were Moey's Grocery, from which I stole candy, Izzy's produce stand, where my mother squeezed fruits and vegetables, and the bakery that made Charlotte Russe, the sweet confection, which I devoured in huge quantities. Finally there was the dairy where I stole eggs on a daily basis so I could throw them down the stairs onto the landings in our apartment building.

Despite living in an actual neighborhood and supposedly having other children to play with, my childhood was a very unhappy and lonely one. I cried myself to sleep most nights. In 1949, there wasn't much help available from counselors or child psychiatrists for an eight-year-old refugee girl whose experiences as a Holocaust victim had left her with powerful feelings of impending doom.

My mother's reaction to the horrors she'd witnessed during the Holocaust caused much of my loneliness. Overprotective? It's hard to describe just how much she tried to control my life. I know now that she was trying to keep me safe and shield me from harm, but at the time all I knew was that she wouldn't allow me to have any friends. The first thing she would ask me once she became aware of any new playmates was "Are they Jewish?" The answer had to be "Yes," or my mother would do her utmost to smother the friendship at birth. My school was filled with other immigrant children, most of them Puerto Rican Catholics. Alba, one of my first friends there, was not allowed in the house because she was Puerto Rican.

Being Jewish, I therefore learned, made me different even here in America. No longer a prisoner of labor camps, I found myself instead, in my new country, a prisoner of loneliness.

Holidays emphasized the feelings of isolation. Other families around us would gather together—cousins, grandparents, aunts, uncles. The Zelkowitzes were different: we were not surrounded by relatives. I think my parents tried to hide their sadness on the holidays, but it didn't work. The holidays reminded them of everyone they'd lost, especially my two brothers. The only memento of them my mother had managed to bring from the old country, a little crocheted woolen hat, was kept in a chest in my parents' room. Whenever she saw that hat, life in the apartment turned into a waking nightmare. She would break down and begin weeping and sobbing uncontrollably.

My mother's weeping would last the whole day; the memories made her crazy with grief. As any child would be, I was naturally curious about this solitary reminder of my brother, but it was nothing we could ever talk about: I couldn't stand to see Mom fall apart. To this day, my sister and I don't know how old our brothers were when they died, or how they died. We did our best not to remind our mother of them, and had a pact between ourselves that we would never ask.

My parents both came from large families. My father had nine brothers and a sister. My mother was a twin. Our family had been financially well off in Poland before the war. It wasn't being poor that caused my mother's grief, but guilt: she had made it out of Poland and survived the Holocaust, and the rest of her large family had not. They had all been killed in the concentration camps. The torment she must have felt is unimaginable—and it was unbearable.

My older sister Helen has a complete mental block about her childhood before coming to the United States. Doctors have told her it's better that way, keeping her memories locked up inside; they said she didn't have to face them, so why should she? She has the scars of about

150 stitches on her neck from being hit by shrapnel—her head was nearly blown off. A soldier who saw my mother holding her grabbed Helen and took her to an army doctor, who sewed her up. Those are all the details I know of Helen's childhood. Again, we had a sort of code of silence on the subject of her injuries, and it's one I've never broken.

Taken together, the bits and pieces of memories I had and my inability to get any real information about our family from our parents meant my life was filled with anxiety and uncertainty. My mother's guilt and fears were thrust upon us continuously, and this made me even more nervous and scared. How could she console me when she couldn't even console herself?

My own terrors grew day after day, year after year. Even simple things could set off further cascades of terrifying memories. Once my mother took me with her to purchase a chicken for a holiday meal. The kosher slaughterhouse was under the Williamsburg Bridge on the New York City side. As I stood next to my mother, I watched a man beheading chickens. The chickens ran around headless for a long time. I cried and tried to hide my eyes in my mother's skirts. She wasn't affected by those headless chickens in the slightest—all she cared about was whether or not the birds were kosher—but I wasn't concerned about how Jewish the chickens were: I was just horrified. I'll never forget the sight of those headless chickens running around.

I remember one awful dream in particular. I walked into a room and found my mother sitting on a high stool. As I got closer, I told her I loved her. She looked right through me, with no expression on her face. I said, "I love you" again, but she didn't hear me. I shouted and screamed to her that I loved her, and still I got no response. I took out a knife and started stabbing her over and over again, all the while shouting at her that I loved her . . . and then I woke up crying. I sobbed for days because of that dream, and the memory of it still causes me pain. It's no wonder I was on Valium by the time I was eleven years old.

Even before then, others had noticed my distressed state. When my mother took me to the doctor because I was having nosebleeds, he kept asking her, "Why is Goldie so nervous?"

She told him, "I don't understand. She has food and she has clothes. I give her everything she needs."

At the time I blamed my mother for my misery. I held her accountable for all my unhappiness because I could never seem to please her. I learned not to go to her for comfort, even when I was scared: she had nothing to give. Like most unhappy children, I dreamed of running away, of leaving Rivington Street forever. If only I could get away from my mother, I thought. I believed she didn't really care about *me*, just about whether or not I behaved myself. Children don't fully understand adult motivations, so how could I know the effect the Holocaust was still having on my mother?

For years Helen and I shared a bedroom, and indeed the same little bed. My feet soon started to hang over the end of the mattress (I became the tallest member of the family). The room had no closets. We shoved all our clothes into one chest of drawers, because one chest was all we needed. We didn't have enough clothing to fill it up, not even between the two of us.

I had to go to bed earlier than Helen. I used to turn on my portable A.M. radio very low and glue my ear to the tinny speaker. I thought one of the D.J.s, Danny Stiles (also known as The Cat Man), was my personal friend. His radio station, which was somewhere in New Jersey, barely came through, but I didn't care that the reception was terrible. The Cat Man would come on, I'd hear his theme sound—a bunch of cats howling—and I'd settle down and listen for hours. This was my first introduction to music, and I was hooked from the get-go.

Songs like "Wind" (by the Diablos), "God Only Knows, He's Gone" (by the Chantels), and "Sincerely" (by the Moonglows) lulled me into a dreamlike state. I loved listening to Baby Washington sing "Time." Even though I was young, I understood the link between music and pain. I *felt* the words. My ears were in training. I even learned how to speak better English through listening to the radio. The radio and the music saved me in so many ways. I did not feel so alone because the words kept me company.

I went to P.S. (Public School) #4, located right across the street from our tenement. Looking back, it seems all we did was drink milk and take vitamins, and have long naps in the afternoons. The main purpose of the class specially designed for refugee children was to nourish us and make us healthy. I spoke lousy English as a kid, but soon I could curse fluently without a trace of an accent. I suppose that came from the neighborhood, listening to all the people talking in their apartments as I walked down the street.

By the time I was ten or eleven, in 1951, all the girls I knew had roller skates. When you're a kid and everyone else has something, you must have it too. Day after day I begged my mother for a pair of skates, weeping as if the world were ending when she said no. I jealously watched all the other kids skate by: it seemed they were flying in the wind. Of course, my mother did not want me to have any skates—I would get hurt, I would fall down, something terrible would happen to me, she just knew it. But I carried on for weeks—I *had* to have a pair of skates!

My mother finally gave in and bought me a pair. Then she handed me one skate. Just one.

I said, "Mom, where's the other skate?"

"No. Only von skate. You von't fall dat vay."

This story illustrates my mother's defensiveness of me better than any other I could tell. She tried to protect me in her own way. To a kid, it made no sense. Why would having only one skate protect me, keep me from falling? All I could recognize was my disappointment. Not having a pair of skates made me stand out from the other kids, which—yet again—made me feel isolated and different from the others.

The truth of it is, I feel as if I've been rolling around on one skate ever since.

• • • • • •

Each year in the early 1950s, Grand Street Settlement House offered poor East Side kids the chance to go to a summer camp, Camp Moodna, for chump change. The camp was run by Dr. Tom Horowitz and his wife. I liked Camp Moodna, and went there two years running. I even remember winning a "Most Popular" contest, a big deal for someone who felt as alienated as I did. At Camp Moodna I could play with kids my own age. The curious thing is that, even though I was having fun for once, I always missed my mother. The same thing happened when, as sometimes happened, my parents sent me to the Horowitzes' home for the weekend. I couldn't understand it. I guess I felt abandoned because I never knew when it would happen, or why.

Despite the fact that I felt like an outcast most of the time during my school days, there was one part of my life at school that always brings me good memories: Mr. Levinsky's class. Mr. Levinsky put me in some of the school musicals—which were really more like interpretive dancing than anything else. He would have the students dance to records of operas and operettas like *Carmen* and *Billy the Kid* or, my favorite, *Slaughter on Tenth Avenue*. For the first time in my life I felt I was part of a group—I *belonged*. Mr. Levinsky told my family I had talent, and even my mother approved of my participation in those musical presentations. He would always stress that we should "feel the music." I did. I swayed and danced to my own inner beat. I didn't know it then, but I was preparing for my future.

I was never comfortable in my own skin, but when I was on-stage in those musicals I could be somebody else. I liked the person I was when I was there, even though I thought the other kids hated me.

Off-stage they constantly picked on me and made fun of me. I dressed differently—my mother used to put big bows in my hair—and that sort of thing makes you stand out as a kid. I understood that. I wanted to fit in so badly, but I always felt like a square peg in a round hole.

One day, in a desperate attempt to become part of the group, I decided to set fire to a bathroom trash can so I could yell "FIRE!" and save the school. I thought I would become a hero. Unfortunately, everyone knew I was the one who'd done it. Instead of getting a parade in my honor and riding down Fifth Avenue in a Cadillac convertible as I waved to the cheering crowd, I ended up at the police station with my parents.

The police and the school recommended that my parents take me to a psychiatrist. The psychiatrist told my mother I was apparently not receiving enough attention at home. Talk about a scheme backfiring! Now my parents watched my every movement to make sure they knew where I was every second of the day. The overprotective mother I had so resented in the past was nothing compared to this new version. She insisted we were cursed, that a black cloud hung over the Zelkowitz family. Yes, we were doomed. To add to my misery, the teachers told my parents I was a dreamer, that I would stare out the window all the time during school. To that my mother said, "Oy, vat else can I do vit her?"

● ● ● ● ● ●

My mother never prepared us for our periods. Talking about that kind of stuff was taboo in my house. I knew something was "going on" with Helen, but no one told me what. So when I got my first period at age twelve, I had no clue what was happening. I ran to the living room in a panic to tell my mother I was bleeding.

She was on the phone with my father. She screamed to him in Polish, "Goldie just became a woman!" and hung up. Then she came over to me with a big smile on her face, slapped me, spat three times, and finally kissed me. Mystified, I thought either she'd gone nuts or she believed I'd done something to myself. Later on, I found out that's what they do for good luck in the old country. It would have been nice if she'd warned me.

The ritual over, she handed me a Kotex and asked if I needed any help.

"No," I said to her. "You've done enough. I can figure this out."

Soon after that she told me, "Goldie, now that you're a woman, you stay away from boys or you'll get pregnant." That was the sum total of sex education so far as my mother was concerned.

Her behavior in general still bothered me. I did most of my drilling for information from my father when he was drinking. It was the only time he would smile and open up, go back into the old days and talk about our lives before the war. One of the questions I asked him was: "Ta Ta, was Mommy always like this? Was she always afraid?"

"She is vurst now . . . more than ever," he would say. "She is more nervous. She vas a beautiful vooman."

Then my father would tell me about their lives before the war—how they had a great marriage and a successful business, with family everywhere. Such a big family—nine brothers and a sister. And he told me about how he had made ice cream. I would dream about that ice cream. My father looked like the actor George Raft. He always wore a hat on a slant, very dapper. He rarely smiled. He looked tough, in a handsome way. He and my mother made an attractive couple. She really was a beautiful woman.

Unlike Ta Ta, my mother had only horrible stories. I didn't want to hear any of hers. I wanted more information about our family in Poland, about the time before the war, about the happy past. My sister and I knew nothing about our relatives in Poland. According to my parents, they had all died. Our past still remains a mystery to my sister and myself.

I wished Ta Ta would tell me something different about the war—like maybe it was all a lie. I suppose I kept asking because I hoped the stories would change, hoped that maybe I still had two brothers, and grandparents, maybe some aunts and uncles too. I really wanted him to tell me that none of it had ever happened. I wanted to hear that Jews had not been killed in gas chambers.

* * * * * *

Rivington Street was a noisy and violent place to live. The door that led out to the back of our building was right next to the garbage cans.

People communicated from there by screaming up toward the windows, trying to see through the laundry lines and hoping to catch sight of the person they wanted sticking their head out the window to yell back. If the person on the ground level were lucky, no one would throw garbage out the window while they were down there yelling up.

The music streaming out of the windows sounded like a street fair. You could hear the sounds of every ethnic group in the world. The whole place vibrated, night and day, to different rhythms and beats from all over the globe. But it was not only music that filled the air—you could also hear the bloodcurdling screams of men and women fighting. Sometimes I knew what I heard was women being beaten by their spouses. The sounds of domestic violence—the crying and the wailing—those were the sounds of everyday life on Rivington Street.

Garbage lined the thresholds of the apartments and piled up on the ground near the back door. Dead animals stayed there for days, especially cats. Katy, our superintendent, didn't clean up much of anything. I had a theory that most of the animals committed suicide—jumping from the high windows, anything to get out of those hot boxes we called apartments. There were nights in the summer, when it was ninety degrees outside, that Helen and I slept on the fire escape above the dump. Times were tough then, and my parents had a hard task making the thirty-five-dollars-a-month rent.

By the time I'd reached fifteen I had become an expert in the art of lying. Like most teenagers, I snuck out of the house and went where my parents forbade me to go. I also wore jeans; girls were not allowed to wear jeans in our family, but on the Lower East Side they were part of a girl's survival gear: your panties didn't show when you got knocked down. So I hid a pair of jeans at the back of the hallway in my building, beside the steel garbage cans, and put them on once I got out of my mother's sight.

One of the first "dates" I ever went on ended in disaster. A friend of mine fixed me up on a double date with her and her boyfriend. It seemed like a good idea at the time: they had booze. We were in a park somewhere in the Bronx when the guy jumped me. I tried to push him off, but he slapped me around and tried to get my pants off. The only thing that stopped him was my telling him I was a virgin. I drank too much whiskey on the way home and threw up out the car window.

By then I'd become part of a gang, hanging out and dancing and drinking with a crowd of kids. Sometimes I'd sneak out of the apartment or cut class and join them at a place we called "The Club." It was in an abandoned apartment building on Clinton Street. We had to cross a roof to get in there. The Club had hardly any furniture—just a few couches—plus a turntable with speakers. It was where all the gangs would meet and hang out and drink beer. Some of the guys were junkies; they'd stop there to shoot up. On occasion I wasn't allowed in because the guys had a whore in there with them.

I just wanted to dance. Like most teenagers, I'd begun to discover my body, and dancing the fish helped me do just that. It awakened my sexuality. The best way to describe the fish is this: it's a vertical clothes-on fuck. You rub and grind against a guy to songs like "Lonely Nights" by the Hearts with Baby Washington. (That was the best grinding song.) Guys got real excited, girls learned about being excited, and that's the way it was. Even so, despite my dancing, my sister and I really didn't know anything about sex except what we had heard on the streets, in jokes, and what we read on walls. This ignorance made Helen especially vulnerable.

In 1956, I introduced Helen to a twenty-three-year-old gang member from The Club called Jack India. I have always felt rotten about making this introduction. He was a bad guy but, having nothing to compare him to, Helen fell in love with him. He was her first boyfriend, and she had her first sexual encounter with him.

There was hell to pay at home when my parents found out about them. My father had always said he would know if we were doing anything "wrong"—meaning sex. He found out about Helen and Jack.

I believe my father's behavior and the stranglehold he tried to exert on us were what made my sister eventually marry Jack India. Everyone knows that kids do the opposite of what their parents want, just to show their independence. There was a war in my house over that boy. My parents disliked him for many reasons, one being that he was only half-Jewish. My father forbade my sister to see Jack again and even hit her. But Helen kept seeing him, and I used to lie and cover for her so she could. She stuck to her guns and married him. For his part, my guess is that Jack married Helen to spite my parents; he hated them.

Helen had three babies with Jack, one right after another. I swear she got pregnant if he so much as looked at her. I nicknamed her "Fiona Fertile." They lived on South Third Street in Williamsburg, Brooklyn. Besides giving her babies, he gave her grief. One night he went out while Helen and the three kids were sleeping, leaving a cigarette burning in an ash tray by the bed—we're not sure whether or not this was on purpose. A fire started, and the fire department had to be called. Luckily, only a couch was lost. Jack India was nowhere to be found that night. Helen salvaged all her belongings but wound up broke and on welfare.

Even before the apartment burned, I had come to hate Jack and what he was doing to Helen and my family. I was the baby sister, but I had always felt a need to protect Helen. I went to see my friend Babaloo in Brooklyn and borrowed a gun from him: I wanted to shoot Jack India.

I remember that day like it was yesterday. I walked from the water yards in Brooklyn feeling the weight of the .45 in my jeans pocket. I hid almost all day under the stairs of the building where Jack and my sister lived, the gun cocked ready, my finger on the trigger, waiting for Jack to come home. Every time the front door opened, I pointed the gun at the person coming through it. Jack never showed that night. I think some kind of guardian spirit must have been watching over me because I would have shot him—I know I would.

The next day I returned the gun to Babaloo. Jack India eventually wound up in jail and on the front pages of the newspapers; he had robbed a detective's home. The court sentenced him to ten to twenty years for that. The bastard died in jail.

∙ ∙ ∙ ∙ ∙ ∙

A few years before Helen's horrible marriage to Jack India, my parents had sold the candy store and bought a restaurant, which they turned kosher and named Nathan's Delicatessen. Located at Three East Broadway, it was just across the street from the edge of Chinatown. Hot dogs, corned beef, pastrami—my parents served delicious food, and the Asians loved the place. (For some reason, the Asian men also liked to expose themselves to me in doorways.)

While Dad was running Nathan's Delicatessen, he hired a black man we called Uncle Louie to work for him. Uncle Louie—whose real name was Luther Highsmith—became a part of our family. He would come to our apartment every Friday night for Sabbath dinner. Having someone else in the apartment made me feel like we had kin; it was nice to have more than just us at the table.

Uncle Louie bought me my first record player and my first record, "Shake A Hand" by Etta James. He would pick me up in his car and take me to see his family in the Bronx. His mother would serve me homemade lemon meringue pie and bacon and eggs. They fed me all the stuff we were not allowed to eat in our kosher kitchen on Rivington Street.

Bacon in particular was so good that I managed to "un-kosher" the apartment on Rivington Street one day. Playing hooky from school, I stole a packet of bacon, cooked it, and ate it all. I think I got sick.

We did a lot with Uncle Louie. He took Helen and me fishing. I spent a good deal of time in Harlem, because that was where Uncle Louie lived. The best occasion was when Uncle Louie took me to see Santa Claus! My parents freaked, and didn't stop yelling at him for days.

Nathan's Delicatessen began to prosper, and my parents started doing well. They worked very hard, leaving around four-thirty a.m. every morning and working into the night. But something happened; no one would ever tell me the details, but my parents lost the restaurant to a couple they had befriended and taken in as partners. I know my parents fought in the courts unsuccessfully for years.

Losing the restaurant devastated my father. He began to die a little each day, and watching it happen was painful. All he did was sleep, get drunk, and fight with my mother.

Mom and Dad were now broke. Even when we were children, if my dad drank, he would get physical with my mother, sometimes even with Helen and me. Sometimes it got so bad we had to leave the apartment in the middle of the night and sleep at a neighbor's. These are the kinds of things you try to block out as a child. I adored my father—he was strong

Refugee meets Santa, 1949.

and he was my hero. I didn't want to think about him hitting my mother. It was terrible for us girls to watch Mom get slapped around. I wanted to believe that somehow my mother deserved it, that she had made him hit her. Otherwise, how could my Ta Ta still be my hero?

Once the restaurant was gone, my father became even more abusive. My mother didn't make things better by calling him names and yelling at him when he was drunk. I used to beg her to shut up, to stop screaming.

● ● ● ● ● ●

In the summer of 1957, I decided I wanted a job. I thought that I could run away if I made enough money. I was seventeen years old. Helen knew someone who worked for the telephone company in their Fourteenth Street and Second Avenue office. They hired me as an information operator. The large room I sat in had four rows of women operators lined up in the middle of the room; the supervisor who walked up and down the aisles listening and checking up on the operators wore a big gold ring in the shape of a telephone.

I used to answer the switchboard by holding my nose and shrieking, "In-for-mationnnnnnn!!" When the supervisor heard me doing this, she warned me to cut it out.

One day a woman asked me for the number for American Airlines. I misunderstood and said, "I'm sorry. There is no listing for American Nylons."

She said, "American Airlines, stupid."

"Fuck you! Look it up yourself!" I answered.

I got fired. There went my "running away" money.

By then I was sleeping on a secondhand couch my mother had picked up somewhere. It came with bedbugs. No matter how much my mother cleaned and changed the bedding on that couch, the bugs were still there. They were in the mattress. Whatever we tried, we couldn't get rid of them. I would lie awake scratching all night, and in the morning there would be welts on my skin from the bites. The bugs were ugly, little, brown, flat things that stuck to your skin.

That couch was the straw that broke the camel's back. I really did have to get out—and it had to be soon.

CHAPTER TWO
Getting In—To Get Out

DESPERATE TO GET OUT of my parents' apartment, at the age of sixteen I felt I had no choice but to marry Irving, a twenty-eight-year-old Jewish man from Brooklyn, even though I couldn't stand him. My parents loved him. Of course they did—he was Jewish and he came from a wealthy family.

It all started after Helen married Jack India. Jack and Irving were friends, and Jack was showing the wedding photos to him. Pointing to me in one of the photos, Irving asked, "Who's that?" Jack informed him that I was Goldie, Jack's new sister-in-law. Irving told me later it was love at first sight, that he fell in love with me through that photograph. I often wonder if it was the photograph he fell in love with— and stayed in love with it—not the real me.

Jack brought Irving over to Rivington Street to introduce us, and my parents went crazy over him. After that introduction, my home could never be the same. Irving would kiss their asses. He would bring cigarettes and booze for my father and, I later found out, even give my parents money. It was, of course, a conspiracy to get to me. He thought all he needed was their approval and he'd be able to have my hand in marriage.

The first part of his scheme worked. He became my parents' obsession. Right away they knew they had a mission—for me to marry this guy.

Irving used any excuse to come over to the apartment just to look at me and hang out. My mother kept promising him, supposedly secretly, "She veel fall in love wit you. She veel merry you!"

And it wasn't just that he was Jewish, like us. Irving had *all* the right credentials. His father was the creator and manufacturer of the Garrison belt; in the 1950s and 1960s, just about everyone wore a Garrison belt and buckle. Irving, as eldest son, would be sole heir to the beltmaker fortune. This alone would have been enough to make my mother think Irving was God incarnate.

Even God can have some serious flaws, though. Irving used to go to a strip joint in Greenwich Village regularly enough that all the strippers knew his name. I suppose he thought this would impress me, a 16-year-old girl, so the night he took me there he made sure they all said "Hello, Irving!" just for him. It was that night in the strip joint that I figured out alcohol could be used to ease pain. I drank and drank there, but it wasn't just for fun anymore. It was to kill the pain of depression and make me forget what was going on around me. All of a sudden, things didn't look so bad. I got giggly and loose. I felt bigger, better, and free. Wow, I'd found the Magic Elixir!

By the time I got home, I was sick, dizzy, and nauseated. What's a girl to do when she lives on the fourth floor? I stuck my head out the window and threw up on the garbage and dead animals below.

I started enjoying the alcohol part of being with Irving. I didn't want my parents to hear or see me when I'd been drinking, so I would use Irving to get me out of the apartment hellhole and into a bar.

After a while, I decided I'd never be free unless I learned how to drive a car. I convinced Irving to teach me. He'd pick me up late in the evening and we'd go to the business section of Manhattan, where streets like Canal Street and Broadway had virtually no traffic at night. I told him I liked the noise an automobile makes when it really roars, so he got under his car and broke the muffler. Another whim of mine was wanting to learn how to ride a motorcycle. Irving bought a ridiculous-looking scooter. I tried it, fell off, and said, "Fuck this. Where's the Harley?" By this time I'd worked out that he'd do just about anything for me. I held all the trump cards, and I wasn't afraid to use them.

However horrible I was to Irving, he continued to come over every day to see me. One day I asked him, "What is it you love so much about me? I'm so nasty and mean to you."

He replied, "Oh, Goldie, I just love you, your eyes, your lips, your body."

I thought, *You mean you love my ass.*

I wanted to be going out with boys my own age, but there was no way Mom and Dad were going to let me date anyone from school; they wouldn't even allow me out of the house unless it was with Irving.

My father started following me everywhere I went unless I was with Irving. He'd duck into buildings so I wouldn't see him. I got so mad I started calling Dad "Dickless Tracy" behind his back.

Whatever I might think about Irving, I knew he represented the only way I was ever going to be free of my parents. And so, sitting on the front stoop with him one evening, I said, "Look, OK, I'm willing to marry you on one condition. You don't touch me—not until I'm ready."

"Really? Oh, baby! Really? Really? Do you mean that?"

"Yes. I can't stand it in my house anymore. We have bedbugs."

We went upstairs and told my parents. Oh my, such happiness on their faces! They were thrilled to pieces, even when I told them, "Now I wanna quit school. And no more sneaking cigarettes. From now on, I smoke in front of you."

I think much of the relief I could see on their faces must have been because from now on I would be Irving's problem, not theirs. But there was more to it than that: he was rich and he was a Jew. All in all, this was a great marriage as far as they were concerned.

A few weeks after I'd consented to wed Irving, I told my mother I'd changed my mind. I explained to her that I was too scared to marry him, that I didn't love him. Her response was to yell, "It's too late, and the invitations are out! You veel get married!" The only way I could get her to quiet down was to agree that, after all, I'd go through with it.

Irving asked me if I'd like to go to Europe for our honeymoon. My reply was forthright: "Europe? Why would I want to go there? I was born there and I hate Europe. What about Florida?" He said Florida was fine. He didn't care where we went, just so long as we got married.

He paid for everything—the wedding, the gown, the reception. Right before the wedding, Uncle Louie tried so hard to say something profound to me, but all he could come up with was: "Girl, you is a woman now." Then he kissed and hugged me.

I said, "Uncle Louie, I hate him. I don't want to be with him. I want

Kenny to be my boyfriend." Kenny was a boy at school I had a crush on, even though he didn't so much as look at me.

Uncle Louie stared into my eyes and said, "Woman, you is still a girl." Upset, he shook his head and walked away.

My family was joyous all through the ceremony and the reception. Irving's family sat there with long faces, and you could hear them thinking, *Oy vey! Our poor Irving* . . .

When we got to Miami for the honeymoon, I refused to have sex with him. I wasn't ready, and I reminded him that he'd agreed to leave me alone until I was. When I think of it now, it must have been nightmarish for him to be in bed with someone he cared about and was desperate to have sex with, and not get any. Irving was plenty horny, as you can imagine, and he didn't find my blithe jokes along the lines of "Willie and the hand jive" very funny. I even told him he could go find someone else to have sex with if he wanted to, but he wouldn't do it.

However much I disliked him, I started to feel really bad on his behalf. After a few days I decided we should try "it." I didn't know if it was Irving not turning me on or what but, when we finally made the attempt, "it" proved to be a disaster. Irving thought there might be something wrong with me physically, or that I was frigid. For a week he bugged me about seeing a doctor. I finally told him I would, but only if the doctor was a woman. We found a female gynecologist in Miami and made an appointment. This would be the first time I'd ever seen a gynecologist.

I went into her examining room and sat on an examining table. She came in and asked me to get undressed. I wouldn't take off my panties.

She looked at me in disbelief. "You'll have to remove your underwear."

I said, "I can't." I was so embarrassed.

The doctor said, "If you can't, then there's no way I'm going to be able to examine you, is there?"

"Um," I said. I told her I would come back some other time, and we left. I was so embarrassed, red in the face. Irving was disappointed.

Two days later, he talked me into making another appointment with her. When she came into the examining room, I got as far as taking off my top but then, again, hesitated and started to put my clothes back on.

She said, "Oh, come on. I've seen it so many times it just looks like a face to me!"

That's when I said "okay" and took my panties off.

She examined me and said, "Nothing's wrong with you. You're just a virgin."

She asked if I wanted her to do minor surgery. I said no, that I would use the natural method of coping with the obstruction. Irving and I accordingly tried again, but we never really got anywhere together.

After the honeymoon we went back to New York. Irving's mother found us an apartment in Brooklyn, not far from her. His family didn't like me, and I think his mother thought I would kill him or torture him. In a way I did torture him, I suppose: because I didn't know how to cook anything else, I fed him spaghetti with butter for a week.

Irving was employed at his father's factory. He didn't want me to work; he was very jealous, and was afraid I'd meet someone else. When other guys would look at me, he would say things like, "I want to put a paper bag on your head." Another gem of his was: "There are more eyes on your ass than on the New York Thruway." I guess he was so jealous because he himself wasn't getting anywhere with me sexually. To put it crudely, he couldn't get it in. And, after a few times, I wouldn't let him try anymore.

Every day while he was at work I stayed in the apartment and sang. This is when my singing voice really first came into play—when it all started for me. I had a funky little tape recorder, so I'd record the songs I loved and then sing along with the tape. In effect, I made my own karaoke, recording myself as I sang. I listened to the replay and, wow, I sure loved how I sounded. I knew then that singing satisfied me more than anything else I knew how to do.

One night when Irving got home from work we had a big argument. He knocked me onto the bed, held my arms down, and climbed on top of me. Then he said the worst thing he could have said to me: "I'm your husband, and I can take you any time I want you, whether you like it or not. I wouldn't get arrested because you're my wife. It wouldn't be called rape."

He was right. Back then, there were no laws protecting wives from spousal rape. I started to scream and hit him. He called my parents and told them I had not consummated my marriage yet.

My mother and father came over. My mother looked at me and said, "Vat a sin dis is . . . a vooman is supposed to do vat a man vants ven she is merried. I didn't vant to do it vit your fadder either." She was telling me I had to put out. My father had a smirk on his face. I bet he thought it was great that his little girl was still a virgin.

After they left I realized I had only two options: I could put out or get out.

I wanted to get out.

I still had my fantasies about Marlon Brando and running away, like in *The Wild One*. I was in love with the idea of leaving on the back of a Harley-Davidson motorcycle. Before my marriage, I would sneak out from time to time and hitch rides with bikers as they went past me on the street. There was a guy called Bullet I sometimes rode with. For a while I'd even had a black leather jacket with gold studs and "Goldie" written across the back, but my mother had found it and taken it away from me.

A few months after I'd married Irving, I was on Essex Street when I saw this big bike roaring down the road. I stuck out my hand for a pick-up, and the biker stopped. I went over to him and said, "Can I take a ride with you?"

He said, "Sure."

I jumped on this beautiful Harley-Davidson with its big leather seat, chrome edging, and high stirrups. I was on top of the world. This was freedom.

The guy's name, he told me, was Ralph. I would creep away from Irving whenever I could to go riding with Ralph. I complained to him about how miserable I was at home—although I didn't tell him it was my married home I was so unhappy about.

A few weeks after our first meeting, I called him and told him I wanted to run away. He told me that in a month he was planning to go to Manhattan Beach, California, to meet friends there. *Great*, I thought, *this could be my ticket to ride, to get away from here. I'll find my freedom on the back of a Harley.*

"If I could get some money, would you take me with you?" I asked Ralph.

He told me he would.

We made plans to leave together. I hocked my four-carat diamond wedding ring for four hundred dollars at a pawnshop in Carnarsie, Brooklyn—$400 was a fair amount of money back then. I met Ralph in Brooklyn with only a small suitcase; he'd told me to pack light, and so that was what I'd done. I didn't take anything Irving had bought me, but I left him a note:

Dear Irving,

I'm so sorry, but I gotta go. I'm miserable. It's not you, it's me. If I ever come back to you, I will try and be a better wife to you. Promise.

PS: The car is parked on the corner of Skank and Skidmore. Here is the pawn ticket so you can get the ring back.

I sat on that big, beautiful, shiny Harley, straddling Ralph, for three thousand miles. We took our time. To this day, I regard that motorcycle ride to California as the most fabulous trip I have ever taken. I sang in his ear all the way. Ralph kept asking me to sing again and again, and I did! I knew by then how good I sounded. We rode through rain, sun, and clouds. Freedom.

When we got to Manhattan Beach I skipped out on Ralph after he'd introduced me to some of the guys he knew. And it didn't take me too long to get into trouble with the guys I met in California. It was the first time I'd had any freedom at all. I got involved with two brothers, George and Jimmy, simultaneously, each without the other's knowledge. Of course, it wasn't too long before they found out; and when they did they beat each other up over me. Their mother called me that night and said, "Why don't you screw me and then you'll have had the whole fuckin' family." It never crossed her mind that I'd not been having sex with her two sons, that I might still, in fact, be a virgin.

I slowly got more and more broke. I couldn't get a job; not only did I not know how to apply for one, I hadn't even graduated from high school. I started getting scared of being alone out there on the West Coast. It took me a while to admit it to myself, but I wanted to go back to New York.

I called Irving and told him I'd like to come home. He thought this meant we'd be getting back together, and sent me a plane ticket. When I met him at Idlewild Airport, the first thing I told him was that I wanted an annulment. Poor Irving. Though he was bitterly disappointed, he nevertheless got me a room in Brooklyn. I stayed there for a while, and then my parents asked me to come and live with them. I told them I would on condition I could come and go as I pleased, and they agreed to this.

I'd been married. I'd ridden a Harley from New York to California. I was only seventeen, but I knew I'd earned my freedom.

• • • • • •

She looked like a slut sitting on that train. Her tar-black hair was piled high on her head, bigger than a football helmet, coated thick and heavy with hair spray; you knew if you bumped into it you'd be concussed. She wore bright orange lipstick way above the lip line, and cracked her gum so loudly you could hear her at the other end of the train.

Come to think of it, I probably looked just as much the slut as she did. My hair was piled as high as hers, my lipstick was above my lip line, and I was cracking gum! We were both riding the "D" train into Brooklyn. I could tell right away she was a flake, probably even flakier than I was.

A few days later I saw her on the train again, and this time we nodded to each other. The third time we saw each other on the train we started talking. Her name was Jeannie. We had a lot in common and became tight really fast. We both loved bikers (though only if they drove Harley-Davidsons, of course!), soulful music, and dancing. Both of us wanted to get away from our parents and have our own places. And we were both bored. It didn't take more than a few minutes of conversation for me to know Jeannie would do anything for kicks—just the kind of girl I wanted as my friend. We both hungered for excitement, and we knew we could find it together.

By then, even though I wasn't yet eighteen years old, I'd begun posing semi-nude as a cheesecake model. I'd encountered the photographer at an Italian restaurant in Bensonhurt, Brooklyn, as I sat eating stuffed clams with a girlfriend. The really good-looking man sitting at a table next to us—I thought he looked just like the actor John Derek—was staring at me and smiling a lot. I knew he was flirting with me, and I flirted back. Soon he came over to our table and told me by way of introduction that I was very beautiful. Always a good way for a man to start a conversation, so far as I'm concerned. My head thoroughly turned, I suggested he bring his food to our table and sit with us. He explained he was a professional photographer but that his day job was as a pilot for United Airlines.

My girlfriend finished eating and left, but the pilot and I stayed on, talking about all kinds of things, like movies and how I wanted to meet Marlon Brando. Then he offered me a hundred dollars to do a few face shots for him. He kept telling me I had the most fabulous almond-shaped eyes and beautiful long neck. I got really excited; images of Hollywood and Marlon racing through my mind, I said yes and gave him my phone number.

Wow, I thought. *Maybe I am beautiful!* I'd never really believed I was pretty. Indeed, I'd never thought too much about my physical appearance at all. It wasn't a subject my family ever thought to give me any reassurance about. I started to fantasize about maybe becoming a star one day. Anything was possible.

At the first session, Joe (the pilot) took some basic head shots. He started our second session by showing these to me. I'd never seen 8 x 10 head shots of myself before. To me they seemed very professional—and I thought I looked great in them! He began taking some more pictures of me, but before long I could see he was getting fidgety.

Then came the inevitable question: "Could you take your top off?"

I thought about it. I supposed I was flaky enough to do that. I had a bra on, anyway, so what harm could it do?

"Semi-nude modeling—cheesecake modeling, we call it," he said. "You have the body for it." He went on to explain: "Cheesecake is when you're nude but you don't show any pubic hair. So, if you're interested in being a cheesecake model, could you take off your bra as well?"

I'd never been called a "model" before and it felt good, made me feel special and beautiful. One hundred bucks an hour for posing and feeling like I was the most beautiful girl in the world—how could I say no? A hundred dollars was a lot of dough for a young girl in the 1950s. (Hell, I'd take that now!) I also, to be honest, had an exhibitionist streak in me. I had no shame. I didn't mind showing off my body.

Cheesecake modeling (may Mom rest in peace).

Joe—who really was a pilot—called me whenever he flew into town. I was always ready for the money, and being told I was beautiful didn't hurt either. During all of our photography sessions, he never touched me, or made an overt pass. This was a good thing for our professional relationship, because he never would have gotten anywhere with me. I was still, despite all my carefully cultivated appearances to the contrary, a virgin.

One day he took me to a low-class New Jersey motel, just outside the Lincoln Tunnel, for "a quick shoot." On the way he stopped at a hardware store to pick up a spray can of gold paint. When we got to the room I promptly stripped down to my panties—I knew the drill by now. This time, though, he didn't start taking photos right away, but first sprayed me all over with the gold paint, Goldfinger-style.

In a matter of minutes, I started to sweat. I felt lightheaded, dizzy, and nauseous. In a panic, Joe got me into the shower and started washing the paint off me. I didn't know it then, but what was happening was that I was suffocating: the paint had blocked all my pores and my body couldn't breathe. Sometimes I think that if Joe had been a bastard, he could just have left me there in that motel room to die; remember, I was underage, and he would have been arrested if someone had found us. But luckily he wasn't a bad guy, not really. He kept washing me until the paint was all gone and I started to feel more or less normal again.

It was a close call, and I've been claustrophobic ever since. I guess that's when I first really *earned* the name "Goldie"!

• • • • • •

I was making enough money from my cheesecake modeling to afford to move out from my parents' home and become roommates with Jeannie. We got an apartment—really more of a crash pad than an apartment—on Coney Island Avenue. This is where life started for me. We had barely any furniture; just a bed, a dresser, and a couch in the living room.

I started doing some more modeling, this time for what were called Beginners' Photography classes. Actually, I think they should have been called Beginners' Pervert classes: the way it looked from my angle, the classes were a cheap way for Peeping Toms and sickos to get their thrills. Most of the men in the "class" would focus through their little lenses in the hope of getting better views of forbidden territory. In short, it was all about the sneak peek. But so what? I got paid. And there was never any

Before I knew I could sing, circa 1957 (may Mom rest in peace).

touching. Fortunately, because if any of them had tried anything they'd have been flying toms, not peeping ones.

The classes did turn out to be useful, though, not just for the money. I met many genuine photographers and other artists there, including Shel Silverstein. Shel was then a cartoonist for *Playboy* magazine; it wouldn't be until later that he became a hit songwriter and children's author. We struck up a friendship.

One day Shel called and asked me if I'd be interested in doing a shoot at a nudist colony in Maryland. The money would be good, he assured me. I asked if I could bring Jeannie with me, and he said that'd be fine.

We drove to the nudist colony in Shel's car. When we got there, we found the place had a tent for us to undress in. After I'd got my clothes off I discovered I was too self-conscious to come out of the tent. There were just so many people there. Yeah, they were naked too, but as was all too obvious to me on my way here, this was *really* nude, not cheesecake nude. And it was so strange to see naked men, women, and children just going about their business, having fun, playing ball, swimming and just, well, letting it all hang out. One advantage, I told myself, is *I'll be able to tell right away if someone's got the hots for me.*

Shel and Jeannie laughed at me struggling in the tent, and kept saying, "Get out here! Get out here!" Finally I peeked out at them and saw Jeannie's bush, then Shel's bush and associated appendages. If Shel wasn't worried about showing his all, why should I be? What the hell—if they could do it, so could I. After all, people in nudist colonies generally were, well, nude, weren't they?

"Please, please don't take any pictures of my face," I begged Shel as I extricated myself from my tent. "You can show my ass or anything else, but not my face! My father has a candy store, and he sells these magazines. If my parents saw my photo in one of them, they'd kill me!" So the pictures Shel took of me showed me lying face-down on a mat in the pool.

Jeannie and I got bored and wanted to leave the nudists early. We'd seen enough men and their three-piece sets for one day: big guys, small guys, fat guys, tiny guys, three-balled guys, you name it. We were all laughed out. Shel wanted to stay longer, so we decided to hitchhike home.

A man picked us up just outside the camp. The three of us sat in the front seat of his car. Within a few minutes his hand went into his pocket and stayed there a while. Jeannie and I looked at each other for a second, totally paranoid, and then started to yell, "Let us out! Let us out right *now*! Pull over!" He obediently stopped the car, scared out of his mind, and we jumped out.

Now I think back and wonder if maybe this poor man was just digging in his pocket for change—there was, after all, a tollbooth up ahead.

Months later, when the magazine came out, all you saw in the photos were Jeannie, Shel, and my ass. Shel went on to write some great songs in the 1970s for a group called Dr. Hook and the Medicine Show. Among many others, he wrote a hit called "Sylvia's Mother" as well as "Carry Me Carrie," a song I would eventually record.

∗ ∗ ∗ ∗ ∗ ∗

It was the Coney Island Avenue apartment that saw another important development in my life: I finally lost that pesky virginity of mine. The guy who assisted me in this endeavor had the unprepossessing name of Pinky, and he was married. He took the day off work specially. I stayed in bed with him for six hours, and the first five of them were spent trying to enable him to boldly go where no man had gone before. When he finally succeeded I sort of liked it because it didn't hurt—I'd anticipated it would. Ever the romantic, I flapped around yelling, "You got in! You got in!" Pinky was exhausted, but quietly proud.

Of course, the first thing I did was call a girlfriend from bed to tell her the news. She congratulated me, which was exactly the right thing to do under the circumstances.

I was extremely happy to have got it all over with, even though for days afterward walking was painful. Pinky had the same problem, and another as well. A few weeks earlier I'd done some cheesecake modeling in the country and, asked to lean against some trees, had been attacked on the abdomen by poison ivy. Ever since, I'd been itching and scratching. Even though I'd kept my belly thoroughly slathered in calamine lotion during my encounter with Pinky—told you this was romantic, didn't I?—he'd still managed to get infected. I've often wondered how he explained it to his wife.

※ ※ ※ ※ ※ ※

And so the years turned on. Jeannie and I continued to do cheesecake modeling from 1959 to 1961. Together, we had a few different apartments and went through the usual teen things—flirting, partying, trying out drugs and new drinks. We were experimenting.

One night in 1960, Jeannie and I decided to go to the Brooklyn Paramount to hear some live groups. One of my favorites, The Chantels, was going to be singing, along with The Drifters, Fats Domino, Mary Wells, and a bunch of other R&B artists. It promised to be a good show. The place was mobbed; we had to stand in line for tickets.

All the performers involved were black until, about halfway through the show, out onto the stage came a white woman, Lillian Briggs. When she sang I couldn't believe it: her voice had such power. A strong white singer!

She sang a killer song, "I Want You to Be My Baby," that had these amazingly rhythmic lyrics. I realize now it was almost like something by

Lambert, Hendrix, or Ross, but at the time I didn't know their music. (I would learn, though—man, how I would learn!) I was mesmerized by her performance. The singing absolutely blew me away. And then, just to cap it all, she played a solo on the alto saxophone.

That was it for me. I saw my destiny that night. I had to do this thing myself. I stood there listening in absolute awe of her. I have never forgotten Lillian Briggs and her performance that night. I wanted to *be* her. I wanted that kind of energy and sex, and all of that control.

From my mother letting me go on-stage in grade school for Mr. Levinsky's musicals, to my singing in my kitchen while the spaghetti boiled, to my being in front of cameras doing cheesecake modeling—all this time my road was being paved.

I wanted to be up on that stage.

I wanted to sing!

CHAPTER THREE
Music Music Music

THE FIRST TIME I ever performed on-stage was in 1962 with Richard Perry and his band The Escorts. Richard went on to become one of the most renowned record producers of the 1970s—he worked with Barbra Streisand, Carly Simon, Art Garfunkel, Diana Ross, Harry Nilsson, Johnny Mathis, Ringo Starr, Leo Sayer, Fats Domino, Captain Beefheart, and a host of others—but at the time he was a student at the University of Michigan. The other band members were all in school with him.

I'd gone with Jeannie and a couple of our girlfriends to the Lollipop Lounge, a club on Coney Island Avenue in Brooklyn. The place was known for its live music, and that was what had drawn us. The Escorts were playing oldies and everyone in the club was singing along. For us, the evening was filled with dancing and drinking, drinking and dancing. I got rowdy, and loudly declared my fervent desire to get up and sing. Jeannie dared me to go to the stage and try to get the band to let me sing with them. Naturally, I accepted the dare.

Once I'd reached the stage there was no stopping me. I pulled on the lead singer's sleeve right in the middle of a song. He ignored me at first, so I yanked his arm again.

"What do you want?" he asked, understandably pissed off.

"I wanna sing!" I told him.

"Can't you wait until this song's over?"

I went back to the table, drank, danced some more. Then one of the band somewhat surprisingly waved to me to come and talk. I made my way over to the stage and he stuck his arm out to pull me up beside him.

"What do you want to sing?" he asked.

"Do you know 'Stupid Cupid' by Connie Francis?" I screamed.

"What's your key?"

"What's my *keys* gotta do with this?" I said, ratty. "Why do you want my keys?"

He looked at me like I was a complete idiot and said, "Ah. Okay, then. You start singing and we'll just follow you."

I grabbed the mike out of his hand and began singing: "*Stupid Cupid, you're a real mean guy . . .*"

The band jumped right in, and I was off and running. I had a real microphone in my hand, and a real live audience. I knew heaven for the first time! When the song was over, the crowd yelled, "More! More!"

I turned to the tall, lanky guy who'd asked for my keys and asked if the band knew "Lonely Nights" by The Hearts. He nodded and started to

The first time I heard my voice at the Lollipop Lounge.

ask me, "What key?" before catching himself and saying instead: "You start, we'll follow."

After we'd done the song my head was reeling. I had to sit down. The audience was roaring for another, but I couldn't sing anymore. I think I was in shock. The Escorts continued without me but, when they'd finished, the tall guy came over to our table and asked for my phone number. The girls kicked me under the table, a signal for *Give it to him, give him your number.* I figured what the hell, so I did. I thought he was just coming on to me, which was flattering even if he wasn't cute—that preppy look wasn't what I was looking for. (In those days I still went for the biker type.)

A few days went by and then I got a phone call.

"Goldie? This is Richard Perry."

"Who?" I asked.

"Richard, from the other night. The Escorts, the Lollipop Lounge, the band you sang with . . . "

"Oh, yeah," I said. "The you-lead-we'll-follow guy."

"That's me," he answered.

He told me the band had fired their lead singer and he wanted me to consider singing with them. I didn't believe him. I thought, *This schmuck just wants to get into my pants.* Then he told me the band had a recording contract, and my defensive skepticism suddenly evaporated. I gave him my address.

A couple of days later he showed up at my apartment, wanting to make arrangements for rehearsal. He couldn't have picked a lousier time: We'd had a big party the night before, and four guys were sleeping in the living room—one on the couch, one in a chair, a couple on the floor. When Richard came in, all preppy and neatly dressed, the Brooklyn mafia-wannabe guys were just waking up, hungover. As they drifted out of the apartment they gave Richard some really heavy-duty testosterone looks. I could tell they were making him nervous and uncomfortable.

We sat in my living room, and he told me the band's contract was with Coral Records, a subsidiary of Decca. I still found it hard to believe they actually had a contract, and even weirder that he wanted me to sing with them on the record. We decided to rehearse the next week. Richard said he would give me a lift to the rehearsal.

When he arrived in his cute red Fiat a few days later, I still thought he might be hitting on me—that the whole record deal was just a come on. We drove through Flatbush, Avenue M, a neighborhood full of mansions, an area of Brooklyn I'd never seen. When we pulled up in front of his house, he jumped out and opened the car door for me. *This guy is wealthy!* I thought. We went inside and he introduced me to everyone, even the maid. He called his parents by their first names.

How strange, I thought. If I'd called my parents anything but Mom and Dad they'd have slapped me. Calling them anything else would have been seen as a sign of disrespect.

The Perrys had a Steinway grand piano in their living room. Richard began to play "Somewhere" from *West Side Story.* He told me this was the song we were supposed to record. I remember thinking to myself, *What kinda white shit music is this?*

We rehearsed a lot over the next two weeks. I started looking forward to hanging out with Richard—or Richie, as I came to call him—and we wrote some songs together, the ones we'd eventually record on the B sides. His preppy look, which had so turned me off originally, started to seem attractive. The supposed glamour of the rich kid/poor kid romance, shown in a thousand Hollywood movies, probably influenced us, but pretty soon we were falling for each other.

Goldie and Richie makin' out.

Our relationship got pretty heavy. Eventually there came that inevitable day in any serious relationship when we had Our First Big Argument. I almost walked out of the band when Richie made a remark that really hurt. He said, "How unfair it is for you, Goldie. What a shame you were a refugee. You could have done so much more with your life if your parents had known better. If they'd had money you could have gone to college."

That cut me like a knife. "Oh yeah?" I shouted. "And if your parents had been in concentration camps they'd probably have left you there to die. Who needs college, huh? College? For what? Just watch me—I don't need no fuckin' college. And watch what you say about my family!"

I was very protective of my family. Even though they put me through hell, they'd done something beside which that consideration paled: they'd saved my life.

Richie's parents began to get nervous about our relationship. He was wealthy and had a good future; my family, the refugees, were illiterate and poor. I was a peasant, and they sure didn't want their beloved son marrying a peasant like me! Nevertheless, Richie and I continued to rehearse and see each other.

(Clockwise from lower left): Goldie, Richie Perry, and the Escorts. No groupies for these guys.

A month passed and the summer was going by fast. We had to move quickly on the recording front because the boys had to go back to college in September. Sometime in the fall of 1961 we met with the record-company executives at Decca in one of their piano rehearsal rooms and talked with the artist relations (A&R) department. They wanted to see and hear the new singer—me—and asked us to perform some of our songs.

We sang "Somewhere" and then the B-side song, "Submarine Race Watching" (a song that Richie and I had written about parking and making out). Next we sang a gospel song, "Back Home Again." During the latter the eyes of Henry Jerome, the music director, lit up. He looked pleased. After we'd finished the song, I told Henry I could go for singing lessons if he'd like, but he immediately said, "No, no, don't do that! It would ruin your sound!"

I had no idea what he meant by my "sound" but I knew I liked his praise! We went ahead and recorded "Somewhere" and three other songs. I was so nervous I sang terribly off-key, and you can hear my voice trembling on the track. I guess they thought that was part of my "sound" as well.

Bernard Purdie was the drummer on the first session with Richard Perry and his band. The association with Bernard is something I'm proud of. He drummed on just about all the hit records being played on the radio. His nickname was "Pretty Purdie" and he was known as "the most recorded drummer" back then. Whenever he played a session, he would hang a "Pretty Purdie" sign in front of his drum kit. He was what I call a "pocket drummer," meaning he was always in a groove. Eventually he played drums for most of the best, including Aretha Franklin, King Curtis, B.B. King, and Miles Davis.

The single of "Somewhere" was released in the late summer of 1962 and soon started to climb the charts in Ohio and Canada, then hit #1 in Michigan. At first I didn't know anything about the success of that single, though: I was in New York City, and no one told me what was going on in the Midwest until I got a phone call one day from Henry Jerome.

"Guess what, Goldie? You have a No. 1 record. The boys are waiting for you in Michigan to do some record hops."

I thought, *What the fuck is a record hop*? "Well, I don't know . . ."

Henry said, "It will be with Marvin Gaye."

Aahhhhaaaa! Marvin *Gaye*? That was all I needed to hear. I started packing as soon as I'd hung up the phone.

Goldie and the Escorts at the hop.

Coral Records made all the arrangements for me. They picked me up and took me to the airport, where I boarded a plane to Michigan. When I landed in Detroit, I took a cab to meet Richie at his dorm on the University of Michigan campus in Ann Arbor. The wildest thing happened during the cab ride. The radio was on and suddenly I heard my voice. It was singing "Somewhere."

I started whooping at the driver. "Hey! That's me! That's me!"

It was the first time I'd ever heard myself on the radio. Then it hit me: I *did* have a No. 1 record! The DJ was yelling about a record hop that night. *My* record hop! Wow, what a feeling! I will never forget it. It didn't seem real.

The DJ kept going on and on about the hop. "And of course the number one group The Escorts—with Goldie Zelkowitz!—will be there."

I couldn't believe the DJ was actually saying my whole name. Zelkowitz? How did *that* happen?

"That's me, that's me! I'm Goldie!" I cried to the driver.

"Oh yeah?" he said, giving me a withering just-another-loony look in the rearview mirror.

The hop was very exciting. Here I was, seeing Marvin Gaye in person and singing on the same stage. Back in the early 1960s all recording artists lip-synched on-stage to their records. There was, in fact, no live music at record hops. We had to mime our songs, and this business of just pretending to sing made me feel silly. In the end I always sang along with my own voice—probably loud enough for everyone to hear that I could really sing, not merely lip-synch.

After our set at this first record hop, I went out into the audience to watch the rest of the show. A girl recognized me and came over. She looked straight into my eyes and then, with a shaky voice, asked "Are you Jewish?"

"Yeah." I was ready to fight.

Her face lit up and she said, "So am I."

I stared at her for a moment. After a few silent seconds I asked, "Are we the only Jews in Michigan?"

The girl just sort of laughed.

Richie told me later the radio D.J.s thought I was a black singer spoofing on the name Goldie Zelkowitz—they thought this was so hip. When I did some interviews over the next few days they couldn't believe I really was a white Jewish chick.

Since, with the exception of me, the Escorts were all college students, we could do only summer gigs. So after this first success there had to be a hiatus. During the time the boys were at school, I continued to earn money as a "model."

When summer finally rolled around again, Richie booked The Escorts at Trudy Heller's, a club on the west side of Greenwich Village, on the corner of 9th Street and Sixth Avenue. I was getting tired of modeling for slut magazines, and very much looked forward to the resumption of my musical career. We were now billed as Goldie and The Escorts; putting my name first was the record company's decision, not my idea. I felt sort of funny about it, but you didn't argue with your record company.

Trudy's was right across the street from a women's detention center. Some of the inmates would holler down at me from the windows as I walked past on my way to and from the club.

"Hey, Mama! How are ya?"

I'd look up. "Fine."

"See ya when I get out, baby!"

In the early 1960s, clubs hired dancers to do the twist. The girls wore teeny bikini outfits with loads of fringe and glitter everywhere. At Trudy's there was even a gay boy, dressed very campily, twisting on the wall. The walls had handles on them for the dancers to cling to, and even ledges for them to stand on. Between the dancers and the patrons, everyone-doing the hully gully, the swim, or the line dance, the place was one big sweat box, a real circus, loud and hot.

Trudy's didn't have dressing rooms, so everyone, even the dancers, had to change in the bathroom right along with the customers. We could hardly breathe in there. The girls were constantly running to the bathroom to fix themselves up and get ready for dancing. Women on dates kept coming in and spraying their hair, and the fumes from the aerosols were enough to knock you out. It's a wonder we didn't all choke to death.

Trudy Heller owned the club. She was gay and didn't care who knew it. In the 1960s in general, though, being a lesbian was not something anyone talked about. Times have changed for the better, but back then no one came out of the closet. Trudy was a tough cookie and I liked her. One thing for sure, I didn't ever want to get on her bad side. She required rockers to rock—no ballads. She'd go crazy with rage whenever we sang a ballad. I'd look down from the stage and see her getting angry, then she'd run over to the light switch and start flicking it on and off, screaming, "C'mon! C'mon! Let's twist already! Let's twist the night away! Come on, baby, let's do the fuckin' twist!"

To say she was intimidating would be an understatement. Much later, with my next band, I finally worked up the nerve to make fun of her on-stage; by then we knew each other well enough. She'd get off on that, my teasing her, but she never did get over being angry when someone played a slow song. All she wanted was action and for the place to rock.

The Escorts did six forty-five-minute sets a night, with half-hour breaks in between. Today I have no idea how I sang that much—not just at Trudy's, but for so many years thereafter. I'm surprised I still have any voice left.

One night on a break at Trudy's, Richie asked me to walk over with him to a club called Cinderella on Eighth Street, just around the corner. He was going to see Mickey, a friend of his from Brooklyn. Mickey Lane was a keyboard player and a songwriter, supposedly very talented. Richie and I had been "going steady" for quite some time by now. He'd even bought me a Pekinese puppy, probably so I wouldn't forget him while he was away at college. I named the puppy Van, Richie's middle name. His mother wasn't too pleased about that.

Mickey was playing this little dive. He sat at the piano, eating a sandwich with one hand and playing the keys with the other. He sang between bites, spitting some of his mouthful of food out onto the piano as he sang. It didn't matter; aside from the bartender, we were the only ones in the club.

The place was dark. I could see Mickey all right, but the shadows were deep enough that I could barely see his drummer, behind him at the back of the stage. I started watching the drummer nevertheless, admiring the foot action and the beat. And then I realized, after doing a double take, that the drummer was a girl!

They took a break. Mickey came over and introduced both himself and the drummer, whose name was Ginger Panabianco. They sat with us at the table while Mickey talked. Ginger, by contrast, was incredibly shy and withdrawn; trying to get a word out of her was like pulling teeth. As we left, Richie invited them to come over to Trudy's during their break.

At the end of the night, Ginger and I exchanged phone numbers. She lived with her parents in Valley Stream, Long Island, but she said she needed to get out, that she was going to run away soon.

"Really?" I said. "Call me. Maybe I can put you up."

"Good," she said. "I don't have much. I won't take up too much space."

A few days passed, and then Ginger phoned me. I remember thinking, *Wow, a girl drummer. I'd love to work with a girl drummer. Maybe we could have an all-girl band.*

Over the next few days, Ginger and I spoke several times on the phone, and sometimes she came over to the apartment. When she did, we'd talk for hours about how great it would be to put an all-girl band together and about everything band-related—names for this putative group, where we'd play, what we'd wear on-stage. One day I said to her, "We both have fantasy names, like from fairytales—Goldilocks and the Three Bears, the gingerbread house . . . Why don't we call the band Goldie and the Gingerbreads?"

"Fine," Ginger responded.

We decided it was time to start turning our ideas into more than just idle dreams by looking around for players to be the rest of the band members.

"It's not going to be easy," Ginger cautioned. She didn't yet know what a determined person I am.

"Maybe not," I answered. "But it's going to be fun trying. We can do it."

Those days I felt like I had the world by the balls. I had this feeling I could do anything and succeed. Now that I was no longer under my parents' thumb on Rivington Street, the sky was the limit. I could do anything and go anywhere. What a great feeling!

It didn't take long for Ginger to want the freedom I had. She had a strict Italian family, and yearned to be out of the Panabianco house. One night she called and said she'd like to come live with me. I warned her that all I could offer was a couch in the living room, and no closet.

"No problem," she said, and told me once again, "I don't have much—just a few things."

I hadn't said anything to Jeannie about the possibility of a new roommate coming to live with us. We were so loose I never thought it would matter to her.

The next morning the doorbell rang. I opened the door; Ginger was standing on the landing surrounded by shoeboxes—at least twenty of them. *Okay*, I thought. *There's room in the closet for the shoes.*

Then Ginger said, "I'll be right back."

A few minutes later, she came up the stairs carrying a suitcase filled with more shoes. *What the fuck?* I thought. *Maybe she has a thing for shoes.*

Ginger put the suitcase in the living room, turned to me, and said, "I have just one more thing. I hope you don't mind. I brought Beaumont, my monkey."

I must have stood there with my mouth hanging open for ten minutes as I stared at my new roommates. I had met Beaumont once before, when I'd gone to Ginger's parents' house. I liked him okay, but our apartment was in a no-animals-allowed building, and I was already treading on thin ice with Van, the Pekinese. Nonetheless, Ginger, Beaumont, and all the shoes moved into the apartment.

Beaumont was kept in a cage. I found out rather quickly that he screeched all day because he wanted out of it. One night when I was baby-sitting him I released him from his cage. I'd made spaghetti for dinner, and he sat at the table on my lap eating all my spaghetti. He threw the stuff on the ceiling, the floor, the walls. Afterwards, he didn't want to go back behind bars, so I put him on the couch with me as we watched television and waited for Ginger to come home.

Beaumont sat on my stomach, staring right into my eyes. This went on for so long it was disconcerting, to say the least. After a while, still looking straight at me, he started to unbutton my blouse, one button at a time—slowly and deliberately. He never took his eyes off mine. At first I just sat there, stunned, almost transfixed by that monkey's stare. It was at this stage that I got totally creeped out. Leaping off the couch, I began shrieking. "Back to the cage, baby!" I yelled. I picked him up and dragged him to his little jail. He screeched back at the top of his lungs.

When Ginger finally came home and I told her what had happened, all she said was, "Well, you do have great boobs." After that we laughed about it for hours, but I never trusted that monkey again. I made a point of not walking in front of him unless I was fully dressed.

A few days later Jeannie told me she was moving out. She said something was wrong with her health and she needed to go back to her family. Actually, I think she was jealous of my new friendship with Ginger. I was upset she was leaving, but I knew there was nothing I could do to convince her to stay.

Meanwhile, The Escorts finished a two-week gig at Trudy's. The summer was almost over, which meant it was time for Richie to go back to Ann Arbor to finish college. I told him I was going to try to form another band to sing in, but just until the next summer, when he'd have his break from college and The Escorts could get together again.

I lied.

CHAPTER FOUR
Goldie and the Gingerbreads Get Started

GOLDIE AND THE GINGERBREADS was going to become a reality. No more daydreaming, no more scheming, no more idle planning.

Ginger and I started to hunt for a piano player—we thought a pianist would be the easiest musician to find. We spent endless hours at the Musicians' Union on Fifty-Second Street looking up female players until finally we found someone who seemed promising. Off we went to Queens to see this girl. Carol O'Grady proved to be very pretty and a good player, although not "rhythm and blues" enough for me; she was definitely a white-sounding musician. However, we recruited her to the band because I convinced myself she could be taught to feel R&B. (Later I found I was wrong about that: if you don't have it you can't get it.)

Pretty soon, Ginger and I discovered that Carol really was different from us. She had different dreams: she wanted to get married, have a home and raise children. It became apparent to us that her membership in the band was going to have to be at best a temporary measure. She would have to be replaced some day, and probably sooner rather than later.

Soon after we found Carol, we started our grueling search again, this time for a guitarist. We traveled all over, auditioning, until finally we

GOLDIE and the GINGERBREADS
Female Twist Band

Direction
Lee Botwin
N.Y.C.
LT 1-1156

Goldie and the Gingerbreads' first members.

met a chick guitarist called Marsha Bendel through an ad in the paper. Marsha was one of those girls you want to smack around, step on her sneakers—you know, dirty her up. She was okay-looking for our purposes—blonde and petite—but she was definitely a Miss Goody Two-Shoes, a real schoolgirl type: that's the part that was so hard to take. I didn't like *nice* girls. I simply could not relate to her. I was foul-mouthed; everything was "fuck this" or "fuck that." She was cashmere sweaters, clean sneakers, and folded clothes. It was a real culture-clash. I wanted to throw up every time she spoke, but I managed to hold my peace. *Something is better than nothing*, I kept saying to myself. I had trained myself, early on, how to go into neutral and just wait.

Marsha was musically trained, and indeed taught music. Everything, all the chords and notes, had to be perfect. This had its pluses, of course, but at the time it was simply another cause of friction: it grated on me.

I loved shocking her and freaking her out. One night, I was driving with her and Ginger on Ocean Parkway when the Isley Brothers' song "You Know You Make Me Wanna Shout!" came on the radio. (I was hypnotized by this song—I loved singing it as loudly as I could. I will never forget how that song made me feel and what it did to me. The next time I would get that feeling was when I sang the ballad "The Time" by Baby Washington.) I slammed on the brakes, tires screeching, and, with the volume turned up as far as it would go, jumped out of the car and started dancing and singing—AS LOUD AS I COULD—right in the middle of the road. I kept up my impromptu performance on the highway next to the car until the song ended, by which time there was a huge traffic jam all around us, complete with horns blaring and guys whistling; cop sirens were headed in our direction. Ginger loved this whole scene, but poor Marsha crouched in the backseat, looking completely mortified.

Ginger was beautiful, as well as sweet (then), quiet, and naive (then). The guys always flipped for her. There were times I thought they were quite literally drooling at the mouth. She was big-breasted, and her face made her look like a young Sophia Loren—the dark hair along with her Italian features. I insisted on Ginger having a platform on-stage for her drums so she could be easily seen as well as heard, and she truly was something to see. I used to love to embarrass her by announcing to the audience that "Omar the tent-maker designs her bras" or whatever. She would get red as a beet and the guys would turn to jelly.

And Ginger could really play those drums. She was so intense. The audience would go nuts when I had her do a drum solo.

What I also loved about her was the chilly attitude she displayed towards people off-stage. It gave her a star persona. Truly cool!

Ginger was great for me. No matter what I wanted to do, where I wanted to go, Gin was up for it.

"Hey, Gin, wanna start a women's band with me?"
"Okay."
"Hey, Gin, wanna stay over at so-and-so's place with me?"
"Okay."
"Hey, Gin, wanna go to Europe and live there for a while?"

"Okay!"

She could also be tough, though, and physically she was very strong. She had the job of packing up the vans with all our equipment, and she did most of the lifting and carrying. In the early years of our career, Goldie and the Gingerbreads didn't have roadies—no drivers or trucks. We had to use our own cars . . . or, I should say, Ginger's car. We would rent a U-Haul trailer, hitch it to her Ford Mustang convertible, and put the equipment in it. As for packing the equipment, the girls would always laugh at me and say, "Oh, here's the supervisor," because I never carried a thing and I always directed, telling them how I thought everything should be packed and where it should go. On the other hand, I always did the majority of the driving—I had to, because otherwise I'd have gone crazy sitting in a car doing nothing for hours, especially if I was doing speed at the time.

When we got to a club, Ginger would also unload. The greatest thing was watching guys run over to us poor helpless girls saying, "Here, let me get that for you!" and then trying to pick up Ginger's trap case or help with the Hammond organ. They'd turn red in the face, like they were going to get a hernia or a heart attack or something. That's when Ginger would step in and grab the stuff back from them: "I'll get that." Then she'd lift the piece of equipment as if it were as light as a feather.

I was living back with my parents in Brooklyn by now, because there was no way I could afford my part of the rent on the apartment Ginger and I had shared. We rehearsed in my parents' basement on Pearson Street, Brooklyn. Mom loved it. She made sure all the windows and doors were open so the whole neighborhood could hear, and she fed us all.

● ● ● ● ● ●

After Goldie and the Gingerbreads had rehearsed a while we got pretty good. I booked us into lots of little bars around Manhattan and Brooklyn. When the clubs advertised in the *Daily News* and the *New York Mirror,* I got a big kick out of seeing our name in print:

> Goldie and the Gingerbreads
> Girls! Girls! All Girls!

(I sometimes wondered why they didn't just say what they meant: "Appearing Tonight: Tits and Ass.") The ads were small, but I liked looking at them because they made the whole thing seem real to me. I cut them out and saved every one of them.

Ginger and I would go to costume-hire shops in Times Square and rent sparkly outfits, some with fringe, some with rhinestones and sequins. The other girls didn't like my taste in costumes, but I made them wear the things anyway.

Marsha announced she could rehearse only on weekends, not during the week, because she needed to make money and teach. I wasn't ready to fire her immediately, because I wanted to continue playing around, so I bit my tongue, cursed under my breath, and went along with all the demands.

Even so, the moment couldn't be indefinitely delayed, and it wasn't long before I canned her. So there we were again, trying to find more females that could actually play instruments. Someone gave us a lead on a guitarist called Mandy Richards, who lived on Long Island. When we invited her to see us in a New York City bar, she brought her mother along. Huh? We asked her to sit in and play with us; she did and it was good. We thought, *Hey, Mandy could work out!*

Wrong. First thing she did was hit me with how she wanted to sing lead. I winced, and spelled it out for her: "Maybe on one or two songs, but I'm the lead singer. You can do lots of background." I could see her point, though. She clearly wanted to front a band; it was just that she'd picked the wrong band. I double-talked her into doing some rehearsals and a gig I'd already booked at Trudy Heller's, the "in" place to work at the time; we had a contract with the club and I wasn't going to screw it up.

Mandy brought her mother with her everywhere, almost as if Mom were another member of Goldie and the Gingerbreads. It was a real problem. They lived in Patchogue, Long Island, quite a distance out from New York City, and Mandy was too young to drive. Accordingly, Mom drove her in each night from Patchogue to the club, and then would sit in her car drinking brandy until four o'clock in the morning. The few times she came into the club, drunk as a skunk, she would call Mandy over and motion for her to sit on her lap—not exactly the image Goldie and the Gingerbreads was trying to project! I sometimes had nightmares that we were performing at a club and I looked out at the audience and could see nothing but mothers.

Trudy's take on the situation was typically in-your-face. "Hey, is Mandy's alkie momma out there in the car getting shit-faced again?" All that was missing to complete Trudy's persona was a big fat cigar hanging from her mouth as she talked. "What da fuck is wrong with dat broad's mother?" she'd yell out. "Get rid of dat player! Get another fuckin' guitar player!" She had no idea how hard it had been to find this one.

In spite of the band being such a motley crew, Ginger and I managed to perform quite a bit with these girls. In the beginning I was responsible for booking our gigs. In practice this was simplicity itself. I had to do no more than walk into a bar and speak the magic words "All-woman band," then listen to them say: "How much youse want?"

The club owners basically didn't care what we sounded like: they just wanted women. We had our own cheap sound system. As long as the bar had a corner, we had a stage where we could set up and play. Word of mouth got us more bookings, club owners telling other club owners about us.

We also worked bowling alleys. The amplifier my microphone went through was fairly small, so during these gigs you could only hear my vocals between strikes. One newspaper ad read: "Goldie and the Gingerbreads—Appearing Live at the Rolling Lanes featuring Burger and Fries."

I was very psyched up about everything that was going on. I saved all our clippings and gave them to my mother, who saved every one. I had her approval at last: she was proud of me!

But of course, with our uneasy mixture of personnel in the band, its future was always a cause for concern. We knew the current lineup couldn't last long. Ginger and I would stay together; that could be assumed. We were in it for the long haul. But finding other Gingerbreads was always going to be difficult. In the 1960s, it was really unusual for girls to pick up instruments unless they were somewhat strange to begin with. What mother would encourage her little darling to play drums or bass or trombone back then? The same went for music classes. Back then the piano, or even the violin, was considered a suitable instrument for a young girl, but the notion of training to play rock 'n' roll was unimaginable. Rock 'n' roll was what juvenile delinquents did, not young ladies.

Nevertheless, even though I knew it would take us a long time to get the right group together, so long as I had Ginger, I felt secure. I loved having a partner, and I thought at the time that a good drummer was the most important thing. I learned quickly enough that all the players are key components in a good band.

Before too long, we found a new guitar player. Shuggie Q was one hell of a rhythm and lead guitar player. Her only problem was that she was such a dyke; she walked and talked like a truck driver. When she'd come up to the stage I'd close my eyes and hold my breath, it was so embarrassing I couldn't watch—not because she was a lesbian, which didn't matter to me, but because she was so obviously butch. In those days you generally had to walk through the entire club to reach the stage, giving the patrons plenty of opportunity to check you out. Believe me, they checked out this all-girl band pretty thoroughly, and many of them stared incredulously at "mega-dyke" Shuggie Q.

Now, almost forty years later, everything's different—attitudes towards gays, abortions, everything. But back in the 1960s, even though the sexual revolution was supposed to be going on, people were still freaked out by anything different. Though nobody would even notice Shuggie Q today, in those days she was definitely an oddity.

Our costumes were gold halter tops with shiny stretch gold lamé pants so tight you could see the panty-lines—very girly. Shuggie, who was also very bowlegged, just to add to the effect, would stomp onto the stage, guitar pick in her mouth, walking as I imagined a guy would try to walk with a Kotex between his legs. I'd try to show her during rehearsals how to walk right; I even put books on her head, because I'd seen this in some commercial about how to get into modeling.

"Walk like a girl, ya' fuckin' dyke, will ya?" I'd shout.

"I'm tryin', for cryin' out loud!" she'd yell back.

But nothing worked. Whatever I tried, she was still the dyke on the guitar, and we just had to accept that.

There was one other thing. Shuggie had broken front teeth. So, in addition to trying to teach her how to walk without looking like a Mack truck, I had to persuade her not to smile on-stage. I would say, "Stay intense, Shug. People like it when you're mysterious and intense. Try to look like you're gonna kill them. Don't even think of grinning!"

• • • • • •

About a year after we'd formed Goldie and the Gingerbreads, an old agent friend, Barry, told me about Margo Lewis, a lovely young Italian girl from Brooklyn who could play the hell out of an organ. I phoned her and arranged for Ginger and myself to go check her out.

Margo's house was in a very Italian neighborhood in Bensonhurst.

When we got there we found it was on one of those streets where all the houses looked exactly the same. We rang the bell and a woman's voice called "Yeah, WHOOOOO is it?" in a thick Italian accent.

"Umm . . . Goldie and Ginger . . . from Goldie and the Gingerbreads," I answered.

We could see the woman through the glass as she started coming down the stairs. She said something that sounded to me like, "*A svagim, adslkdjgj'lds, glsdgkjlds!*"

Ginger, being Italian, understood this and translated for me in a whisper. "These goddamned stairs are going to give me a goddamned heart attack one day!"

When the woman opened the door she looked like she had just stepped out of an olive grove in Sicily. Her black hair was shiny and piled way up on her head, bobby pins sticking out everywhere, and she was wearing this very flowery blouse and a homey apron.

"Aha!" she said to us in a big Anna Magniani voice. "Come on in. I'm Gemma, Marguerite's mother. Come in, come up!"

We started up the stairs behind her.

"Are ya hungry?" she asked as we reached the top landing. "Ya gotta be hungry! I'm makin' peppas and eggs and some bread. Ya gotta eat! Look at youse." She waved her arms in the air. "You're both so skinny! Put some meat on yer bones, for chrissake."

Ginger and I followed her into the kitchen. An old man was sitting in a corner drinking what looked like wine.

"Dat's Marguerite's grandfather, Nonno," said Gemma.

Nonno started to yell in Italian, and Gemma started yelling back, and I looked over at Ginger again.

"It's okay," she murmured. "They're not fighting. He just wants to know what's for lunch."

I left the kitchen and wandered into the living room, where I saw a big Hammond organ with the bass foot pedals sticking out of it—a huge instrument, taking up much of the room. Next to it was a Leslie speaker.

Finally Margo emerged from her bedroom. She had all the Italian features—black hair and olive skin—and a good body, but, unlike Ginger, she seemed very plain. I stared at her and thought, *I'll take care of that look later. Let's see how she plays first.*

After we'd introduced ourselves, Margo sat down to play while Gemma kept cooking away in the kitchen. (Boy, did Gemma's cooking smell good. I was really hoping Margo would turn out to be the next band member if only because then I'd be able to come over to the house all the time and eat! I love Italian food.) As Margo started to audition, with foot pedals and all, I thought her playing was a bit stiff, but she definitely had the chops. She picked organ songs that had been recorded by Jimmy Smith; he was hot at the time, and a great organ player. This kind of music was hard to play.

All in all, Ginger and I were pretty happy, and reckoned we had found our girl, although we knew it would take a lot of rehearsing to integrate her into the group. It's one thing to work as a solo, another to back a singer and know how to work in a group. I still managed to think every scary thought imaginable about what could go wrong. *Let's see . . . does her mother have to go on the road? Does she have to stay in bed for a month when she gets her period? Does she only play on weekends? Is she a nymphomaniac? Does she turn into a guy after midnight? Does she carry dildos? Does she pack a gun?* All these things and more were buzzing around in my head.

We had had so many bad experiences with female musicians by then. Because of my frustration with all the auditions from hell we'd had, there were times on stage when I was not too kind. If a girl fucked up a song, a note or chord, I would stop the band right in the middle of the song and stare at her, then say—into the microphone—"Let's do it again, the right way." The audience would go quiet and of course the girl would be mortified.

But Margo proved to be a find in more ways than one. First, she had a brain. Second, she and I had the same sense of humor. My kind of humor is not always tasteful, but Margo was always inspiring me and egging me on. She would fall apart laughing on-stage when I was funny. I love making people laugh.

We made each other laugh off-stage, too. Many times we would be in a room full of people, look at each other, and not have to say a word, because we knew we were both thinking the same thing. That would always crack us up.

With this kind of close connection, Margo was good for me; she had a calming affect on me. I believe good combinations breed success, and she very soon became an important part of the team.

The blend of the girls in the Gingerbreads was starting to feel right. This good mixture was the reason the group stuck together as long as it did, and Margo was a big part of the glue. I had the balls and made the very bold moves, but sometimes I was too fast with my decisions. Margo would make me look at things before I leaped. Ginger and I were truly partners now, and I needed that back-up from her. In general, the group had become like family. If we had a disagreement, we would never remember later why it was we'd been fighting and arguing. After we'd done a show we would hug each other. There were times on-stage when I know I was performing for the group, not the audience.

• • • • • • •

We understood nothing about the business end of the industry. In the 1960s, if anyone wanted you to sign a contract, you would just ask, "Where do I put my name?" and think to yourself, *Wow! They're giving us a contract. We're gonna make records!* What I guess we should have said was: "Shall I bend over now or would you like to fuck us later?"

At one of our gigs in New Jersey we met the group The Four Seasons. Nick Massi (one of the original members, along with Frankie Valli) fell in love with my voice and with Goldie and the Gingerbreads. Nick said he knew Florence Greenberg, who had founded Scepter Records in 1959, and gave me her telephone number. It was primarily Greenberg's success with The Shirelles and The Platters that convinced us we should contact her.

After we had had a few meetings with her, she asked Luther Dixon (a.k.a. Barney Williams) to come and hear us. It was decided soon after that session that Luther would be our producer. He had co-written and produced most of Scepter's hit songs up to that point; he was also Greenberg's boyfriend. Scepter had the top artists of the time—Dionne Warwick, The Shirelles, Maxine Brown, Chuck Jackson, The Isley Brothers, King Curtis, and Tommy Hunt. What a lineup! We would be the only white act on the label. Obviously it was exciting talking to Greenberg and Dixon. We signed a contract and set a recording date.

The first—and, as it proved, only—record we released under Scepter's Spokane label was "Skinny Vinnie"; it was produced for us by Florence's son Stanley. It was decided that thereafter Luther would be our producer, and we scheduled an early-morning recording session with him. He told Ginger and me we could stay in his apartment the night before so we wouldn't have to get up at some ridiculous hour for the trip all the way from Brooklyn into the city. He had a living-room couch that opened into a bed.

Ginger and I were about to go to sleep when Luther called me into his bedroom. I walked in, not thinking anything about it, to find him lying in bed with his little Yorkshire terrier in attendance.

"I want to make sure you're okay and ask you a few things," he said, patting the side of the bed to indicate I should sit there. He asked me if I was sure I knew the songs well enough to record them, and if I was nervous about the session. Then, after I'd said yes to both questions, he told me how wonderful the session would be and put his hand on my neck, pulling me down. "Kiss me goodnight."

Reluctantly I bent down to give him a peck on the cheek. Next thing I knew, he grabbed me and started to force me to kiss him on the mouth, pulling my head towards his face. He was strong. We struggled for a long while before I was able to pull him to the floor, thinking this would make him give up, but he looked like he was in a trance. He pulled me down with him. Before I could stop him, he had his knee between my legs. I realized he was very close to raping me.

I began screaming. "Ginger! Ginger!" Then I grabbed his Yorkie dog by the throat—it had been licking my face the whole time. I started choking the animal, thinking its yelps might get through to Luther where my own efforts obviously couldn't. But even his dog being strangled didn't faze him any. It was as if he were on drugs.

Again I screamed. "Luther! Stop! Stop!"

Next thing I knew, Ginger was standing over us with something heavy in her hand—I don't remember what: probably a lamp. She said, very calmly, "Luther, if you don't get off her I will break your head." I will never forget how cool she was.

When he climbed off me I was shaking all over. We grabbed our stuff and fled from the apartment. As soon as we could find a phone we called the other girls and told them what had happened.

Goldie and the Gingerbreads never did go to that recording session. I wrote a threatening letter to Luther, telling him that, unless we got a legal release from the label, I would have to inform Florence Greenberg of what had occurred at his apartment. To cut a long story short, we got our release—and quickly. Who knows what Luther Dixon told Florence Greenberg. Who cares?

● ● ● ● ● ●

Every record company we ever had except Ahmet Ertegun's Atlantic label screwed us out of royalties. I think Ertegun's was probably the only record company that actually cared about us. Managers definitely swindled us. I never claimed to be a businesswoman, at least not until it was way too late to do anything about it; all I wanted to do was sing and be a performer. As far as I'm concerned, Goldie and the Gingerbreads were never in the right hands.

But the funny thing is that, when all's said and done, we still made more money than lots of the male rock bands did. We were chicks, and we got paid more just because we were chicks. So the fact that we were working in a male-dominated, chauvinistic industry in fact profited us . . . and we were smart enough to know it. We worked our "chickness" for all it was worth, and laughed about it. This was true at every level, not just the professional. If a guy came over to one of us after a set and asked her out for breakfast at three a.m., we would all jump in and say, "Oh, we'd love to." Then he'd get stuck having to pay for the whole band.

The 1960s were stranger than fiction. If we said "no" to breakfast with one of those guys we'd be called dykes; if we said "yes" we were loose chicks, or sometimes even be dismissed as hookers. It was a lose-lose situation with some of these guys at the bars.

There was even a rumor that we liked S&M and sleeping with midgets. I have no idea how that one started!

● ● ● ● ● ●

In 1962 we got our first big break. The Harold Davidson Agency, a major talent agency, asked us if we wanted to be the opening act for Chubby Checker in Germany and Switzerland. It was the first time that Ginger, Margo, and I would be traveling outside our own country. (We were a trio at this time; Carol and Shuggie had departed and the other Carol, Carol MacDonald, hadn't yet joined us.) Ginger and Margo were scared, but I was ecstatic.

When we arrived in Germany, we discovered that our travel dates had got all mixed up somehow, so that we were two days earlier than expected. There was no one there to meet and greet us, and it was a Sunday night. We ended up sleeping on the floor at the airport.

The next day we found a room in a prostitute hotel. We didn't know when we booked in what kind of a place it was, though we thought it was very strange that the room they gave us had twelve beds in it. A real

Goldie and Chubby Checker touring in Germany.

fleabag kind of place, in other words. Afraid to go anywhere in the hotel alone, we huddled together, glued to each other for twenty-four hours a day. We even bathed together; if one of us had to go to the bathroom at any time, then we all went. We made numerous calls to the agency in the United States before finally getting their attention. Eventually we were picked up from that dumpy hotel on the Tuesday after we'd arrived.

In spite of the weirdness factor, we laughed our way all through the experience. We always had good fun, no matter what—and, hey, this was an adventure! We were finally out of the grip of our parents. We were young, free, and getting paid!

Goldie and the Gingerbreads played all the major towns in Germany and Switzerland, and we had a ball. What a trip! We loved our hotel rooms, after that first place; they came equipped with fluffy duvets and, exotically, bidets. I still haven't worked out how to operate one of those. We bought leather coats and pants and went into all these really cool stores. The food in Germany and Switzerland was unbelievable. We felt like stars.

Most of the time we traveled by bus. This was the hard part. Some days there were pretty hairy mood swings on that bus. We would travel for seven to ten hours straight. Cramped, we would beg the driver to stop and, when he didn't, we'd get really pissed off. If you got your period—it seemed one of us was always having a period—you couldn't stop to change your Kotex. If you wanted to shower and clean yourself up, forget it. You had to wait until you finally hit a hotel. I used to look at Margo and say, "I smell! Smell me." She would assure me I didn't. Then we would laugh so hard we would wake up everyone on the bus.

It was always rush, rush, and rush. Arrive, sound check, quick change, perform. We were so happy when we finally reached our hotel each night.

Given my family history, I had major issues about being in Germany. "Of all places for me to have my first tour!" I kept saying. Before we'd left New York, I'd had this giant ring made: a white gold Jewish star with a huge cubic zirconia in the middle. Wherever we went I would show off my ring. Every chance I had, I would go into a jewelry store and ask for a Jewish star. In one small town a proprietor said, "You vill not find a Jewish star in dis store," and I started to curse and yell. The girls had to pull me out.

I was being pretty prickly—I'd come to Germany with an attitude, all right. I soon realized, though, that there wasn't much point in this sort of behavior. Also, as Margo pointed out, I needed to remember that the Germans were paying us. We were *taking* from them, not them from us. Good old Margo: she knew the way to soothe me, even when she was jiving me.

And she was right. With very few exceptions, the Germans we met were lovely people. Germany is a heavy music country. The Germans love music, especially rock and roll. We ended up having a hell of a good time.

At some points in the tour we played to crowds of as many as five thousand people. That was a first for us, and it was magical. I remember thinking how lucky we were that this was our work and we got paid for it! I will never forget that feeling: I had the control, the strength. Playing in front of thousands of kids, I knew I had arrived! I finally understood what my life's journey was going to be, that this was what I'd been waiting for. Everything before that moment had been preparation. The audiences went nuts. We did encore upon encore.

I saw teenage hysteria at firsthand, and it was scary. Fans would attack our buses and want to grab anything—a part of you, your hair, buttons from your clothes, anything, all the while shouting in a language we did not understand. The first time it happened, our bus driver came to our rescue, grabbing us and pulling us into the bus. We were really getting to know what it felt like being rock stars.

Chubby Checker, with whom we were touring, had a problem in that he thought of himself as a serious singer, even though his big hit was with this new dance called the twist. He would try to do a ballad in the middle of his show, and the audience would start to boo or begin screaming, "Da tvist! Da tvist! Vas is das? Da tvist!" It really pissed him off. More than once he walked off the stage and refused to continue; the rest of us would have to talk him into going back on stage to sing. We really wanted this tour to continue.

Tony Sheridan was the German headliner for the tour. The girls went crazy over him. He was very, very handsome, and his fame in Germany was truly enormous. Moreover, he could really play the guitar.

After a few chats with Tony, not to mention some judicious flirting, I talked him into playing with Goldie and the Gingerbreads on a few songs. His manager—"Horst the Nazi," as we called him—didn't like that: The audiences were there to see Chubby Checker and Tony. We were just the opening act, and Tony was supposed to appear *after* us, on his own: The Superstar. Tony ignored Horst and came on-stage with Goldie and the Gingerbreads. Horst had it in for me from that point on.

Even though Horst the Nazi was on top of Tony twenty-four hours a day and watched him like a hawk, Tony was on all kinds of drugs. He mostly did speed—and lots of it. He was nuts to start with, and the pills definitely made him crazier. To add to Horst's problems, Tony had a crush on me, and soon we were sleeping together. I think our affair interfered with Horst's German control issues: "You vill do vat I say and enjoy it!"

Tony kept telling me all these stories about Liverpool and the Beatles and how he had once been a part of that group. Before long I got really bored with this. I couldn't have cared less, and let him know it, telling him to save the stories for someone who would be impressed.

All I sought from Tony was a fling, but he wanted more. One day I tried to break it off. It was over between us, I told him. He got mad, saying things like: "Then I can't go on."

I thought he meant "on-stage."

That night—I don't remember what city we were in—he tried to overdose. Ginger and I were in our hotel room when suddenly there was an almighty banging on the door. Ginger opened it, and there was Horst with his horrible German accent. "Vere is Goldie?"

When I appeared at the door he started shrieking, "Tony is trying to keel himself because of you! If Tony dies I vill keel you! Dis is all your fault!"

He walked off and Ginger and I just stood there, staring at this crazy German as he vanished down the hall. Then I turned to her and yelled, "What the fuck are we gonna do! If Tony dies, the tour is over and the Nazi'll kill me!" You can tell what my priorities were, I guess.

I called Margo, and soon we were all three in my room, panicking.

"We have to do something," I said.

"I know," said Ginger. "Let me go to Tony's room and see if this is baloney. He might just be full of shit and trying to scare you into taking him back."

Ginger and Margo accordingly went to his room. Horst had not been putting us on. Tony was spread-eagled on his bed, totally out of it, staring blankly up at the ceiling.

Instinctively Ginger jumped on his stomach and started to smack him in the face. *Whack! Whack!*

"Get the fuck up!" she yelled. "Get up! Get up, you stupid fuck!" Then another smack, and another one, harder this time. And another, harder still. "Get up, you son of a bitch! Get up!"

Slap!

"Get up!"

Slap!

Margo and Ginger managed to pull Tony to his feet. Margo got a cup of cold water and threw it on his face. Then they dragged him under the shower. Ginger went on smacking him. "Again!" Margo kept crying. (Maybe she was getting off on this!)

The whole time this was going on, I was scared out of my mind. Finally, after about two hours of slaps and showers, Tony snapped out of it. Throughout this ordeal, Horst didn't check on Tony even once. I guess he was in the bar drinking, devising the method he would use to kill me.

The next day, Tony looked really bad, with a definite yellow hue to his skin. Sitting by me on the bus, he begged me to stay with him. So, in the end, I continued sleeping with the fragile doper, just to keep the peace. While he got a piece. The girls and I thought it was the best thing to do. There were only two more weeks left on the tour.

CHAPTER FIVE
Back in the U.S.A.

IN EARLY 1963 we were home in New York, still high from our German tour.

We started looking for female musicians again. I wanted a larger band—a trio was just not enough for me. After a series of gruesome auditions, we found Nancy Peterman, a bass player. Nancy was part Indian, part French, part silly. She was also very pretty and, most importantly, a superb bass player; I called her Thunder Thumb because to hear her play you'd think she was a 250-pound guy, even though she was the most feminine, petite girl. When she climbed on-stage and got behind that bass, she was amazingly powerful. She blew most male bass players away, and many of them watched her in awe.

Nancy wore her hair in an upsweep (a hairstyle popular in the 1960s: your hair was piled on top of your head and held in place by ugly bobby pins), and always looked like she had just had a manicure and pedicure. She used way too much eye makeup; I swear you could see your reflection in her lip gloss. I always told her that if she fell on her face she would slide all the way to Florida. And I often made fun of how Dainty Nancy wiggled when she walked.

GOLDIE and the GINGERBREADS

Goldie wanted glam.

So now we had a four-member group: Ginger, Margo, Nancy, and myself. Margo was not too happy at first about having a bass player in the band; she was used to playing the bass on the organ's foot pedals, and would get lots of raves about her ability to play bass with her feet. Accordingly, rehearsals were pretty touchy for a while. With certain bass lines, it was made clear to Nancy that she wasn't allowed to step on Margo's feet, so to speak. Eventually we figured out how to divide the bass lines, and the music sounded better than ever.

* * * * * *

Being the only all-woman band in those days made us quite a novelty, and we were much in demand in the clubs. We were also booked in some very strange places, among them Air Force bases and Naval bases from Newfoundland to Goose Bay, Labrador. We would do two- or three-week gigs at each base, and we made so much money that I remember coming home after one of them and paying cash for a new 1964 Pontiac Grand Prix.

There was no opportunity to spend money when we were on the bases: There were no towns to shop in, the meals were free, and we never had to buy any drinks because the guys would always be sending drinks to our table. Whenever someone bought us a round, we would look over to their table, bow our heads, and say thanks. I think this is where I really learned how to drink. My tipple was Southern Comfort. I remember our sitting there so many times with all these shots lined up in front of us. The servicemen would send me drinks while I was on-stage performing, too.

At the beginning of each night, when we would get the drinks sent to us at our table, Nancy would giggle and say, "Oh, I don't really drink." Then she would knock the shots back like a trooper while the rest of us just sipped ours. I was still sipping then.

Being an all-female band on an army base, surrounded by thousands of horny men, was quite an experience. At night there would be guards posted outside our bedrooms. At one of the bases I got something of a crush on a guy named Carlos, and flirted with him a few times. In a way, he taught me never to underestimate the military: Late one night an emboldened Carlos came climbing in through my window. His sudden arrival scared the hell out of me! I quietly chased him out, and was a bit more sensible about flirting with servicemen after that.

Sometimes we would take along a female twister from the Peppermint Lounge especially for the bases. That made *five* women for the soldiers to look at. We did lots of R&B, and I would end the show with Ray Charles's song "What'd I Say." I usually had the audience join in; "What'd I Say" was a perfect audience participation song. I would take my mike into the audience as far as the wire would allow me to go and shove it in someone's face so they could sing with me, and they usually did. The song would last at least twenty minutes and usually the place would go nuts.

We noticed there was no racial mingling between the soldiers in these places, and this caused us definite problems—aside from the fact that we just didn't like it. The white soldiers sat with the whites and the black soldiers sat with the blacks. Some of the white guys would get very upset when black guys came over to our table. Initially we never gave this a thought—it was *our* table, after all, and we were the ones who should choose who we invited to sit with us. Any caustic remarks made by the white soldiers had no effect on us other than to really piss us off. Besides, the black audiences were always the best audiences, no matter where we played: they loved our music and showed it. Whether the soldiers were black or white, we really appreciated them all.

One night in Goose Bay (where it was always daylight) we got called into the sergeant's office. He said, "You girls will start a race riot if you're not careful. Please watch who you speak to." It was obvious what he meant, and we let him know in no uncertain terms that we weren't happy about it. In fact, we were so mad and upset by it all that we simply stopped talking to *any* of the men. We just did our shows and then went to our dressing room between the sets. Really boring—and a particular drag because I loved the flirting.

● ● ● ● ● ●

I wanted a back-up singer. God knows, Margo couldn't sing—even Margo knew she couldn't sing, and used to make fun of it herself. She screeched when she tried. Ginger was no better: far from being able to sing, she could barely talk, just mumbled.

One day we got a call from someone who had spotted a female guitarist named Carol MacDonald. I'd wanted a guitarist for a while; the big attraction of this particular guitarist was that, according to our informant, she could also sing. At the time she was working in the West

Village at a little cabaret club, the Page Three. Tiny Tim was also on the bill. Ginger, Margo, and I went downtown to hear her.

When Carol came on-stage after Tiny Tim—who we thought was great—I wasn't at all impressed by the way she looked or sang. She played rhythm guitar, which was what we needed, but she looked like she came from Pennsylvania Dutch country (it turned out she did, in fact) and she had a *straight* voice. What I mean is that she sounded like Brenda Lee—not that there's anything wrong with Brenda Lee, you understand, it's just that it ain't my kinda soul. Carol also was a bit on the chubby side, though I told myself this was probably because she was wearing a flared flowery dress. But by now I wanted a guitar player so bad that I swore I could change that look somehow, even if I had to sneak speed into her drinks to starve her on the road.

The three of us spoke among ourselves while listening to her. Finally I said, "Let's talk to her and check out her personality. We also need to see if she's even interested in joining us." The truth is that I didn't care if she was interested or not: I'd decided she was going to. I was relentless in getting what I wanted.

So, after her second show, we introduced ourselves to Carol, and Carol, in turn, introduced us to her friend LillyMae, also from Pennsylvania. I had a feeling they were gay. I found out I was right, but they weren't a couple: just close friends.

Back then—remember, this was the 1960s—I was very sensitive about any risk of Goldie and the Gingerbreads being labeled a "lezzy group." My concern had nothing to do with anyone actually *being* gay—I had no problem with that—it was just that I didn't want anything to stand in the way of success for the band, and I knew all it would take was one gay band member coming out of the closet for us all to be *branded* . . . and that would be bad for business. After all, this was long before being out was in. The idea was to get guys to fantasize about sleeping with the band; they weren't going to dream those dreams—well, probably not—if they thought we were all lesbians. In the 1960s the club owners and managers in New York City all knew each other; half the clubs were owned by the same people. It was a tight little Italian clique. I wanted to make musical history, not become history. If we got a reputation for being a "lezzy group" our bookings would dry up, and it could be the end of us.

Let me stress the point. This was fifteen years before Studio 54. "Ride Sally Ride" was a lyric in an R&B Song, not an astronaut in a Space Shuttle. There were no women in space yet—hell, I'm surprised we could vote. It was harder for women to do anything, especially something as notorious as playing instruments. We were supposed to be at home making babies, not music. The early 1960s was no time for anyone to come out of the closet, however much we might now think of it as an era of social freedom and revolution. It was commonplace for the club managers to call gays things like "that homo cocksucker" and "that pussy-eating lezzy"; they didn't think twice about it. Society had not yet accepted lesbians. There were some small gay movements starting but even so, unfortunately, homosexuality was still taboo. I couldn't take chances with the future of the band. I wasn't ready to make some kind of political stand; all I wanted to do was sing.

Carol's lesbianism aside, we were anxious to have her join us. We raved to her about the trip to Europe we'd just done with Chubby Checker, and told her how successful we'd been there. I showed off my leather pants as an example of the leather coats and shoes we'd bought, trying to convince her that she too could have all this if she joined us. I came on very strong.

But Carol was iffy. As she spoke to us she looked uncomfortable in that flowery dress she was wearing, and at one point she actually said, "I hate dresses." I kept quiet about the stage costume we were wearing then—gold lamé pants or fringe dresses—and thought: *not as much as you'll hate what you're about to wear if you join this group*. In the end she rather reluctantly agreed to come by the club we were playing to check us out. We were going to be performing at the Headliner Lounge on West Forty-fourth Street for the next two weeks.

The night Carol and LillyMae came to see us, Carol looked like a different person. Her blonde slick hair was combed back, she had on jeans and a white shirt, and she looked pretty butch. She brought her guitar.

While we were playing I could see she was in absolute awe of us—she had this big goofy grin. You could tell we had our guitar player on board. We asked her up on stage to sit in with us, with Margo calling out the chords to her during the songs, and as soon as she started to play . . . well, it was unbelievable. It was as though she had worked with us forever—she fit like a glove.

We went into two weeks of rehearsals with our new band member. Carol asked on at least a weekly basis if it was really necessary to wear these tight lamé pants, and each time I'd reply, "Yes. What would you like to wear—a bomber outfit? We're a female band. We need to look sexy."

A potentially more serious problem arose when she expressed a desire to sing lead on some of our songs. I told her she could sing lead sometimes—but only sometimes. I was the lead singer of this band, and I was going to remain so. I was gentle with her, though, because I knew this was a sore spot for her and it was definitely a sore spot for me; after all, she was a lead singer herself.

Carol had a persuasive, strong personality, almost threatening at times, and it made me wonder if she would be a problem in the future. She played wonderful rhythm guitar, though, and she knew her harmonies. She also had a great sense of humor, just like Margo, and we had really good times when we were all together, which was pretty much twenty-four hours a day. Ginger stayed herself, of course—"quiet, intense Ginger." I loved her. I could not have done this without her. She was my soul sister, my partner.

From the very beginning of Goldie and the Gingerbreads, it was fun to watch people's reactions when we pulled up to a club we'd never played before, especially when we traveled out of the New York City area to places where no one knew anything about the band. We would see the owners or managers of these bars getting more and more nonplussed as it dawned on them that we really were an all-female band. Most of these guys were Italian, and they never knew how to act around us. When they saw us dragging in our equipment, they'd blurt out stupid things like, "Uuhhh, did youse eat? Wanna have some pasta? Can we get youse anyt'ing?"

At the time we all looked like Annette Funicello after a rough one-nighter, except Ginger, who, carrying her trap cases and her drum equipment, always looked fresh and pretty. For some reason, carrying our own equipment into the joint made the men really nervous and awkward. And, boy, did we love to goof on them. Sometimes when we'd be setting up our equipment I'd whisper to the girls, "Let's do *the heart attack sound check.*" This was the cue for us to do a phony sound check with all of us playing in different keys at the same time. Of course, the result was the most god-awful noise. The guys would usually stop whatever they were doing and exchange horrified looks. We could come to a stop and speak to each other as if we were satisfied with how we'd sounded, then say to the guys: "Okay, what time do you want us to start playing tonight?"

One guy really lost it. "Deeze broads can't play!" he screamed. "Geez, deeze broads can't play tonight! Call the fuckin' agent!" Another club owner was smoking a huge cigar when we started our heart-attack sound check; he let his cigar fall to the ground and started cursing loudly in Italian, yelling that he'd close the joint down rather than let us perform there.

I loved to do this. These guys didn't know whether to let us go onstage or give us money *not* to play—or just to shoot us.

For hours after our "sound check," while the club was filling up with patrons, the bar managers/owners would be getting more nervous by the second, sweating bullets. Then, when we would get on-stage and start to play—*really* play—I would look down from the stage at a bunch of frowning, sweating men and see them suddenly smile in relief. Sometimes they would stare at us in total incredulity, and I could tell they were saying, "What the fu'?" and then, right afterwards, they'd fall in love with the band and our music.

We worked New York City and the northern states quite a lot, but we refused to work the southern states. This aggravated our agents, who said it lost us lots of gigs and money, but we insisted we didn't want to work for segregated audiences. Our friends in the group The Rascals felt the same way. We were happy working around the northern towns and Canada.

But even so we couldn't escape the whole race business entirely. Once we were introduced to a very important program director of a major black station. We started to talk to him and I asked him why he didn't play our records. He told me, "You women are white. We play music *by* blacks *for* blacks." Meanwhile, of course, we had white program directors saying to us, "You're too black-sounding for white stations." It was a bit of a dilemma.

Our first gig with Carol was one of the Canadian ones. As soon as we got there she started to come on to me—coy and flirty, relentless. I kept smiling and flirting back at her, but refusing. She said things like "What are you afraid of?" and "Don't knock it till you try it" and "What's the matter? Think you'll like it?" So one night I figured, "What the hell? I'll try makin' it with a woman." So we made it. I had my one-nighter with a woman. But I found it really wasn't my thing—although, drunk and on a dare, *anything* could be "my thing."

● ● ● ● ● ●

When working in New York City, we would finish playing at about four a.m. and head uptown for breakfast to a place called Ham 'N Eggs, on the corner of Fifty-second Street and Broadway, that was open twenty-four hours a day. It was always packed with music people; at four a.m. you would meet other performers as well as radio disk jockeys. Ham 'N Eggs was across the street from the Brill Building, which we called the Music Building because anyone who was anyone in the music business worked there—all the managers, agents, and publishers under that one roof. (We, too, were in and out of the Brill Building on almost a daily basis, seeing our managers, agents, or publishers.) The Brill even had recording studios.

Sitting in Ham 'N Eggs, I would watch a steady progression of sidewalk drug addicts. I called them "nodding junkies" because their heads would slowly slump down, almost hitting the ground, then they'd wake up just enough to jerk back upright. For drug money, these guys would sell their music to producers and publishers right there on the sidewalk in front of Ham 'N Eggs. The junkies knew that's where the music people hung out and they could make a few bucks for the songs. Whenever you hear a hit from the 1960s you can never be sure who really wrote it, because anyone who bought a nodding junkie's song would claim the credit for writing it.

* * * * * *

When we had out-of-town gigs, I was always the designated driver. On one occasion we had a gig at a ski resort that was a ten-hour drive away, with a good deal of the trip driven on the hypnotizingly boring Ohio Turnpike. We always left at night, so to stay awake I would take some speed. Soon I was pretty buzzed. We would sing, do three-part harmonies, and learn new songs. We always laughed a lot. Then the other girls would usually fall asleep while I drove.

On this particular trip we'd been about nine hours on the road when the sun began to come up. The past three hours I'd been driving at a steady ninety miles per hour. I'd been following a truck for quite a while, so when it slowed down considerably I swung into the left-hand lane to pass. What I didn't know was that the truck I'd been behind had slowed because it, in turn, had gotten stuck behind *another*, even slower truck. The driver of "my" truck pulled into the passing lane, right in front of me. Because I was in a trance—perhaps I thought the brakes had locked—I couldn't get the car to slow down. We were going to crash into the back of him. I pulled hard to the left, and we went slamming down into the median, a deep gully that separated the highway. We hit wet grass on an angle, sliding fast. Out of the passenger window I could see us passing the truck; we would certainly have hit it if I hadn't pulled out.

Then I looked up and saw a concrete bridge just ahead. I screamed to the girls to wake up: "Jump! Jump!" And that's what I did myself: I opened the door and leapt out onto the median. Rolling down the hill, I saw the car wheels pass my face.

Inside the car, Ginger woke up, swung her foot over the middle hump of the car and hit the brakes. Margo hurled the upper half of her body forward from the back seat and grabbed the steering wheel. The car came to a stop, and the girls jumped out and ran over to me.

They didn't really know what had happened. They'd been sound asleep and then all of a sudden I'd started shouting, "Jump! Jump!" and had disappeared out of the car.

Ginger screamed, "Goldie, are you all right?"

Margo said, "What happened?"

Carol added, "You stupid fuck. You coulda killed us."

"Why didn't you jump?" I asked them. I think I had control issues even back then.

The police arrived soon after. I stood there shaking all over while the girls described what had happened. I didn't want to get into a car again, much less drive it, but the cop said, "If you don't do it now you'll never drive again." Good advice. Then he added: "You need to go to the hospital."

He was right. Shaking and nervous, I drove the girls to the hospital. After my checkup, the E.R. physician told me, "You don't need a doctor. You need a shrink. No one jumps out of a car doing sixty miles an hour. You ought to be thankful you came away without a scratch."

After that, I never really enjoyed driving.

Still enjoyed speed, though.

● ● ● ● ● ●

It seemed to me the band was getting to be some kind of bait for the freaks to come out of their homes. One time, as we played at yet another Italian-owned club, Ungano's, on Seventieth Street off Broadway, a short, chubby girl walked in surrounded by her friends. She was probably in her teens. I could tell right away these were Italian girls; they had what you could call the Mott Street look. (Mott Street is in the part of Manhattan called Little Italy.)

The girls sat very close to the stage and stared at us with their mouths open as if they were amazed the whole time we performed. The chubby one gaped at me so hard while I was singing that I began to wonder if she was counting my teeth. When we took our break she came over to our table at the side of the stage, stuck out her hand to shake with me, and introduced herself.

"My name is Jo Jo," she said. (I'm changing the names to protect the innocent—me.) "Youse are so fucking good! Youse wanna drink?"

Our first groupies! A menagerie of Italian closet lesbian groupies! They were so macho-looking you just knew that some of them had to be carrying weapons. I had never heard any girl talk like Jo Jo; she sounded like one of the "wise guys" in a mob movie.

I soon found out that Jo Jo's father was indeed a well connected, big-name mobster, and that she had a few brothers who also worked in the "family business." One of those brothers was found shot in the head in the trunk of a car at the corner of Mulberry and Mott Streets. This was, obviously, a rough family. And a God-fearing family—they had so many crosses around their necks, it's a wonder they didn't fall over.

Jo Jo and her entourage started to show up at all of our New York City gigs—wherever we performed, there they'd be. And they *always* had a good table. Our bookings were generally for three weeks at a time, six days a week. We usually played at the Wagon Wheel or the Peppermint Lounge, both on Forty-fifth Street, but we also did the Headliner, and, any time a new Italian-owned club opened in New York, we would perform there, too.

I'd been worried about the number of cigarettes I'd been smoking, and so, as a way of trying to cut down, I'd started to use little cigars called "Hav-A-Tampas." The next thing I knew, the cigars had become the latest craze among the Gingerbreads. It wasn't just that the whole group was smoking them, our Italian fan club was also. It was something to see—and smell.

One night in the summer of 1964 we were playing Ungano's when one of Jo Jo's surviving brothers came into the club with his crew. A really tough guy, he just stood in a corner staring at us—no smile, no reaction, no expression except the one that looked like he was thinking, "I could kill youse if I wanted."

I wondered if he thought I was responsible for Jo Jo smoking cigars, staying out late, and cutting her hair really short. After our show, as I was walking off the stage to my table, the tough guy waved me over. I pointed to myself as if to say, "Me?" and he mouthed, "Yes."

Shit! Here we go! I thought.

When I got to his table, everyone with him stood up, and they stayed up until I sat down.

"Wanna drink or something?" he asked.

"Southern Comfort," I answered.

"I'm Sal. Youse are pretty good for broads."

In those days I took that as a compliment. I smiled.

"Youse looking for management?" Sal asked.

Wow, perfect, I thought to myself. *With the mob managing us, we could make loads of money and be protected too.*

"No, actually, we're not," I said nonetheless.

"Ya know, my father, Bernie B., he's sort of in the entertainment field, but he wants to get more into it," Sal said. "Ya ever hear of Bernie B.?"

"No," I answered, wondering what "sort of" meant.

"Look, here's a telephone numba," Sal went on. "Bernie B. knows about youse, we seen ya around. He'll be waitin' fa ya call."

I took the piece of paper from him and got up to leave. Again, as I stood the guys stood as well. *What gentlemen,* I thought. Then I saw Sal give Jo Jo a look, and she began moving really fast—she said goodnight to us and left. You could see she was frightened of her brother.

I told Ginger what had happened and said I was going to give Bernie B. a call and make an appointment; I wanted her to come with me. The next day we went to see him in his office in the Brill Building at 1619 Broadway. He told us he had an associate, Sonny Z., who would tend to everything for us. Bernie B. himself would be more of a silent partner, he said. He spoke of Las Vegas and record contracts, and Ginger and I were thrilled.

We met our new "manager," Sonny, a couple of days later when he showed up at a gig we were playing at the Headliner Lounge. He was surrounded by men wearing hats, all of whom seemed likewise to be called "Sonny"—or maybe that's just the way I remember it.

Over the next few months we met all of the "wise guys." Sonny was proud of us, and brought them to our shows, especially at the Wagon Wheel, so he could show off "his" girl band. From the stage I could see the waiters falling all over Sonny and his friends like they were gods. The "wise guys" left great tips, but I think Sonny also had some ownership in a few of these clubs, like the Wagon Wheel, the Headliner Lounge, and the Peppermint Lounge.

Every night Sonny was at one of our performances I dedicated a number to him. "This one's for you," I'd say, pointing at him without saying his name. He would look proud as a peacock—an Italian peacock.

While Sonny was our "manager," Goldie and the Gingerbreads also had an agent, Associated Booking (A.B.C.)—a big booking agency headed by a guy named Joe Glazer. Joe loved the group. We were his little darlings, and he booked lots of gigs for us. Eventually he had to give the booking part of the agency over to his sons, because in those days you couldn't manage and be an agent for the same acts. He managed Billie Holiday and also some heavyweight boxers. He was a wonderful person with a lot of heart.

Being managed by the mob did have its downsides, though—like the time we drove up to Canada for a three-week gig. Neither Joe nor Sonny had thought about work permits, and we didn't know we needed them. When we got to the Canadian border the first thing we were asked was: "Are you here on vacation or for work?"

"Work," we answered. What else could we say? We had a U-Haul trailer behind us filled with our equipment. Since we couldn't produce the work permits we didn't have, the border patrol wouldn't let us cross into Canada.

It was eight o'clock at night and I'd been driving (and speeding, not in the miles-per-hour sense) for two days. I was tired and a mess. There we were, stuck at the border, five girls cursing, yelling, and getting nowhere.

I had to call Sonny.

"Hi, Sonny. It's Goldie."

"DON'T TALK MY NAME!" he yelled.

"Wha . . .?"

"DON'T TALK MY NAME ON THE PHONE!"

I couldn't believe this. "Sonny?"

"DON'T TALK MY NAME!"

I started to say "What?" again but he yelled, "Hang up and call me back in one hour. And DON'T TALK MY NAME!"

Not having the patience to wait an hour, I decided to call Joe Glazer at home. (He liked Goldie and the Gingerbreads enough that he'd given us his home number.) When I told him our problem he started cursing his son-in-law, who was working on our gigs for A.B.C. Entertainment, and told me it was all *his* fault. After Joe had made some calls, we were allowed into Canada. I did not call Sonny back that night.

* * * * * * *

One night, about a year after Carol had joined us, we were back at the Headliner Lounge when I noticed the girls were acting weird toward me. They would stop talking every time I walked into the dressing room, and they were sort of skirting around me, whispering. Nancy, in particular, wouldn't look at me. None of the girls were making the usual jokes. It started to drive me nuts. Obviously, something was up.

Finally, in our dressing room, Margo and Ginger turned to me and told me to sit down. They had something important to tell me.

Oh-oh, what the fuck is it now? I thought.

"Have you noticed that Nancy is acting funny?" Ginger asked.

Margo piped up. "And that she's been sick a lot, and crying between songs?"

They were taking it in turns to prepare me.

"Well, come to think of it, yes," I said. "She's been looking kind of green . . . and acting dumber than usual."

Then came the bombshell. "Nancy is pregnant."

"What?" I screamed, leaping off my chair. "What did you just tell me? Oh my God! Why, why, why?"

All I was thinking about was Goldie and the Gingerbreads' future. We were supposed to play Vegas in a few months; it was a very big deal.

"How are we going to go to Vegas?" I yelled. "And what am I going to tell Sonny?"

I tried taking several deep breaths.

Margo was—as usual—the one who managed to calm me down. "We'll get there," she kept saying. "We'll play Vegas."

I tried to figure out how to cope with the situation. I knew there had to be some way of sorting this out—after all, we were managed by the mob.

"Abortion!" I said. "We'll tell Sonny, and he'll take care of it. But we have to get the money from somewhere." Abortions were still illegal in those days, of course—an added problem.

Nancy had been waiting outside our dressing room, and now the girls told her to come in. At first I just stared at Nancy, but then I couldn't control myself anymore.

"How could you do this?" I shouted. "We're going to Vegas soon! Look what you did! Look what you went and did!"—pointing to her stomach. "Why, why, *why*? How *could* you? How could you go and get pregnant?" All of a sudden I was my Jewish mother.

"I was so-o-o-o-o lonely," she said in her high-pitched voice.

"Lonely? Lonely!" I yelled. I couldn't believe what I was hearing. "Why didn't you play with yourself, or call *me*, or go to a movie, or go out and dance, or practice the fucking bass?"

But all Nancy could keep saying was, "I was so-o-o-o-o lonely!"

When I'd calmed down a little I managed to stutter, "Wh-wh-wh-who did this to us? Who *was* the fuck?"

"The organ player from the other band," she mumbled.

In those days, Goldie and the Gingerbreads would alternate sets with another group. We played forty minutes, they played forty minutes, and so on until four o'clock in the morning. The other band was on-stage while we were having this discussion in our dressing room in the basement.

"Get upstairs right now," I said to her. "Go over and say to him, 'I'm pregnant and I want money for an abortion!'"

"While they're playing, Goldie?" she moaned.

"When else are you gonna tell him? While he's getting off the stage and you're getting on? Yes, *now!*"

I didn't think she would take me at my word. I was not so rational at that moment.

We followed her upstairs and watched as she wiggled her way onto the stage and between the musicians. She bent down and started talking into the guy's ear, and as she did so his playing got all screwed up—you could hear the organ getting slower and slower, and he started hitting wrong chords. Then he turned to talk into *her* ear, and after about three minutes she shimmied off-stage and we all followed her downstairs again.

"Well, what did he say?" I asked.

"He can't," Nancy answered sadly. "He's paying off his organ."

This comment brought total silence. Disbelief. Ginger, Margo, and I looked at each other for quite a while, half-stunned, and then we all burst out laughing at the same time. Poor Nancy just stood there looking green, obviously with no idea what we were laughing at. As usual with Nancy, the lights were on, but no one was home.

"You tell him," I said at last, "that if he doesn't take care of this little problem he won't have any organ to pay off—and I don't mean the one he's playing right now."

To our astonishment she marched right upstairs—the rest of us in tow again—and told him exactly what I'd said. He looked like he'd seen a ghost. As it turned out in the end, however, the threat didn't scare him enough to make him pay for the abortion; we never did manage to get the money out of him.

Sonny set up Nancy's abortion. The procedure was to be performed by a doctor on Park Avenue early in the morning, before his regular office hours began. "Be real careful and nice wit dis guy," Sonny warned me. "It's a favor he owes me. Don't talk too much."

The morning of Nancy's appointment, I got up at four-thirty so I could give her a lift from the hotel she was staying in to the doctor's office. At the time, I was staying back with my parents in Brooklyn. As I was making coffee, Mom appeared in the kitchen. She took one look at me and was completely horrified. With a kerchief on my head and no makeup, I must have looked like a refugee again.

"Oy!" she yelled at me. "Vere are you goink! Vy you look so bad?"

I told her I had a rehearsal. I still wonder if Mom really believed all the stories I used to tell her back then.

I got to Nancy's hotel at six a.m. It was a good time in New York City—no traffic yet. There she was, the French Indian, all made up and dressed to dazzle, her hair piled high in her usual upsweep. She looked like a lost hooker.

"What the fuck are *you* doing all made up?" I asked her.

"I don't look good without makeup," she whimpered.

"Nancy, you're not *supposed* to look good this morning," I hissed back. "Get in the car. We're gonna be late."

We arrived at the doctor's office, and he opened the door. He looked at me, then at Nancy, then at me again, and waved for me to come in.

"It's not me, it's her," I said, pointing at Nancy.

He stared at her for a long time and then, shaking his head, led her off to a room. I tried to get comfortable in the waiting area. My body was still in shock from having had only two hours' sleep.

Just five minutes later the doctor and Nancy came back out. All I heard him say was, "Good luck! Goodbye!" in a very loud voice. Then he sort of shooed us outside.

On the pavement, I turned and asked Nancy, as nicely as I could, "What the fuck happened?"

"I don't understand, and I don't really know," she whined.

"What did you say to him?" I asked, trying to stay calm but not succeeding.

"Well," she replied, "he asked if anyone else knew I was here besides you. So I said, 'Oh, not *too* many people. There's Sonny, Margo, Ginger, Frank, Ed, my mom, our agent, and the guy who got me pregnant.' And that's when he took me by the arm and led me out."

I sat on the curb and put my face in my hands. So that was that. Nancy was going to have to leave Goldie and the Gingerbreads. She would have this organ player's baby. There went our Thunder Thumb. *Here we go again,* I thought. *More auditions to look forward to, in search of another fucking bass player!*

Oh shit.

* * * * * *

Ginger and I soon knew we were going to have to shed our mob connections. Sonny wasn't really doing anything for us. Scared to death, we went to their office and told them we wanted out.

I will always remember that last conversation with Sonny and Sal B.

"If youse weren't broads, youse would be in a lotta trouble right now."

"Yeah," added Sal. "Some heads would be broken. Go on, get outta here."

Then Sonny said, "All youse broads are the same. 'Buy me,' 'Give me,' 'Get me.'"

Ginger and I left, looking down at our feet as if we were kids and our parents had been scolding us. We did our best to look chastened. As soon as we got out the door, though, we started laughing, and we giggled all the way to the car, even though we knew this could have been really bad.

Whew! Thank God that was over. A few months later Ginger confessed to me she was very nervous about Sonny at that time. He'd apparently come on to her "strongly." That made me sick.

* * * * * *

I met Adrian Barber at Joey Dee's Starlighter Lounge (which used to be the Headliner Lounge) on 48th Street in the fall of 1964. Adrian was an electronic genius. He built sound systems for clubs. The bar, set up like the Peppermint Lounge and the Wagon Wheel Lounge, was at street level, and had a neon sign in the window. Inside, it was the same, too: full of dancers and just plain craziness, and a stage by the bar where voyeurs stood staring at the fringed girls while the music blared.

Adrian was a skinny, gaunt guy with that English "I've never been in the sun, which is why I'm so yellow" appearance. I thought he was good looking, with his square-chiseled jaw and high cheekbones (*à la* Clint Eastwood), and I was anyway a sucker for guys who looked as if they hadn't had a square meal for a year. He smelled like all the musicians in Germany, though, which was a bit of a drawback. The first time I went to his place I knew why he stank so badly—he had no shower! The bathroom had just a washbowl, and his toilet was in the hallway. It was like a boarding house in Manhattan.

He worked on sound systems, and had wires all over the place. Much later he custom-built the multi-recording board for the Atlantic Records recording studios. At the time I knew him he did too many pills. Amphetamines made him look like a deer blinded by the headlights. He stared a lot.

About four times, either because I was horny or I'd had a fight with my mother, I went to his apartment (it was a way of getting back at her), but then I tried to cut the relationship off. By his reaction, you'd have thought we'd been together thirty years rather than a few weeks.

At the time, Goldie and the Gingerbreads were performing at the Wagon Wheel. We were without a bass player, but that was okay because Margo could churn out the bass lines on the organ with her fabulous feet—and her big smile to go with them! (There were more nodding junkies in that club than customers—it felt like the emergency room at St. Claire's Hospital in Hell's Kitchen. I wondered why our music was putting so many customers to sleep until I found out they were junkies.) While performing one night I noticed skinny, pale-faced Adrian walking very slowly towards the back of the room. He was directly in front of me, leaning against the back wall. I stared at him as I sang, and he stared right back, never taking his eyes off me. He reminded me of Beaumont, Ginger's monkey. Adrian kept up that blank stare, watching my every move, all the while walking around in front of the stage and down the side of the room. And he had his hand tucked under his jacket, in the upper left corner. As I sang this beautiful Mary Wells soul ballad, "Little Boy," I had a horrible thought: *He has a gun and he's going to shoot me!*

Continuing with the song—"Little boy, what have you done to me?"—I ran around behind Carol and tried to hide. When she saw him, too, she turned and ran behind me. We started behaving like something out of a Three Stooges movie: we kept moving around the stage as Adrian stared at us, his hand still in his pocket.

I shortened the set and, when I got off-stage, went looking for our bouncer, Frankie Knee. (Frankie had a trick knee from a bullet wound, which is why we called him that.) I found him in the kitchen and told him we needed help, now! But when we came out of the kitchen we found Adrian had disappeared.

I knew where he worked—at Joey Dee's—and so all of us, including Frankie Knee, went over there on our break and spoke to one of the owners who'd hired Adrian. They knew us, of course. I explained to them that I was scared and this was serious, and they promised they'd speak to him and make sure that in the future he stayed away from the Wagon Wheel and me.

At this time, I was still living in Brooklyn with my parents, my sister Helen (by now divorced from Jack India) and her three kids. It would have been crazy for me to have kept my own apartment, because the group was on the road so much. My parents' house was basically a storage place for me.

Adrian called me there at midnight one night when I was off work. I told him I was going to hang up on him and I didn't want to talk to him or see him. He said he was going to come to Brooklyn and burn the house down. The threat scared the hell out of me; I knew he was nuts, and I believed he might do exactly as he said.

What was I to do? First I called Ginger, who said she'd come right over. Waiting for her, I thought a bit, then decided I had to wake the family and let them know what was going on. Ordinarily, I would never have told my father about that phone call, but in this case my family and their home were being threatened. What if Adrian did come to burn the place down? What about my sister and her three babies? I had to tell her, too.

Helen was dating a guy called Doc then. (He later became my brother-in-law. I'd introduced them.) He was a Boy Scout leader. When she called him he came running over dressed in his Boy Scout outfit. He looked ridiculous in his Boy Scout shorts. I wondered, *What are you planning to do—scare him with your shorts? Pull out marshmallows when he starts the fire?* I couldn't hold back a laugh. Here we had a dirty English maniac who could even be a killer—a guy once managed by the mob, who worked in mob-owned clubs—and Doc was coming to our rescue looking like a giant Cub Scout.

Before I knew it, it was three a.m.. The doorbell rang. Adrian was there. Son of a bitch, he'd really come to the house.

Well, you didn't mess with my father. Dad had been in the Russian and Polish Underground and had been a boxer in his younger days. He was pretty tough.

When Dad opened the door, Adrian came in looking whiter and pastier than ever.

My mother's first words? "You vant breakfast? You look hungry."

I couldn't believe it. She was going to feed the guy who wanted to kill us all.

Adrian said, "That would be nice."

I must have stood there with my mouth open for about two hours. They all sat at the table while Adrian ate eggs and drank coffee. As he did so, my father laid down the law to him, "If you ever come around Goldie or our home again, you vill not make it to the next day." He repeated this over and over.

Adrian, still eating, kept nodding his head in response. "Yes, okay, I understand."

And all the while Boy Scout Doc sat there and repeated what my father said, as if he were an interpreter.

"Don't go near Goldie or mine house again."

"Don't go near Goldie or the house again," Doc echoed.

"I knew punks like you in mine old days."

"He knows punks like you," came the echo.

"More coffee?" That was Mom.

"I vill keeeel you if you ever come here again."

"He will kill you if you come here again."

It was truly a nerve-racking night—one I will never forget. After Adrian had finished his meal my father grabbed him by the scruff of his neck, took him to the door, and said, "Now go home and don't come here again, you understand?"

"Yes," said Adrian humbly. He looked at me and left. I did not see him ever again.

Later, I wondered if maybe he only came over to the house because he was hungry . . .

• • • • • •

It's a funny thing, but sometimes it seemed every other guy who met us wanted to be our protector.

Lots of times, while taking a break from playing at the Wagon Wheel, we would go next door to the coffee shop on Forty-fifth. We always sat at the same booth, talking to the go-go girls and others from the club. I had my eyes on the guys, of course, but unfortunately most of the time they were really nothing special—just a mix of junkies and hustlers. Next to the coffee shop was a hotel where hookers hooked and dopers doped.

We had an over-protective junkie groupie whom we nicknamed "Jimmy-No-Teeth." One time I invited this good-looking guy to sit with me, and we talked and drank coffee together. He was facing the window onto the street, and after a while he noticed Jimmy-No-Teeth standing there glaring at him through the glass. This vision must have scared him, because mid-sentence he abruptly got up and went.

Goldie and the Gingerbreads at rehearsal, 1967.

A few minutes later, I left the coffee shop and had a few words with Jimmy-No-Teeth. "Hey," he said. "Want me to run after that guy and beat the shit outta him? He looked like he wuz bothering you."

"Jimmy, stop fucking up my dates," I replied wearily.

● ● ● ● ● ●

By 1964 we'd become the talk of New York City and the darlings of the jet set, and we were really pulling in the crowds. I had the Gingerbreads in new costumes: stunning, tight, black velvet skirts with a long slit up the left leg all the way to the panty line, silver-blue halter tops, and fishnet stockings. My own costume was always a little different—same theme but, where the girls' skirts were black, mine was gold lamé. Also, I didn't wear a bra. That's nothing now, but in 1964 going braless was pretty radical. I wanted the audience to drool for us. I wanted men *and* women to want us.

It worked. We packed the clubs. Everyone came to see Goldie and the Gingerbreads.

One night while we were performing at the Peppermint Lounge, Ahmet Ertegun of Atlantic Records was in the audience. He just fell in love with us, and pretty soon we were signed to Atlantic.

Ahmet had the best ears in the business. When we recorded in the studio at Atlantic he gave us the freedom to be ourselves. I discovered then that I had the ability to produce as well as perform. We recorded some singles at the Atlantic studios—"Sailor Boy" and a few others—and had a great session. Ahmet says today that some of our best-recorded songs are in his vault, and that might be true. It was really *us* in there—no outside influence because there weren't any producers.

Ahmet was always a big part of the New York social scene, and he'd boast about us, describing Goldie and the Gingerbreads as his "prize find." He seemed so proud of us. We were a great band, not just the only female rock band in town at the time, and we were signed to his label. Ahmet's praise brought us to the attention of a whole new public.

Jerry Shatzberg, a well known photographer, turned out to hear us at the Wagon Wheel. After we'd come off-stage, he asked us if we'd perform at a private birthday party he was going to hold for the model and celebrity Baby Jane Holzer in his large duplex at 333 Park

Avenue South. Baby Jane was mentioned in all the society columns of the day. Oh, added Jerry, and the Rolling Stones would be there. The money he offered was great, too. Of course we accepted the gig. The party was called the "Mods and Rockers Ball," and was sure to be the biggest social event in New York City that year.

As always, we set up our own equipment when we got there. It was what we were used to doing, but as you can imagine we found it hard to look like ladies while dragging equipment. The setting up completed, we got into our costumes and started to play.

Soon a crowd gathered in front of us. Baby Jane and Jerry were always hanging out with people like Andy Warhol, Diana Freeland (editor of *Vogue*) and David Bailey (who photographed models like Jean Shrimpton). Anyone who was anyone was at that party. There were blondes with boas, blondes with bangs, blondes with beehives and, oh yes, Goldie and the Gingerbreads, covered in tight lamé from stretch pants to halter-tops.

We performed our usual popular cover songs, such as "Baby Baby Where Did Our Love Go?" (always our most requested number). The crowd danced, and from where I stood on stage the scene looked like something from a wild Fellini movie. The clothes were all outrageous. Some people had purple hair, others had sparkles splashed on their faces. Some wore masks and had tiaras on their heads. Fingers, earlobes, and wrists glittered with diamonds.

As the night wore on and the champagne flowed, the dancing became wilder and the floors started shaking—I thought we would wind up in the apartment below. Everyone there loved Goldie and the Gingerbreads.

Tom Wolfe wrote about that party in *The Kandy-Kolored Tangerine-Flake Streamline Baby,* and said of Goldie and the Gingerbreads: "Goldie, the leader, is a young girl with a husky voice and nice kind of slightly thick—you know—glorious sort of *East End* features, only she is from New York—ah, the delicacy of minor grossness, unabashed. . . . Goldie and the Gingerbreads are on a stand at one end of the studio, all electric, electric guitars, electric bass, drums, loudspeakers, and a couple of spotlights exploding off the gold lamé."

The evening certainly was a success. Although the Stones were somewhere in that duplex, we did not actually see them, but later we were told they saw us and went nuts over us. The socialites knew they were at the best party of the year. We would have played all night, but around four a.m. we were asked to pull the plug, so we ended our show, changed back into our jeans, and quickly packed up our equipment. We were asked out to breakfast at the "in" after-hours restaurant, The Brasserie, on Fifty-third between Park and Lexington. Baby Jane and Jerry and a few others joined our table.

All in all, it was a party no one would ever forget—or ever stop talking about.

CHAPTER SIX
Goldie and the Gingerbreads Take Europe by Storm

PERFORMANCES by Goldie and the Gingerbreads were always loud and raucous. They were made more so by the comedic flair I found I had: I could make audiences laugh. And not just audiences: There were times Margo couldn't play the organ properly because she was laughing so hard. We had some crazy people in our audiences too—one night someone offered me and Carol $1,000 to go home with him and have sex in a menage à trois. Carol was up for it, she said, but my response was: "No way!" I was into romance and physical attraction. (Today, on the other hand, I'd take the cash!)

When we played at the Wagon Wheel there were lines around the block. We were the toast of the town and I wanted it to stay that way. I was very ambitious, and pushed us hard. Mixing my metaphors, I hoped the toast wouldn't get burned out. To cope with the pressure, I kept taking uppers. (Everyone called the capsules Green Men because of their color. Sometimes, if supplies ran short, we would cut them in half to make sure there were enough for the whole group. It was very hard doing six shows a night.) At the end of a night of performing, I would be speeding my ass off, and I had to have a few drinks to get myself down.

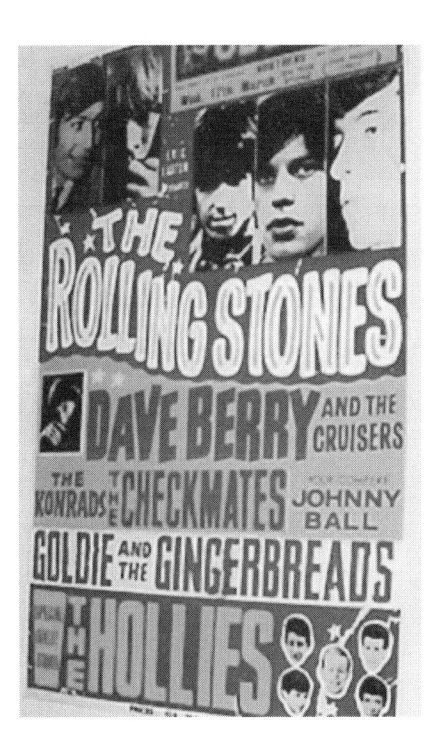

Goldie and the Gingerbreads' first tour of Europe.

The pressure of dealing with the business end at the same time as keeping everyone happy took its toll on me. I began to lose it, and at one point I think I had a nervous breakdown. I knew something was wrong one day. My mother had forgotten to put salt on the table. I screamed and cried, "You know I love salt!" then started to break the furniture in her kitchen, still yelling, "I love salt!" She just stared at me and got scared. Later I bought her new kitchen furniture.

Adding the stress of going on a long and complicated tour might have seemed the worst possible thing I could do . . .

✱ ✱ ✱ ✱ ✱ ✱

One night in 1964 at the Wagon Wheel we were in the middle of a loud raucous gospel song called "I Can't Stand It" (originally recorded by the Soul Sisters) when two of the Animals—Eric Burdon and Hilton Valentine—plus their manager, Mike Jeffries, came into the club. Their single "The House of the Rising Sun" was a big hit at the time. The three guys stood out from the rest of the audience because they dressed differently. Mike Jeffries in particular appeared very refined in his pinstripe suit—a sort of brittle, very uptight look. (Brittle/British—the two words could be related.) They sat down at a table right in front of the stage, stared at us, and started talking and laughing.

The guitarist, Hilton Valentine, stared at me the whole time, and I stared right back at him. *Cute*, I thought. I was singing the Sam and Dave song "Hold On, I'm Comin'." We finished the set and the audience wanted more, as usual. As an encore we sang "Goldie and the Gingerbreads, Yeah," based on the tune of "Mashed Potatoes, Yeah." (I did that song to introduce everyone in the band and announce the next act. It became our signature piece. Not infrequently we would be walking down a New York street when somebody would sing out, "Hey, Goldie and the Gingerbreads, Yeah!")

Finally we got off-stage. I felt a tug at my arm.

"Excuse me," said Mike Jeffries in his English accent. "Could we talk to you?"

I looked at the three of them and said, "Yeah, sure."

He pulled out a seat and I sat, all sweaty and still dressed in my glitter. He introduced himself, and then asked, "Have you heard of the Animals?"

"Do I look like I just got out of prison? Of course I've heard of them." I had that *fuck you* attitude.

"Well, this is Eric Burdon, this is Hilton Valentine, and I'm Mike Jeffries, their manager."

I said, "Really?"

"We thought we were hearing a black group," said Eric. "That's what it sounded like from the street. That's why we came in." He added, "I could hear that tambourine all the way from Broadway."

They went on to tell me they were performing at the theater down the block; they'd been on a break and had decided to stroll down Forty-fifth to check out the popular Peppermint Lounge. Eric said, "But then I heard that soulful voice and an organ. We never expected to find an all-woman band in here. We think the U.K. would love you."

I called the girls over to introduce them, and we all sat together. Hilton and I began flirting. I already knew I was going to make it with him; it was just a matter of where and when.

Mike was trying to dazzle us with descriptions of how wonderful it would be if we went over to the U.K. He told us that he and the well known rock entrepreneur and producer Mickie Most (his partner at the time) would manage us and the Animals would produce us. He said he had an incredible organization—a great press agent (Annie Ivil), and the best accountants and roadies—that could all be put to our service. Mike was really persistent about impressing us, at one point saying, "We also manage a group called Herman's Hermits, who are likewise very successful."

It all sounded very promising.

Mickie Most was a musician himself, which further attracted me to the ideas Mike was presenting. Mickie's was a name to conjure with in those days, of course. He produced, among countless others, Lulu, the Nashville Teens, and Donovan; he also produced Jeff Beck's hit singles "Beck's Bolero" and "Hi-Ho Silver Lining." Before that, when he'd still been called Mickie Hayes, he'd been half of a singing duo, the Most Brothers, the other half being Alex Wharton. He'd then spent a few years in South Africa, where his band Mickie Most and the Playboys had eleven Number One hit singles with cover versions. He won a Grammy in 1964 as Producer of the Year. He wasn't really able to adapt, though, when pop music progressed out of the straitjacket of the three-minute single, which is why his later career is much less distinguished. He died in 2003 of a form of lung cancer.

Back in 1964 in the Wagon Wheel, I was trying to act cool, but inside I was busting—almost jumping out of my seat. I told Mike that the band obviously needed to discuss a move like this before giving him an answer. He said, "We leave in two days, so try and get back to me soon." I agreed to call him the next day. (I already knew the answer was going to be yes; we were going to the U.K.) Then, right before the three of them left, Hilton looked at me and said, "I hope I see you in London." That answer was *definitely* going to be yes.

The other girls were nervous about taking this kind of a trip. We were doing so well in New York, they said, so why change things? We talked and talked about it. But I was adamant. "We *have* to do this. We *have* to take this shot! What could we lose?" I didn't envision myself working on Forty-fifth Street for the rest of my life. I kept saying, "Let's go for it. Let's go for the gold!"

I called Mike, as promised, and told him we were interested but that although the girls had agreed they were still very iffy, so he should move quickly before they had a chance to change their minds.

Soon everyone we knew in New York was aware that we were planning to go to Britain. The owner of the Wagon Wheel kept saying to us, "Youse broads goin' abroad? Youse better write." The fans were telling us much the same.

A few weeks later Mike called us from the U.K. and said, "We're having problems with your work permits." Already the girls had started getting cold feet, and this news didn't help. Mike and I had some long phone conversations—we spoke almost every other day—and I kept emphasizing the need for him to move quickly. He explained it was not that easy: He needed to find an exchange group for Goldie and the Gingerbreads. (The laws were different then. If an American band went to work in the U.K., a U.K. group—an "exchange group"—had to play in the States at the same time. Hold-ups would always occur as people wrangled over money.) Later on, because we remained in England so long, we would be the exchange for many English groups: the Stones, the Yardbirds, Herman's Hermits, and the Moody Blues worked in the States in exchange for us.

One of the times I spoke with Mike, I spelled things out: We were getting bookings for various gigs, and pretty soon we'd be booked up right into next year. In the 1960s, we didn't do one-nighters; when I booked a gig the contract would be for three to six weeks. I always had jobs lined up six months to a year in advance.

That scared him, which was of course my intention. So he came up with a temporary solution to his problem which kept us safe in his grip. He made the travel arrangements for us to go to the U.K., booking us on the Cunard liner the *Mauritania,* which would take us right from New York City Harbor. The voyage would last about four weeks, so everything should be sorted out by the time we arrived. (We found out later that this was also the cheapest way of getting us there!)

The *Mauritania* was old and fucked up by then; in fact, this proved to be her last trip across the Atlantic. To make matters worse, Mike had got us really cheap cabins, near the boilers at the bottom of the ship. We promptly made a deal with the ship's captain: if he upgraded our cabins, we would perform a few times during the voyage.

And so, after weeks of travel, we finally arrived in England. The 1960s has to be the best time to have been in that country. We were very well received: the press's new American Baby, an all-woman rock and roll band. At my insistence we wore matching outfits everywhere we went, something the British weren't used to. We also had our "Apollo moves"—synchronized dance steps done while we performed—down pat. Audiences loved us.

When we first arrived Mike didn't have a place for us to stay, so we were put up at "The Animals House"—the members of the group were all living together at the time. This was a beautiful duplex on a cobblestoned alley—or, in English parlance, a mews.

After we'd been there a few hours, I walked into Eric Burdon's room. What a shock! It was filled with World War II memorabilia, almost like a museum. He wasn't a Nazi or anything like that, but he was really fixated on Nazi stuff: There were books about Hitler everywhere, and uniforms, clothes, and war helmets hung on the walls. For obvious reasons this made me really uptight, and I never went into his room again.

Hilton Valentine and I saw each other almost every night. He showed me all the hot spots in London's Soho, sometimes with the other girls. We loved that area of London: It was alive with music.

In one of my letters home to Mom I mentioned I was dating Hilton Valentine of the Animals. She boasted about this to her neighbor: "Mine daughter is going mit an animal."

"Don't worry, Goldie's a smart girl. She'll know how to handle him," the woman replied.

※ ※ ※ ※ ※ ※

Eric and his preoccupation with Nazi paraphernalia started getting to me very quickly, and it wasn't long before I needed to clear out of there. I wasn't all that friendly with Eric himself, although for the band's sake that obviously had to change: We would be working with the Animals and I'd be running into him all the time, especially in the clubs. So I had to be at least civil. His Nazi stuff was something else, though; I didn't have to live with it and I wasn't going to.

Luckily, after a week Mike announced he'd finally found us space in a hotel. My first thought was that anything was better than the "Nazi Hut," but then I saw the Aaland Hotel. It was a dark, musty place, funky and depressing. Mike assured us it was safe, and told us that lots of musicians stayed there, but all I could think was that they must be very down-and-out musicians. So this was stardom?

The rooms were small and there were two of us to a room—Ginger and I in one and Carol and Margo in the other. You had to put money in a slot for the gas heaters to work or you'd freeze; we hadn't even figured out the British coins by then. Another weird thing was that the kitchen was downstairs. We were so freaked by the place that, if we wanted tea or breakfast, we would all go downstairs together. None of us wanted to venture down there alone.

The Aaland Hotel was the home of one of the most popular British disk jockeys, Jimmy Saville. He was definitely a character: He had long platinum hair and always wore what looked like pajamas, sort of Hugh Hefner-style. Also at the Aaland while we were there was the Irish band Them; their lead singer was this quiet guy called Van Morrison. I used to cut my own hair in those days, and everyone loved my hairstyle, which was called a shag. (This was long before Austin Powers, so Americans weren't familiar with one of the other English meanings of that word.) I used to cut the girls' hair too, and soon all of the musicians we were meeting wanted my style. I wound up giving Van Morrison a haircut.

By this time we were getting an enormous amount of press. We were Annie Ivil's press dream come true. Annie reminded me of Alice in Wonderland: a petite Englishwoman with long blonde hair. She set up interviews one after another, and we seemed to be in the papers every day: *New Musical Express*, the *Daily Mirror*, you name it. Even made-up stories started to appear: "Goldie Was Really Discovered by George Harrison" or "The Gingerbreads Forgot to Bow for the Queen."

We were invited to tons of parties. At one of them I met Ringo Starr and George Harrison, who was so good-looking then; he kept staring and smiling at me, though. I got nervous and turned away. I started talking to Ringo, and we became friends. He told me about this restaurant he knew that he reckoned had the best Indian food in London. A few nights later he and Harry Nilsson picked me up from the Aaland Hotel and took me out for my first Indian meal ever. I didn't know what to expect. Ringo ordered for me. He asked if I liked spicy food, and I told him that sure I did. Big mistake. Ringo got me the hottest curry dish ever imagined; I took one mouthful and spat it back onto my plate. I thought I was going to die! He laughed and ordered me something else instead, something much milder. Later in my life I'd get used to Indian food, and now I love it. But not then!

(It was Ringo who, much later, got Goldie and the Gingerbreads our first TV show—a spot on the Peter Cook and Dudley Moore comedy series *Not Only But Also*. I was coming off a morphine habit I'd acquired after a dental nightmare in Germany (see p. 101), and so I don't remember much about the experience except that my face was all swollen up. I do recall that Dudley Moore was cute. He winked at me just before we went in front of the cameras to sing "Can't You Hear My Heart Beat?")

By now Mike Jeffries and Mickie Most had split up their partnership; the Animals would stay signed with Mike and Herman's Hermits would go with Mickie. Goldie and the Gingerbreads would stay with Mike, but there was a problem. The song he was saving for us to record, "Can't You Hear My Heart Beat?" was also in Mickie's possession, for Herman's Hermits to record. Now both groups had access to the same song.

Chas Chandler and Eric were to produce us, and so we went into the studio with them to record "Can't You Hear My Heart Beat?" In truth, we girls actively disliked the song, which we thought was sappy. Chas and Eric didn't understand us at all, not musically. We were a soulful band. We weren't pop: We were R&B, more Spencer Davis than the Supremes. Chas and Eric tried very hard to make us sound like a girls' pop group. When it came to my vocals, I fought them all the way. I resented them trying to make us sound like something other than what we were. Eric kept saying, "Sing it like Diana Ross would sing it," to which I'd reply, "But I'm *not* Diana Ross." It was a struggle.

The recording wound up having an edge to it because of the atmosphere in the studio, so I suppose all was not lost—and the single charted for us. I know if Chas and Eric had understood our sound they'd have come up with a better song for Goldie and the Gingerbreads and we could have made it bigger than we did. Still, charting at No. 13 wasn't bad.

• • • • • •

The U.K. immigration laws were strange. Like I said before, you needed to make artist exchanges if you were going to work in that country. We were signed up for the U.S.A. with Frank Barcelona's Premier Talent Agency, the biggest U.S. agency; Frank had all the major U.K. groups signed to Premier Talent. This was good for everyone concerned, because Goldie and the Gingerbreads could be used as exchanges for many big U.K. groups to come to the U.S. and perform. The first group to be set up as an exchange for us was, in fact, the Animals.

About a month after we'd arrived in Britain our work permits still weren't in order, so Mike decided to send us off to Germany for a mini-tour. Among the venues we played was the Star Club in Hamburg—and I loved that place. One night we played there a German R&B group was on-stage; they were pretty good. When they started to play the Ray Charles song "The Night Time Is The Right Time" I sat in with them. It felt really good to sing the high-voiced Raylettes part. When that bit of the song was over I tried to leave the stage, but the audience wouldn't let me go. I had to do it all over again.

After I'd finally left the stage a stunning violet-eyed German guy walked over to me, stared into my face, and said, "You are so good I could keel you."

I looked back at him and said, "What a nice compliment for a singing Jew in Germany."

He followed me to the table where the rest of the group sat. As we talked, he told me his name was Jurgen Otterstein. His English was very broken, but not so bad I couldn't understand it. I don't remember what the conversation was about, though, except that he said he hated being a German because of all the atrocities of World War II; I just kept staring at him and melting. I'd never seen a guy with lavender eyes before. We made plans to meet again.

Jurgen and I started seeing lots of each other. At one point during the relationship I went back home to Brooklyn for a break. While I was there, Jurgen called the house one night. My mother answered the phone to hear him saying, in his heavy German accent, "Let me speak to Goldie, *ja*?"

My mother said, "End who is dis?"

He answered, "Jurgen Otterstein."

My mother gave me her "Nine months I kereed you" look, handed me the phone, and said, "It's a Jurgen Otterstein from *Germany*."

Jurgen and I talked for a few moments and then he dropped his bombshell. "Goldie, my love, I have done it! I am now a Jew! I have gone to Hebrew classes and I have converted! I have even had a circumcision!"

I thought, *Ouch, he's carried this thing a bit too far. Pretty heavy thing to do!* So Jurgen was now a Jew. And I felt terribly guilty. Was it my fault his penis would now and forever look like it had a fireman's hat? How had I led him on? Then I thought, *Wow! He either really loves me or he's nuts. Either way, I must never get together with him again.*

We stayed in touch over the years, however, despite my guilt feelings. Jurgen became a successful record executive at a large German record company. It was hard not to run into him. Later I even joked with him about his circumcision. "What did they do with the extra penis skin? Bury it to grow more Germans?"

But the most important thing that happened during that mini-tour of Germany was that I got really sick—and almost died. It started much earlier, before we'd left the U.S.A. for London. I was having dinner one night when I heard a crack in my jaw. Nothing hurt and there was no bleeding so, after I'd eaten and chewed a while longer and everything seemed fine, I paid it no further mind. But a few months later, in Germany, while we were gigging in the small town of Kiel, I began to feel very tired and feverish the whole time. After a while it was obvious something was wrong with me. I went to a doctor, who did some blood tests and told me my white- and red-corpuscle counts were way off. Somewhere in my body there was a serious infection. He thought it was probably my appendix, and suggested I should have it out. I refused to get operated on in Germany—and that proved to be a good thing! By the time we got back to the Hotel Dusseldorf I was really sick. The whites of my eyes were getting yellow. This new doctor asked me if I'd had my teeth checked lately, and suddenly everything fit into place as I remembered that cracking sound in my jaw.

So that same morning I went with Margo to see a dentist the hotel clerk had recommended. The dentist took some X-rays. As we stared at the negatives he said, "Aha! There it is!"—an impacted and infected wisdom tooth. The dentist, who could barely talk English, told me, "It must come out." He had to draw Margo and me a sketch of what he meant to do, because we couldn't understand him.

Finally I said, "Okay, if it's gotta be done, let's do it!"

He got to work. I recall hearing a snapping noise at some stage, but I didn't think much about it at the time. After an hour of struggling with my tooth, he stitched up my gums and sent me back to the hotel.

The next day I was in terrible pain. The girls called the dentist, who sent a regular doctor to my hotel room to give me a shot; I didn't know it then, but it was morphine. Thereafter the doctor came to my room every day to shoot me up. There were times I couldn't wait for him to give me my morphine—I started to love it.

The girls did some gigs without me—after all, the show had to go on—but after a while they stopped performing, saying they couldn't go it alone. They kept calling Mike Jeffries and giving him reports on my medical condition.

Here we were in a small German town; I was getting a morphine habit; my right cheek was totally swollen; I couldn't eat; and my skin was yellow. I looked like a chipmunk storing nuts, but at least I didn't feel any pain. I remember smiling the whole time because I was so high, and thinking I was going to die there. I thought my parents would not be too happy with me dying in Germany of all places.

Finally the girls called Mike Jeffries yet again and yelled at him that they didn't care about the fucking U.K. work permits, I needed to be brought back from Germany. He made arrangements for us to catch a train to London.

The girls were nervous not just about my health; they were concerned over the daily morphine shots. I don't even remember the train and ferry trip back to the U.K.. By the time we got to London my infection had gotten even worse, and it didn't help that I was going cold turkey from a morphine habit. The only way I could get any nourishment was through a straw, because my jaw wouldn't open properly. Not surprisingly, I was on the verge of a nervous breakdown.

When Mike saw me he got scared. He made me an appointment with one of the best Harley Street specialists, who concluded that not only had the dentist left part of his drill in my jawbone—that snapping noise I'd heard in the man's operating room had been the drill breaking—but also the stitches he'd given me weren't the dissolving kind, so that my skin was growing over them. In addition, I was suffering from a form of lockjaw, and needed to be treated immediately. He said that, if I'd waited another week, I'd have been dead. The first thing they did was start radiation treatments on my jaw.

And then guess what the doctor said? I had to have *another* wisdom tooth removed—the one on the other side. It too was impacted. Oh, the horror! I screamed, "*I wanna go home!*"

He promised me I wouldn't feel anything, and he was right. He put me under a general anesthetic for the surgery, and I spent a week in hospital. I couldn't recuperate in the Aaland Hotel; I needed real care and attention.

* * * * * *

By this time we'd become friendly with Vicki Wickham, the editor of one of Britain's most popular and important rock TV shows, *Ready, Steady, Go!*. In fact Vicki was more of a producer than an editor; she was the one who picked the talent. All the big stars were featured on *Ready, Steady, Go!*, including the Stones, Dusty Springfield, and Madeline Bell, all buddies of ours. We appeared on the show many times. Cathy McGowan was the hostess, the co-host being a very handsome Michael Aldred.

Vicki came to the hospital to visit me. When she saw what I was going through she decided her apartment would be a better place for me

Goldie and the Gingerbreads getting their wigs styled before going on *Ready, Steady, Go!*

to recuperate than the Aaland Hotel; it would be warm, and she could look after me. Obviously, I thought this was a good idea.

The Gingerbreads would, of course, carry on at the hotel, and this created a certain rift between us. They became jealous and insecure, and I know that a good part of this was that they were upset with me for staying at Vicki's apartment. But the truth was that I just couldn't stand the prospect of being in that hotel room while I was so sick. It was depressing, damp and cold—the last place anybody should be trying to get over surgery. And popping out of bed every hour to keep putting coins in the heater—I couldn't imagine doing that. The girls eventually got over it but, for my part, I found it hard to reconcile the fact that they could become that jealous. I'd never seen that side of them before.

Vicki was a good caregiver. She used to come home from the show at lunchtime with soup and food for me. She made sure I ate and took my medicine. She was a good friend.

Eventually, Goldie and the Gingerbreads got a two-bedroom flat in London's Bayswater: 30 Palace Court. Ginger and I roomed together as usual, while Margo and Carol shared another room. You had to walk down some stairs from street level to get to our flat. Yes, it was another of Mike Jeffries's cheap moves: a "basement apartment." He put us on a very low salary, saying he would take care of the rent and all the other bills, and that made us bitch a lot. But at least now we finally had our own space in London. It felt good to have a home of our own.

The "in" drug at the time was hashish, and we had lots of it. I was not into smoking marijuana as much as the other girls were because I'd had a bad experience with it in the past: An allergic reaction, probably to something someone had added to it, had made me almost stop breathing. So grass wasn't for me. But hash—ah, that was another story. I rolled the best doobies (or "spliffs," as the British called them). I would roll them on record album covers, of course.

I'm glad I don't smoke anymore; I don't know how you would roll a joint on a CD cover.

● ● ● ● ● ●

1964 was a great time to be a musician in the U.K. The clothes were incredible, and Carnaby Street was the place to buy them. We had our clothes designed by the famous designers there—including beautiful pin-

Goldie and the Gingerbreads looking hip in London.

stripe suits made especially for Goldie and the Gingerbreads. We had wigs made for us out of real hair—long beautiful hair. Our press agents wanted us to look Mod. Little did they know how Rocker we were!

We started touring all over England, Ireland, and Scotland. Soon we began to attract our very own groupies: gay, straight, boys, girls. I still don't know how they found out where we lived, but they used to hang out by our basement apartment door and we had to chase them off. Sadly, some of these girls were running away from home and wanted to move in with us; of course, we couldn't let them. We did our best to talk them into moving back with their parents.

There was a big demand for Goldie and the Gingerbreads to tour as a support act for major groups. We were good for the Hot Seat—which is to say we were a strong enough act to go on immediately before the headliner and still hold an audience. We even managed to get some encores, which for obvious reasons is pretty rare for an act that's in the Hot Seat. Those were truly great times for me: Not bad for a girl whose childhood had never taken her far beyond the confines of Rivington Street.

It was in 1963 that we got our first tour with the Rolling Stones.

At the start of the tour we got on this long bus that had no bathroom; naturally we were the only girls aboard. Over by the window I saw a guy crying his eyes out. Sob after loud sob. His nose and his eyes were running. He was a mess.

I went over to sit near him. "Why are you crying?"

He said, "My guitar got stolen . . . my favorite guitar." I could hardly understand him between his crying and his heavy English accent. Then he added: "And my wife has left me."

I handed him a tissue, and he started to calm down. "What's your name?" I asked.

"Jeff Beck."

"What band are you with?"

"The Yardbirds."

"Oh yeah, the Yardbirds," I said. "Look, you'll get another guitar."

He sobbed louder. "Never!" He spat out the word. "Not like this guitar."

"Maybe your wife will have a change of heart and come back to you one day."

"This guitar was *special*."

Ha! Musicians!

I'd taken a small record player and about fifty 45s to England with me. I had to have my Ray Charles and my Buddy Guy records. I used to

Goldie consoling Jeff Beck (on the left).

listen to them right before I went on-stage; they were my inspiration. Ray Charles put blood in my veins.

One time before the show, Jeff Beck came into the dressing room while I was playing some Buddy Guy. I said, "Hey, you wanna hear real blues?" I put on Guy's "The First Time I Met the Blues," one of my favorites at the time. Jeff freaked. Later on I had to send him a copy from the States. It was me who turned Jeff Beck on to Buddy Guy!

Every show we performed on this tour, Mick Jagger would stand behind the curtain and watch us like a hawk, studying us. We were a great group playing American R&B, and the Stones loved American R&B. After they'd checked us out a few nights, we started to get friendly with them, and quite often the whole band came into our dressing room.

I was attracted to Mick. I just hoped he didn't smell as bad as most of the other British musicians seemed to. None of them used deodorant, and it was pretty disgusting, especially on the tour buses when we were all jammed close together. The girls and I used to say it right to their faces: "Why don't you guys take a goddam shower?"

Goldie and Mick smooching. (I had him when he was young.)

Mick and I started to flirt. He was cute, like in "pretty." We began getting a little closer, and the inevitable happened. To start with we just made out backstage or on the steps of auditorium basements, but eventually Mick and I made secret plans for me to sneak into his hotel room late at night after the show, once everyone else was in their own room. (He couldn't come to my room because I shared with Ginger.) The girls knew Mick and I had a thing for each other, but they didn't know until later how much of a thing. None of the Gingerbreads dated any of the other guys on the tour—not that they couldn't have, because they were attractive girls, but because they just didn't. Brian Jones had a big crush on Ginger for a while, but she didn't want to know.

Mick's sense of humor was like mine, and he loved making me laugh with him at people's expense. He had one idiosyncracy, though: For some reason, he was pretty scared of people in wheelchairs. When he saw them in the audience he'd be freaked, and he was very nervous about signing autographs for them. Odd, eh?

He was going steady at the time with Chrissie Shrimpton, the model, and if she'd found out Mick and I were making it I believe she'd have killed him. He was plenty nervous about that. In fact, we both wanted our relationship to be a secret. I didn't want the Gingerbreads to know and he didn't want the other Stones—and, of course, his girlfriend—to know. But things were too obvious for it to stay a secret during the tour.

Before long the Gingerbreads found out I was making it with Mick. They couldn't understand why I was doing it; they'd make faces, pulling their lips down to make them bigger, and say, "Ugh! How could you?" They thought his mouth was awful. Not me, though. I liked his mouth just fine.

The other Stones were fun too. I liked Bill Wyman a lot; he was a good, solid guy, and I know we'd have become good friends if we'd had the time to hang out. He was a bright guy, a caring person. Keith was another good guy, just wonderful, friendly in his own way and always smiling; he often popped into our dressing room just to say "Hi." Charlie Watts was quiet and very much in the background, which was the way he liked it. As for Brian Jones, he was a very sad and sensitive guy.

We'd all get wild after a show, and it was nothing unusual for us to get kicked out of the hotel we were supposed to be staying in. One night Brian took the fire extinguishers off the wall of some hotel and came into everyone's rooms spraying foam all over the place. A big mess. I think it was the only time I ever saw Brian laughing really hard. He offered to pay the hotel for the damages, but we got kicked out anyway. It was all worth it, though, because we'd laughed so much.

Leaving the theaters after a show was tricky. We all had to sneak out if we could, and then we'd be whisked away quickly to somewhere safe. The problem was that the fans wanted to rip us apart, grabbing anything they could get for a keepsake—hair, clothes, or even your ear, if they could lay a hand on it. One time the fans got hold of Brian's hair and he was in such pain he burst into tears.

Generally, however, touring with big groups was a lot of fun. I remember especially the last night on a tour with the Hollies and the Kinks. We didn't know it at the time, but there was a tradition among the groups that the last night of a tour was called Prank Night: The bands would play weird tricks on each other while they were performing their last songs of the tour.

In those days there were six acts on a bill, which made for some very long shows. The fans really got their money's worth!

We decided not to wear our wigs during the last show of this particular tour. We were in the middle of the closing number—our single "Can't You Hear My Heart Beat?"—when I heard the audience laughing, clapping, and carrying on. I thought, *Gee, they really love this song.* Then out of the corner of my eye I saw Alan Clarke from the Hollies and their drummer, Robert Elliott, coming out from behind the curtain wearing our wigs—and our spare costumes. They started imitating us and the audience fell apart.

They were in trouble now; it was a matter of honor that we get them back. They went on next, and by the time they did so Ginger and I had tied a string around the drummer's seat. When Robert tried to sit down we pulled the string, the chair slid away, and he went crashing to the floor. Later we crept out on-stage and shut the amps off during one of their songs.

A discovery we'd made while touring was that all the guys used to stuff things down the front of their pants so they looked better hung. I wanted to reach into one of the Hollies' pants on-stage that night and pull the stuffing out to see if it was true, but I couldn't get close enough.

* * * * * *

Mike Jeffries decided to send us to Paris to play at the very prestigious Olympia Theater as the Hot Seat for the Animals. The French love rock music: They respect it and they show their respect. In the States, audiences just sort of take musicians for granted, but in France they make a big deal out of the music scene.

The Olympia Theater stage-hands were funny about coming onstage. When there was a problem in the U.K. or the U.S.A., the roadies would always come on-stage and move equipment around and fix things right in front of the audience. They didn't give a damn about being seen. But not the French stagehands, they seemed totally shy about it. That night, while we were performing on this massive stage, Margo's organ stopped playing right in the middle of a song. It was obvious: Goldie and the Gingerbreads had only the three instruments, so when one of them stopped playing you really noticed it. Being professionals, we continued performing. I looked over toward the backstage guys, pleading with my eyes, "Help us! Help us!"

A minute or so passed, and then we saw curtains billowing and bulging and swaying. There were bodies hiding in the shadows, moving behind amps and under cloths. One of the French electricians managed to get under the B3 Hammond organ and, propped on the foot pedals, suddenly popped his head up between Margo's legs. She hadn't seen him coming, and let out a yelp, then started to laugh. From where I was, I couldn't see what was going on and was mystified as to her sudden hilarity. The stage-hand politely said to her, in broken English, "You're unplugged here. I weeeell plug you back in. Please restart your organ."

Since I couldn't speak French, we had a translator write a French "thank you" for the audience for the end of the show. I deliberately bastardized the language as I delivered this message. The audience adored it. We got an encore, for which we played Ray Charles's "What'd I Say," and I got the audience to join in. They wanted another encore, but that was it. We were the hit of Paris.

• • • • • • •

While we were living in the U.K., all of us flew back to the States from time to time to see our families. By now Mom and Dad had a house in Mill Basin, Brooklyn. On one of these periodic trips home, I found my family had stretched this big banner across their terrace: "Welcome Back, Goldie and the Gingerbreads." My mom was proving to be my biggest fan! I got out of the car, arms full of packages and gifts, and this little kid came over to me and sadly asked, "Can I have your autograph?" It sounded like it was such a chore.

"Why do you want my autograph?" I said.

He answered, "Cuz your mom told me to ask you."

I signed it and, mortified, ran into the house to get away from him. For my mom it was always about what the neighbors thought. She was starting to treat me differently. She even put a star on my bedroom door. I was almost uncomfortable with that. I was living her fantasy.

It had always been important for my parents to own a home—part of their American Dream, if you like. With all the money I was earning, I helped them buy the house. House? I should call it a museum. I remember walking into their living room and finding they had a new silk hot-pink couch. When I went to sit down on it my mom screamed, "No! Not till it's covered!"

"Why are you covering this thing?" I asked.

She replied: "Von day ven I'm dead, you veel have this furniture."

I had to tell her, "I don't want this furniture. It's not my taste in furniture." But it didn't do any good. A week later all her furniture was covered in plastic, so that you stuck to it in the summer and froze on it during the winter.

Now, here's a confession: today I have that hot-pink couch, although it's not covered in plastic. It's beautiful. I love it. And, yes, just like Mom I don't allow anyone to sit on it.

I had a Maltese dog called Spunky, and he stayed with my mom while I was on the road. Eventually, of course, it was more accurate to say that Spunky was her dog, not mine anymore. One day I noticed Spunky was walking funny and asked my mother if he was all right. She said she didn't notice anything strange about his walk. Then I saw what was going on. He was afraid to walk on her carpets. He walked fine on the linoleum and the wood floors, but sort of tiptoed on her carpet when I called him! She'd trained him—or, presumably, terrorized him—to keep clear.

When I brought friends to my parents' home my mother used to yell down to me in Polish, even before we'd entered the vestibule, "Tell them to take their shoes off!"

I'd say back, also in Polish, "*You* tell them."

Of course, she would get so mad at us. But that didn't stop her telling them.

• • • • • •

Back in the U.K., we shared everything with the Animals, including the equipment vans. We had two roadies on salary, Terry McVie—a red-faced Scotsman—and Robin. I liked these roadies, and we had fun with them. I used to moon people on the highways, and the two guys would get so embarrassed. We loved teasing them, and I would do anything to shock them. I was constantly lifting up my shirt and flashing them. We asked them to go into stores to buy our Tampax—boy did they dislike that. Of course, we only did it to make them blush. Wherever they are now, I hope they've forgiven me.

Our touring with the Stones always made everyone curious—especially the press. Every time I had an interview with someone from the media, the first question I was always asked was: "How close are you to Mick?" It still comes up! They ask things like, "You toured with the Stones and Mick Jagger. How was it? Were you close to Mick? What was it like touring with the Stones? And Mick?" Sometimes I want to tell them, "Yes, I had him when he was young and cute!" Other times I just want to say, "None of your fucking business!" My answer has mostly been, "I don't talk about personal stuff." I know what they want, of course. Someone actually asked if he was good. I said, "Good at what?"

This prurience was ridiculous back then and it still is today. Sometimes it makes me want to scream. Not only did I fuck Mick Jagger, I fucked Peter Quaife of the Kinks, Paul Jones of Manfred Mann, Hilton Valentine of the Animals, and many, many more. Those were the 1960s. No HIV. So what would you like me to do about it? Sell my IUD on eBay?

There was a great club on London's Wardour Street, in Soho, called the Flamingo. Soho was a popular neighborhood for many reasons—very hip music and people wearing clothes that were pretty decadent—and the club was always filled with the hippest people. They liked all kinds of music: rock, jazz, R&B. The stage was equipped with a B3 Hammond organ and Leslie speakers. It was the perfect place for us to jam. One night we jumped up on-stage and did the songs we could not do on tour, like "Moody's Mood for Love" and "Red Top," and naturally I had to stick in some Ray Charles. The audience had heard those songs before, of course, but we were women and women weren't supposed to be playing that way. Now London was buzzing about us again: Goldie and the Gingerbreads wasn't just a commercial all-woman band, it was an incredibly hip band.

We were doing lots of speed and smoking lots of hash. There was also a pill called the Purple Heart, and when I'd taken one of those I was able to stay up all night and dance my ass off. Purple Hearts also helped my voice—I wouldn't get hoarse however much I sang. They gave me lots of adrenaline. These were the same pills we called Green Men in the States. In fact, they were dexedrine.

We did some hanging out in a place called the Scotch of St. James, a private club for the "in" crowd that you could go to only after hours and only if you were known. There'd be Jimmy Page in one corner while Mick Jagger was over in another there with Chrissie Shrimpton or Marianne Faithfull. Another club like this was the Cromwellian, which was my favorite because it had lots of places you could tuck yourself away and see without being seen. I would hide and watch everyone from the Animals to the Who to Paul Jones of Manfred Mann. It was a place where people in the rock world could hang together to schmooze, drink, and get high.

Another hangout bar I liked to visit on our nights off was the Scene. We performed there on occasion as well, playing with the Who, Them, and the Pretty Things.

Our single of "Can't You Hear My Heart Beat?" was starting to chart. I was also making my own friends in London. I was losing touch with the girls; I guess it was inevitable. I was dating lots of guys, especially the guys we toured with; my social circle really didn't extend much beyond other musicians.

● ● ● ● ● ●

After touring with the Stones, we went on tour with the Kinks. I had a thing for Peter Quaife and would sneak into his room. I wished I weren't the only girl in the band who was doing this sort of sneaking around. I found out later that the others were doing their own kind of sneaking.

The tour with the Kinks was pretty interesting; their song "You Really Got Me" was a big hit at the time.

Speaking of big hits, we were in our dressing room one night after a successful set by Goldie and the Gingerbreads when we heard a big commotion—crashes and bangs. I ran out toward the curtains to find out what was happening and saw Dave Davies lying there on the stage bleeding while Ray Davies, his brother, stood screaming hysterically beside him. The audience was applauding, thinking this was all part of the act. Ray kept shouting, "What did you do to my brother? What did you do?"

The Kinks' drummer, Mick Avory, and Dave had not been getting along too well. They were performing "You Really Got Me" that night when Dave pissed Mick off by kicking his bass drum. Mick must have seen red. He got up, took a cymbal from its stand, and threw it at Dave like a frisbee. The cymbal hit Dave in the head and he passed out, bleeding.

An ambulance came and took Dave to the hospital. Luckily the wound wasn't serious; he was released the same night. Poor Ray was scared so badly that he cried. I tried consoling him. That didn't stop me from singing "He really got him" at frequent inappropriate moments throughout the rest of the tour.

● ● ● ● ● ●

We toured with the Kinks for two weeks, and right after that we went back into the studio, now with Shel Talmy as our producer. He had a great reputation, producing for the Who, Manfred Mann, the Kinks, and more. Talk about us being excited! But, as I always say, "it's combinations that breed success," and we soon found out that Talmy and ourselves didn't make a good combination. He envisioned us as a pop group and kept bringing us the wrong songs. Every song he brought us we nixed. Mick Jagger gave me a song he'd been working on during the time

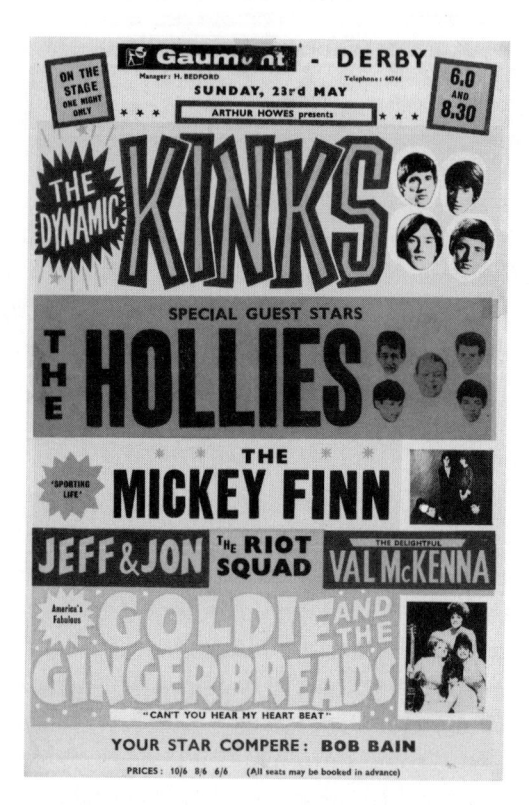

Our U.K. tour with the Kinks.

we'd been hanging out together, but I didn't like that one either. The closest we came to a song that was right for us was "Look for Me, Baby," written by Ray Davies. We recorded it but it was never released.

We were always hunting for material, but no one ever gave us a song we flipped over. Everyone tried, but all we ever got were sappy girlie songs. I was dabbling in some songwriting myself at the time but it was still too early for us to be recording our own material. No one was inspiring us or pushing us to write our own music. Andrew Loog Oldham did the right thing when he forced the Stones to start doing so; it might have been interesting if we'd had an Andrew Oldham to do the same for us. As it was, we had no confidence in our own writing abilities and so we were always at the mercy of someone else—what other people wrote, and what other people thought would be good for us to record. Shel Talmy was a good producer, but the groups he had major success with were groups who wrote their own material, so that they were never being forced into someone else's mold.

• • • • • •

The Gingerbreads were starting to fall apart. The girls became insecure for various reasons, most of which I considered ridiculous. It had started with the friction over me staying at Vicki Wickham's flat when I was sick while the girls were still stuck at the Aaland Hotel. Then, the hotter we got and the more press coverage we got, the more pissed the girls became. The trouble was that, when rock journalists sought an interview, they wanted to talk to only one person, not the whole group. The obvious choice as spokesperson was usually the lead singer. And, after talking to me, they'd often abbreviate the group's name in their headlines; they'd write "Goldie Tours with Stones" or "Goldie on Ready." This made the girls jealous, understandably, but what wasn't understandable was that they started blaming me for it, treating me like some kind of traitor, as if it were my fault.

I was starting to feel separated from the girls. I felt like I was losing them. We no longer had that rapport—that tightness we used to have. I became very uncomfortable. It affected me in many ways. It began to show in my singing and performing. I think it worked both ways: They felt like they were losing me, too, and some of the control they might have had over me. The whole idea of working with them or hanging with them became painful.

We went on for a while longer in what had become a loveless affair. Anyone could feel there was something really wrong between us. We had always had this love for one another, especially through our music, but now it was starting to feel like less and less of a sisterhood.

I knew Ginger loved me, and had known that for a long time. Knowing it put pressure on me. I loved Ginger like a sister; she had become a big part of my life. I knew, too, that she was going through a major depression, but I had no idea how profound it was until she tried to kill herself by cutting her wrists. I lost it when Margo said the suicide attempt was over me. I really had no idea. Even worse, while Margo was obviously feeling bad on Ginger's behalf, she seemed to care nothing about my feelings, and that hurt me deeply. As far as I was concerned, Goldie and the Gingerbreads ended then.

After a lot of thinking and quite a few of those soul-searching nights people talk about, I knew the family I'd spent so much time with—grown with, cried with, eaten and slept with—was falling apart. I had to cope with my insecurities and fears about losing my musical family, had to face up to them.

I made my heart-wrenching decision to leave the group.

CHAPTER SEVEN
Goldie Solo

THE BREAK-UP of our group in late 1967 made headlines in Europe. Countless newspapers called me wanting interviews. Of course, I was always respectful towards the Gingerbreads when I spoke to the press. I did not want to—and, anyway, couldn't—keep the break-up of Goldie and the Gingerbreads a secret, but I knew I had to move on to the next phase of my life.

"We outgrew each other musically and I wanted to explore different directions in music; we are all still close friends."

"It's not them, it's me."

"I want to try to make it by myself—start a solo career."

"We'll stay in touch. The girls and I will call each other. We're so close, we'll always be together in spirit."

It wasn't, in fact, the truth. The rest of the band went back to the U.S. while I decided to stay in the U.K., reasoning that it made sense for me to stay where I had success and a proven track record, that I should be where people knew who I was. Quickly, though, I found out I missed the camaraderie of the Gingerbreads.

Then I met a guy called John Fenton at a press party given for the Moody Blues. John was a music freak who loved jazz and R&B and who'd made a fortune merchandising Beatles paraphernalia; he was also the manager of the Moody Blues. (Mike Pinder of the Moodies was a drinking buddy of mine.) John started calling me, and we went out a couple of times. With so much in common, both being in the music business, we inevitably started to have a relationship.

John had that classic English look: square jaw and thin straight nose. He had impeccable taste in clothes; he was always dressed in expensive three-piece suits with a white shirt (usually without a tie), and had a gold watch and chain hanging in his vest pocket. When I checked him out I thought, *Too very cool*. Although I knew he was married—he was upfront about it and told me—I never met his wife; I heard she had a sweet position working in the film end of the industry. John was forever "getting a divorce." Personally, I didn't care if he was married or not; I knew this was not a forever thing.

He hung around long enough to become not only my lover but my manager. In those days you sold records and got into the charts through being in the daily papers and the music press a lot—especially *New Musical Express*. This form of publicity was right up John's alley; he had a great knack for it. One day he had the bright idea of bribing someone at London Zoo to release a giant eagle named Goldie. It worked brilliantly. Every newspaper's headlines was full of "Goldie Escapes,"

Long John Baldry with Genya in London.

"Goldie Still Missing," and finally "Goldie Found." As a result, I had more interviews that month than anybody else in the music business.

John also found a money backer for us, a posh investor gentleman from the City (the U.K. equivalent of our Wall Street).

With all of the publicity I was getting, I was much in demand. It was time to start touring again. All I needed was a band. John mentioned as a possibility a group from Jamaica—an eight-piece band called Jimmy James and the Vagabonds—so I went to one of their rehearsals to listen to them play. I ended up taking them on the road with me on a tour with Manfred Mann.

On this tour I started my show with a gospel song called "Soulville." I would hide behind the stage curtain while the band gave a long powerful chord. I'd sing the word "Soulville" three times before coming onstage wearing a white, see-through lace, one-piece bell-bottom suit. Then the whole band would kick in. The audience usually went wild.

It was a good tour. I was crazy about Paul Jones, lead singer for Manfred Mann; I cared about him more than anyone I had ever been with—the truth is, I was in love with him. He was married and "somewhat" loyal to his wife. We slept together. I could never have more of him than that.

Bookings meant money, and John insisted I get a house in the posh section of London called Belgravia, telling me it was where the "upper crust" lived. All three bedrooms were upstairs, and that really threw me. I was so afraid of being alone there that I deliberately threw parties every night just so I could have company. Almost everyone I'd ever toured with would come by to drink and hang out.

John knew I was scared to be alone so he bought me a dog, a Silkie I named Britain. But Britain didn't help; he was as paranoid as I was. I'd be in the upstairs bedroom, thinking I'd heard something downstairs, staring in terror at the bedroom door, and Britain would be staring in terror at the bedroom door right alongside me. Or I'd be downstairs listening to creaks coming from the upstairs bedrooms, and all Britain would do was listen to them too. One night I swore I saw a doorknob turning so I grabbed him and we ran out of Belgravia to a girlfriend's house, where we stayed the rest of the night. In the morning I called John and told him I wouldn't go back to this big house, so we managed to rent instead an apartment in a high-rise (not easy to find in those days).

I was also given a Rolls Royce to drive. Imagine me on those narrow winding streets, always wanting to drive on the right rather than the left.

By the time I got it back to John that Rolls had ridges and scrapes on both sides.

Our gentleman investor from the City wound up in jail for misappropriating funds from other investors. I believe lots of that misappropriation might have been for me.

While all this was happening I got a call from Island Records. Bess Coleman—the press person for Island—wanted to know if I'd be interested in doing some background vocals for Chris Blackwell, the owner of Island Records. Of course I said yes; it was going to be a superstar session, with Spencer Davis, Stevie Winwood, and Georgie Fame and his horn section, and I was going to be doing the background singing along with my friends Madeline Bell and Dusty Springfield.

We did a few songs and then, the recording session over, Madeline and Dusty left. I stayed to hang out with all the musicians. While everyone was talking I went over to the piano and began to play a 1950s R&B song. Banging away on the piano, I started to sing. The song was "Disappointed Bride," originally recorded in the 1950s by my favorite group, The Hearts with Baby Washington. Its opening line was "You know sometimes men make you happy . . . and sometimes they make you cry."

The place got very quiet. The musicians started to join in, one by one. I didn't know the microphones were still on. Chris Blackwell was sitting in the control room, and I saw him smiling, enjoying what he was hearing. Soon he came out and said, "Why don't you sing that directly on a mike and let Stevie play the piano part?"

So Stevie Winwood took over my piano line and I went into the booth to sing. The band was amazing. One take—that was all it took to make this single. The recording came out great. Listening back, everyone had a grin on their face.

Chris said, "This is sounding so black that we can't say it's you, Goldie." Another consideration was that I was still under contract to Decca. After giving the matter some thought, he came up with a new name for me, Patsy Cole. I left, went on with my life, and never knew what became of the tape.

Many years later I heard Chris Blackwell had put the recording out with, as B-side, the instrumental version of the same song. I found out it was a big hit in Jamaica—something like #1—but I never heard the finished product and often wondered about it. One day, a few years ago, I mentioned this session to my friend Howard Thompson. A real music man, Howard said he'd do some research; he knew the guys at Island Records. He came through with his promise, and a few weeks later I got a cassette copy. Chris had been right: I *did* sound like a gospel singer. The recording sounds really great.

• • • • • •

Right after that superstar session I knew I needed a break. The collapse of Goldie and the Gingerbreads and the rehearsing of a new band to tour with had definitely taken its toll on me. I decided to go to Majorca, Spain, with Bess Coleman; by this time she and I had become good friends. While visiting some clubs in Spain, I met the famous Flamenco dancer Jose Miguel. Everyone knew that name in Spain. He was incredible—so handsome and such a wonderful dancer. We had a fling. I went home with him and we made love all night; then in the morning he left me locked up in the room until he came back with food. This went on for two days; then I told him, "I have to go. This is kidnapping." Bess had been having such a good time that she'd never noticed I was gone!

Jose and I kept in touch, and we made plans for him to visit me in the States when I was there; when he did, though, the romance had flown. He just didn't make my heart sing in Brooklyn, so I told him I was too busy and couldn't spend time with him.

Speaking of visitors to the States, one of my mother's favorite guests was John Fenton. Mom was so very proud that he would come to her home in Brooklyn when on business in New York. He'd fill her in on how I was doing back in the U.K. I liked him for stopping by to see Mom. She just loved him, and loved his accent (as if she didn't have one herself). She boasted how she gave him at least ten cups of tea.

But my own professional relationship with John was approaching its end. I'd always loved Peter Sellers's films. One week John got a call from the Sellers organization; they'd spotted my photo in one of the music papers, and thought I looked very interesting. They were about to start a production of a film called *The Party*, and I guess they thought my look would fit one of the characters. I went with John to a meeting with them. I was so excited. Not only was I going to get to act in a film, it would be a *Peter Sellers* film. Wow!

The interview went well, but, unknown to me, John wanted more. Without consulting me, he told them, "Goldie either sings the title track or she cannot appear in this film." They said that was impossible; someone was already under contract for the title track. So I never did the film. When I found out about this I was furious. I moved on. No more John Fenton.

● ● ● ● ● ●

Andrew Loog Oldham, the Rolling Stones' manager and producer, really intrigued me. He had a strong character, and was handsome and unique. I loved his look—funky but chic. It was not only the way he dressed but the way he carried himself that generated a sort of aura of star mystique about him. As far as I was concerned, he was more of a star than the Stones themselves! We'd first met when I was on the TV show *Ready, Steady, Go!* with Goldie and the Gingerbreads.

Andrew offered me a recording deal with Immediate Records (his own record label), and I jumped at the chance. He found me a good song—"Going Back," written by Carole King—and did a great production job on it. He took me into a studio called Regent Sound, in London, where the Stones made a lot of their hit records in the early 1960s. Mick Jagger stopped by the sessions a few times to hear what we were up to. The studio was not the most comfortable. The control room was way above the recording room, which was very strange; whenever I wanted to communicate with Andrew I had to strain upward the whole time.

Ready, Steady, Go! with (from left) Goldie, Alan Price, Eric Burdon, and Hilton Valentine of the Animals.

Andrew himself wrote the single's B-side song—which would mean a good deal of money for him if the single was a big hit. (He was pretty business savvy.) His song was called "Headlines," and it mirrored Bob Crewe's sound. Andrew admired Crewe and Phil Spector—anything that sounded black. At the time the U.K. and Germany worshipped the black sound, loving it much more than Americans did. It was sad that Americans couldn't recognize or enjoy their own musical gems. It took British groups to make Americans realize what they had. (Look at what Eric Clapton did for B.B. King!) This was, of course, the reason Goldie and the Gingerbreads had wound up overseas in the first place: we were too black-sounding to be widely appreciated at home.

A few weeks after the session with Andrew, he called me and said Dusty Springfield had been very upset when she'd heard I'd recorded "Going Back," because this was a song she'd been holding onto for herself for a while, although she hadn't recorded it yet.

In my version of "Going Back" I'd changed some of the lyrics without asking permission. This was nothing unusual; singers are always doing it. They make small changes like "he" for "she," while some other minor word-changes just sound better for a particular singer. Andrew couldn't have cared less about this, but we found out later that Dusty had complained to Carole King about it. Of course, the very fact that it had been mentioned to her as if it were significant meant Carole King became curious to know what I'd done, and wanted to hear my version before the single was released. I took this personally, as if I were being asked to prove myself in some way, and I got very bent out of shape about it.

I said, "Fuck this record."

"You mean scrap it?" Andrew asked.

I said, "Yes."

I wish I'd done more singles with Andrew. He was a good producer for me—easygoing, yet he knew what he wanted and how to get it, but let me have the freedom to be me and keep my sound.

• • • • • •

I was still living in my apartment in the London high-rise, Portsy Hall, when one day I got a call from New York. It was Margo, and she sounded very excited. She told me the Gingerbreads had found the perfect situation, and she was asking me to consider coming back so that we could re-form the band. They'd acquired a song they thought was a smash, written by incredible hit writers, new management that had hit artists on their rosters, and an agency just waiting for us. It all sounded so good; no wonder they were so excited. Margo said everything would be different. By this time Ginger had moved to California to become a Playboy Bunny, but she came running back for our reunion. She brought back with her a song she'd found in Los Angeles called "Hey, Joe," later to be a big hit for Jimi Hendrix. We performed this on stage as: "Hey, Gold, where you goin' with that gun in your hand?"

I'd been missing my home and the States, and so I thought about it. Maybe this time it would all work out right. So in the summer of 1968 I came back to give it another try. I stayed with my parents again, in Brooklyn. Back in Britain, Keith Relf of the Yardbirds had taught me how to play blues harmonica, so I spent my spare time practicing the harp to B.B. King records.

But once again Goldie and the Gingerbreads landed a contract with a ripoff manager. Same shit, different contract.

Goldie and the Gingerbreads went into the studio to do another single—still no LPs for us. We released "Walking in Different Circles" and it got some airplay. I always got a kick out of hearing my stuff on the radio, but this was something special: this was in the U.S.!

Something else was starting to brew now.

• • • • • •

Teen magazine's application form for the Goldie and the Gingerbreads fan club.

Carol had always flirted with me and I had always flirted back. My flirting was more out of curiosity than anything else, as had been the time, years earlier, when I'd slept with her in Canada on a whim. Now I slept with her again—one night at her mother's home in Wilmington, Delaware, and this time it didn't turn out to be just a quick thrill. I very quickly became emotionally involved with her. What I'd thought would be a relatively innocent one- or two-night stand soon flew out of control. We became real lovers, and didn't hide this from the other two girls in the group, Margo and Ginger. It made them very uncomfortable.

I wound up staying with Carol for two years, and my relationship with her was the best I ever had. I also had the most fun of any relationship I've been in. It was sensitive, giving, and caring.

At the beginning I told her she could move in with me. I was living at my parents' home in Brooklyn, so both of us stayed in my room. I don't understand how my mother didn't know what was going on between us. After all, it was a four-bedroom house, yet Carol was sleeping in my little room and my single bed. Didn't my mother ever ask herself any questions about this?

Who's butch? Goldie and Carol.

The day came when we figured we'd better find our own apartment. We wanted to live free—no more sneaking around and whispering, no more under-the-table touches. We found a beautiful apartment on East Seventy-second Street in New York City. I told my mother I was moving out and she absolutely freaked, starting to cry and screaming, "No! You're not leaving! Oye! From the vindow I vill jump!"

I remember thinking to myself, *Enough of this emotional blackmail. It worked when I was eight and we lived on the fourth floor, but now?*

"Ma, we live on the first floor so go ahead . . . jump!"

My mother was always very dramatic. I called her from the new apartment a few days later.

"Hello, Ma?"

"Your mother is dead!" She hung up.

Eventually we made up and she got over it.

I wanted Carol and I to have a family. I realized very soon that this would be hard to achieve for two women, so we got a puppy, the cutest little Chihuahua. We named her Chiquita. A small tan thing, she weighed under five pounds and had the biggest bulging eyes I had ever seen on a Chihuahua. This was our little hairy daughter.

Those days we were all on diet pills, Green Men. One day at the apartment one of those little pills fell out of my hand and I couldn't find it no matter how hard I looked. In the end I forgot about it.

I woke in the middle of the night and felt someone staring at me. Chiquita. Her bulbous eyes were even bigger than normal, so that she looked scary. After a few seconds I figured it out. Chiquita had found and eaten the missing Green Man.

I roused Carol and told her what I thought had happened. She looked at the way Chiquita was staring and pacing, and said, "You're right, we have to find a vet, now!"

We called an emergency veterinarian and rushed Chiquita to his office.

"What's wrong with her?" he asked.

"My dog's on speed!" I yelled.

He immediately gave her a shot to stop the racing of her little heart. We took her home, but she could not rest. Chiquita didn't sleep for another three days. Poor little bug-eyed Chiquita.

While Carol and I were living together, a woman named Susan used to come to our concerts all the time. She was a high-priced hooker who had a thing for Carol. (I found out later that they used to perform sexual acts together for money.) I became very jealous. One night we were performing at the Wagon Wheel when Susan came into the club. I was on-stage with the Gingerbreads in the middle of a song called "Knock on Wood." Carol's and Susan's eyes met, and they stared at each other and smiled in a certain way that got me seeing red.

I stopped the song right there and then, grabbed Carol by the back of her neck and said, into the microphone, "If you want her you can have her."

Then I shoved Carol toward Susan and walked off the stage. The audience fell silent. We all went storming to the back room of the club and yelled at each other.

Carol and I made up and went on living together. I didn't want to end the relationship, because I felt it was a really good one.

Then, one night in 1968, she didn't come home until four a.m. and I asked her where she'd been.

She said, "Oh, walking and thinking . . ."

I knew she was lying. I'd received a phone call during the evening from a girlfriend who'd just seen Carol and Susan in a club. That Carol would lie to me like this—well, I just saw red. I picked up a bottle and threw it past her head; something made me shift my aim at the last moment so that the bottle didn't actually hit her.

All Carol could say was "Goldie, Goldie, Goldie."

I broke all the windows. I was very possessive and very jealous and very insecure. I knew we were over, of course. It could never be the same, not after she had lied to me like this. One thing I cannot tolerate from anyone close to me is lying.

I was very confused after the break-up. For the two years of our relationship I had missed being with men, but still I thought I might be gay. I tried sleeping around with other women, but it didn't work for me. Carol was the only one—the right woman at the right time.

I wound up back in Brooklyn at my parents' home. I can remember sitting in my little room there in April 1968 hearing the news that Martin Luther King, Jr., had been assassinated. I didn't answer the phone. I didn't even move around much. I was shocked and horrified. It was a nightmare revisited. Four and a half years earlier I'd listened in this same little room to the news of President John F. Kennedy being assassinated, and my reaction had been the same then.

• • • • • •

Also in 1968, when Goldie and the Gingerbreads were still working with "Mr. Ripoff," we were doing a gig in Chicago when we all got stuck in a hotel. We racked up a bill, but had no money to pay it. The club we were playing wouldn't pay us, because they wanted us to work until their closing time, four a.m., and we insisted, were booked to do only two shows; our contract said we worked only until midnight. When we complained to our manager in New York, he just said, "We're working on it, we're working on it. Don't leave town until they pay you," which was hardly helpful because, since Lenny wouldn't send us any money to get home, we *couldn't* leave town until the club paid us. So we stayed on in that fleabag hotel, totally on edge. I began having the most vivid nightmares.

∎ ∎ ∎ ∎ ∎ ∎

. . . and the ugly pock-faced man has a gun to my head. He's shoving me up a narrow staircase. I trip and fall, but he just keeps pushing me. I fall again, he pushes again.

I scream. It doesn't stop him pushing me.

"Where are you taking me?" I beg. "Please, please tell me!"

"Shut the fuck up, bitch!" he yells.

Now he's starting to touch my ass, sticking his hand between my legs, feeling me up. I'm humiliated. His fingers don't stop doing their work even when he throws up. All over me. The warm vomit clings to me. And he's still shoving me up the stairs, ignoring my pleas, ignoring my screams.

We reach the top.

"Open that door!" He shouts the command.

"No! Please, please no!" I cry. "Don't lock me in!"

But I open the door and he starts forcing me through it into the musty cobwebbed attic.

"I have to go home!" I implore him. "I have to go home! People will be looking for me!"

He just pushes harder.

I half turn, and I can see his face is even uglier now. His nose is running. He has open blisters on his face. He's foaming at the mouth.

And then I'm in the attic. It's filled with blackness. I can see nothing.

"Please don't leave me here!"

I hear the key turn in the lock.

There's just me, alone in the darkness and so terribly afraid.

And then, from the corner of my eye, I see a pale glimmer of light.

"Oh, please," I whisper, "please make it a window."

I begin to run towards the light. It's a long, long way away, and it doesn't seem to come any closer. Cobwebs claw at my face, at my hair. I trip over boxes filled to bursting with forgotten memories, over broken chairs that have grown too small.

And at last I can see something. There's an old lady, flimsy as a wraith, her gray hair like the spiderwebs that still cling to me. She's sitting there under the window, rocking back and forth, alongside a dust-covered trunk.

I stumble towards her. "Oh, thank God, thank God, help me, please help me, I got to get out of here, please, I can't stay here, help me, please, please help me . . ."

She looks up at me. Her eyes are hard.

"Change the script!"

I shake my head, confused. "What?"

Louder this time. "CHANGE THE SCRIPT!"

It takes a moment for what she's said to sink in, but then I realize, Yes! Yes, I can do that! I can change this script—I'll change it right now.

On her lap she's holding a notepad. I haven't noticed it until now. I grab a sheet of paper from it and then start looking around in desperation.

"I need something to write with," I wail. "Give me a pen or a pencil!"

She speaks to me with a sort of soothing malice. "Well, my dear, that's the problem. I don't have a pen or a pencil. That's why I'm still here . . ."

● ● ● ● ● ●

I can remember waking up from this, soaking wet. The glass on my bedside table was still half full of vodka. The ice cubes had melted, making it watery, but I gulped it down anyway.

I was in a hotel room in Chicago.

And it was almost show time.

● ● ● ● ● ●

Carol and I rooming together made things even more uncomfortable. Ginger was upset, because for years I'd roomed with her. Then one day

Margo just skipped, leaving us in Chicago. I was devastated; Margo was a big part of this group. When we finally were able to leave the hotel and get back to New York City, I did everything to try and get her back, but it was over in more ways than one.

I was getting so tired of this all-woman-band stuff. When Goldie and the Gingerbreads had broken up in England they should have stayed that way.

It didn't end quite yet, though. We kept trying to be Goldie and the Gingerbreads. Now we had to find another keyboard player.

We were lucky enough to find Norma LaLane, a really good keyboard player. Also, she was black, and it felt good to me to have a black musician in the band. But I was still getting very disillusioned. I felt I wasn't experiencing any kind of musical growth. The whole women's-band concept that had promised and delivered so much was now degenerating into headaches and heartaches. I yearned to work with male musicians. I wanted to be more creative. I was stagnating. I needed some sort of change.

• • • • • •

We were performing at the Wagon Wheel one night when the group that worked opposite us invited a drummer named Les DeMerle to come up on the stage and sit in with them. Short and smug, Les looked like an elf on drugs, but I couldn't take my eyes off him. And the sound? He was one of the most incredible drummers I've ever heard. I think he wished he was Buddy Rich, whom he somewhat resembled. I spoke to him after we'd played; he flirted with me and, of course, I flirted back. We exchanged numbers, and eventually he called, asking if I'd like to come hear his quartet and possibly sing with them on one or two numbers. I said I'd love to, so he picked me up one evening when he was playing at a Jewish wedding. They almost threw me out of the reception when I arrived wearing my black lace see-through dress and no bra. The rabbi practically had a heart attack. Les had to ask me to sit way in the back.

Later, when we were in his car driving to a restaurant, I told him I was living with my guitar player, a woman, but that things weren't so good. I think that turned him on.

He lived in Queens in a house where he had all his instruments set up in the basement, and we started to hang out there. On Monday nights we used to go to the Village Vanguard to see Thad Jones and Mel Louis—

big band music, and boy did I love that! Les had a vast collection of jazz recordings, and I listened to every one of them. He dressed well, too, in tailor-made suits. I loved it when he wore a tuxedo.

Meanwhile, I took all my belongings out of the apartment I'd been sharing with Carol. No note, no nothing. I just left her for Les.

I started to travel with Les and the rest of his quartet. He introduced me to many great musicians, including the Brecker Brothers and Bill Takas (who wound up later playing bass in Ten Wheel Drive). Singing with Les's quartet, I was doing ballads and straight songs like "What Now, My Love?" and "Sunny Gets Blue." Les arranged to get some charts written for me for the songs we did. I'd never had any music charts to work with before, so when he first asked me if I had charts I really didn't know what he was talking about; I joked that the doctor hadn't said anything! Jazz legend Frank Foster arranged a couple of my songs; believe me, that was a big deal to me, and still is.

There was no denying that Les was a sensational drummer. The trouble was that he had a hard time playing simple rhythms for singers like me; he had to play complex, and it got a little annoying. We used to say, "More music, less DeMerle!"

We played gigs in lounges. One time we got a gig in the South at a very straight South Carolina lounge. We were staying in a small motel and had a few black musicians in the band. We almost got killed by some Southern rednecks. Les had long hair and they hated him for that. I was very loud, both in dress and in mouth, so they had a good reason for hating me, too. It could have been a scene out of *Deliverance,* but at the time we didn't realize the danger we were in.

Les and I had a kind of a crazy relationship going. I respected his playing so much I think I would have followed him anywhere, and I practically did. I went with him to Las Vegas to watch him play with Wayne Newton. It wasn't easy for me to be in the background the whole time, though; it drove me nuts not to be singing, and I got very depressed. Those gigs we did as a quintet were hardly a career-building showcase for me.

Then, back in New York when we were working a club on East Eighty-sixth Street, a well-known record producer who'd come to see Les play quietly said to me, "Why aren't you out on your own? You sound like a female Ray Charles."

No wonder I did! I listened to Ray Charles night and day. He was my inspiration.

Eventually I got very broke hanging around with Les. I hadn't worked in months. Little by little Les stopped coming around, so there we were, me and Bridget, my little Yorkie, in a tiny studio apartment in Chelsea, on Thirty-first Street. Les, I decided, was not a nice person. He used me and everyone else around him. He was self-centered and egotistical. I was so short of money I had to move back to my mother's house again, and she would not allow me to bring Bridget with me—she still had my other dog, Spunky. I cried for days after I had to give Bridget away.

I was not too pleased with Les DeMerle, but I have to admit that everything I ever knew about jazz I learned from him. He turned me on to every great jazz record, and because of him I saw lots of the musicians behind those records play live. The sex bit of the relationship was lousy, but he did teach me some nice drumbeats. All in all, the Les DeMerle experience, as it were, set me up for my next musical endeavor.

I decided to drop the name Goldie and henceforth call myself Genya instead. It was, after all, my given name, and I liked it. In this connection I have to give credit to Les for one more thing. He said, "You sound so *black* when you sing. Why don't you name yourself for something black? 'Raven' or something?"

Hm. "Genya Raven." Yeah. Liked it.

Maybe I would spell it a bit differently, though, and use an "a" instead of an "e."

Yeah, Genya Ravan.

CHAPTER EIGHT
Ten Wheel Drive

IT WAS THE FALL OF 1968, and I needed a new direction. Musically I'd grown stale. The whole music scene seemed to have stagnated. FM radio had come onto the scene—good news for those of us sick of the same three-minute pop songs played over and over ("white shit songs," I called them). Something new, wonderful, and exciting was happening. When FM radio came, real music came with it. The three-minute limit imposed on AM radio began to crumble. Wow! FM didn't care if a song was *fifteen* minutes long. What freedom! Radio at last became interesting. FM gave musicians time to build on the arrangements and to make songs so much more complete. "Finally! Now *that's* music!" I remember saying out loud to myself.

FM sounded fresh. I wanted to become a part of it all. I heard Blood, Sweat and Tears with Al Kooper—they played the full album on the radio, and I loved it. Besides being a horn band, Blood, Sweat and Tears performed soul with a full sound that was well arranged. And their songs lasted more than three minutes!

I still didn't have a clue what I was going to do about my stagnant career. I had just gone through the jazz thing with the Les DeMerle Quintet, but now I was lost. I already felt like a has-been, a very depressed has-been. I'd been halfway around the world and was sort of a star in Europe, but I wasn't well known in the U.S. I had another major problem: I couldn't accompany myself on piano or guitar—on piano I could play a few 1950s-style progressions, but that was it. I played blues harmonica and some drums. I knew my lack of instrumental training didn't help my career. Coffeehouses like The Bitter End were appearing and gaining in popularity, and they were full of chicks with guitars and pianos.

Meanwhile, friends were still calling me and telling me about female musicians they'd found for me; people were always scouting on my behalf, because female musicians were still hard to find. But I was so over the all-women concept by now: Putting female bands together was, I'd decided, a major pain in the ass. More women, more PMS, more complaining, more crap. Still, I figured I had no choice but to put together another women's band, however much I hated the thought. Those were the only musicians who flocked to me—women.

What I ended up with were women musicians who couldn't hold a candle to the old Goldie and the Gingerbreads. They were decent enough to gig with and make some money with, but when I was performing with them I felt like I'd rather find gigs in places where there'd be no one in the audience who knew me: Staten Island, far out in Long Island, anywhere I'd not feel too embarrassed. I also didn't get on with these girls as people very well. There wasn't that old camaraderie I'd loved with the Gingerbreads.

Larry Stagmore, a buddy of mine, recommended Billy Fields as a manager. He said Fields was a good honest guy and was always looking for new talent. So I called Billy and set up an appointment. When I went to his office I found Larry had been right: he really was a nice guy. Billy was very aware of who Goldie and the Gingerbreads had been, and that helped, because I hated having to boast about myself and my achievements. I told him I wanted to be a solo singer, but that I would need an accompanist because I didn't play anything but harmonica and drums.

"Gee, that's too bad," he said. "It's a shame you don't play piano or guitar."

I thought, *Well, that's it. Thanks for nothin'. See ya.*

But he went on, "Let me think about this a couple of weeks."

When I left, it was with the conviction that I'd never hear from him again. I reckoned I'd better stick with this sorry women's band I already had. I was so fucking tired of not having the sound or the band that I wanted.

Surprise! Billy called me about two weeks after our appointment, and thereafter we spoke a few more times on the phone. I could tell he liked me not just as an artist but as a person. He kept saying he thought I was a talent, and this was good to hear; I was so emotionally low that I needed the compliments. Billy made me feel like something would happen for me again musically.

I liked him very much. He was a warm person, and I believe he would have done anything for me. He dealt from the heart. In this business, it's so hard to find someone real. Most managers I'd had were liars: They'd tell you anything they thought you wanted to hear. Musicians have to cope with the sharpest con artists around; if artists deal with the heart instead of the head, they get screwed. Don't get me wrong. In a way managers *have* to be sharp businesspeople, connivers, and cheaters, and I'd always looked for that kind of hustling manager. I sought managers who were good at the dirty business end. For me, I just wanted to be the performer; I didn't want to play those games. It took me a long time to discover that those kinds of managers didn't work for me.

Today it's different. Performers must be business-savvy. The music business is one of the largest money-making industries in the world. Where there's money, there's politics; where there's politics, there are businesspeople; and where there are businesspeople, there are liars and cheaters. It's a vicious circle. Very hard on the creative soul. Today's musicians better have the connections, wrong or right—that's where the strength lies. The modern music industry is too much business and not enough heart.

Like I've said before, "combinations breed success." You're never the only one who makes a hit record. Musicians can be very talented, but, if they don't have the right song, if they're not with the right manager or the right agent, and of course if the timing isn't right, it just ain't gonna happen. Me, I was always ahead of the times, but this was a struggle in itself. I would have to defend myself constantly against questions about my music, my productions, and my women's bands. I was called a pioneer, which was flattering, but flattery on its own doesn't build a successful career.

In hindsight, Billy was not a strong enough manager for me, not a decision-maker. I liked him, but I felt he was temporary. I knew I had the talent to make it in this business.

One day Billy told me he had something that might suit me. Curious, I went as fast as I could to his office, and discovered him with a gleam in his eye and a big smile on his face. "I have an interesting idea, Genya. I got a call yesterday from a friend who knows these two guys who live in New Jersey. He thinks they're talents. They write their own songs and they're also arrangers. They want to start a group, and they've been looking for a singer." He looked at me and put the question: "What do you think?"

Out loud I said, "Well, let's see." What I was thinking was: *Not that promising if they're just starting. What a drag to have to put another band together. All auditions and no income.* But then I added, "Okay. I've nothing to lose."

Disgusted as I was with the women's band, I thought being in a male rock band would be a welcome change. I told Billy I would need to meet these guys, hear their material, and make sure they weren't assholes. Inside, I was praying the material would be good. I knew good material was a prerequisite; without it we wouldn't have a ghost of a chance of success. First-rate songs were hard to find, and, of course, I wasn't yet writing any of my own.

Billy set up a meeting with the New Jersey guys, and I met up with them at a small funky music rental studio on Forty-fourth Street and Broadway. The room was only wide enough for a piano; we barely all fit in.

I stared at the two guys a while. The first, Mike Zager, was very straight-looking. I was used to seeing musicians in tight bell-bottom jeans, teeshirts, leather vests—that kind of thing. Mike's pants seemed too big on him. His shirt was cotton, with short, wide sleeves. He looked like he just got off a plane from a Wisconsin Cheese Convention, and he had this perpetual smile on his face. Aram Schefrin was a bit reserved and serious, sort of cute. He had a mustache (which I hated), long hair, and a cowboy hat. He even wore cowboy boots. Boots! At least he looked a little bit more like a musician—he didn't need a major overhaul. Together, the pair of them remind me in retrospect of Dustin Hoffman and Jon Voight in *Midnight Cowboy*. What a sight!

I smiled politely and said, "Okay, let's hear what you got."

Mike got behind the piano and started to play a song named "I Am a Want Ad." I just stared at them like they were an exhibit in the Reptile House at the zoo. I couldn't understand what the hell the song was about. It used funny words—words I'd never heard before. It sounded to me like this: *I am a want a— bla bla braggle and blattt and I want want want I want . . . things.*

The fact that neither one of them could sing made the songs sound even weirder. Mike played the piano; Aram sang first, then Mike joined in. Both of them sounded like shit, and now they were singing a song called "Polar Bear Rug."

I thought to myself, *What the fuck is this? These songs sound like they should be in a comedy play or something. They're so Broadway—maybe these guys could write a musical. This sure ain't no rock 'n' roll!* I found out later they'd studied with Stephen Sondheim, so I wasn't far off.

I didn't say anything unkind to them, just a long succession of: "Uh huh . . . nice . . . ah huh . . . hm . . . nice."

At last, just as I was thinking they would never stop, they finished playing their songs. They'd given me a headache. Then we spoke. I really didn't know at this point what I could say to them, but I knew it shouldn't be what I wanted to say, which was: "What the fuck was *that*?" The more we spoke, though, and the more they pointed out that I could have all the musical freedom I wanted with these songs, the more interested I became. I could mold these songs to fit my taste in music. I knew I had a lot of work ahead of me because I would have to change so much, but I told myself I could put some soul into these songs. In fact, they weren't that bad. I could alter some of the lyrics. I thought that maybe down the line I could push the guys into writing a little funkier—that maybe, the more I sang with them, the more they would write in my direction.

Even so, I was, to put it mildly, not thrilled. I went home depressed. At the same time, I was ready for the change, ready for anything except what I was doing. Even the Midnight Cowboys would be welcome. I was also tired of calling the shots all the time, always running the show, and having to make all the decisions. I just wanted to fucking sing.

Billy called me that night and asked me what I thought. I told him, "Not bad, but they are really major squares."

He laughed.

"Well, let's see what happens when I've learned the songs," I told him.

Now Mike and Aram needed to hear me sing. I was doing a gig in a seedy Staten Island club with the women's group, and along they came. I was on-stage when I saw them arrive, and I kicked it up and put my energy into it—did a good show. I could see them talking, smiling, pointing. It was obvious they liked what they heard. It didn't hurt that I looked hot. I was always strong on-stage, and sexy. That night I was wearing a see-through blouse with, of course, no bra. I had a tough and confident demeanor to match the R&B I sang—a real rock 'n' roll attitude.

I walked over to their table after the show, and we sat and talked. Mike smiled a lot and kept staring at my breasts. "Great. We'll call you tomorrow," he said. He was so awkward I had to laugh. I decided I liked Mike.

And that was that. They called me the very next day and said I was perfect for what they envisioned for their group. If I was interested, they were ready to start teaching me the songs. So we began rehearsing and getting our sound together.

I went to see them in New Jersey quite a lot, mostly to Mike's apartment, where he lived with his wife, Jane, sometimes to Aram's, where I met his wife, Ettie. I heard the rest of the material and started to learn the songs. I believe it was me who made the songs come to life as I started to make them "mine." The music started sounding good, even with just a piano. We were all thrilled—the two wives as well.

I didn't understand lots of the lyrics. Aram, the lyricist, had graduated from Harvard. I'd learned how to speak English when I was eight years old, and had quit high school at sixteen. Every rehearsal I had to ask him things like "What does that word 'lapidary' mean?" Eventually I bought a dictionary so I could understand at least half the words I had to sing.

We didn't have any other musicians lined up yet. I put the squeeze on both the guys to start this thing rolling; they both tended to procrastinate too much. I think they were scared. I told them about Bill Takas, an excellent upright bass player I'd met through Les DeMerle. Bill had recorded with Judy Collins and Grady Tate. I also had a few horn players in mind. I already knew the Brecker Brothers, because Les (again) had introduced me to them when I was in his quintet. A drummer named Leon Rix was recommended, and when he auditioned for us we knew immediately he was perfect for our group: he nailed a solid beat.

We made the ability to read music a requirement for anyone in the group. I was the only one in the band who couldn't.

Eight weeks went by and still we were only rehearsing. I started to know the songs well enough; now we needed to move on and find the rest of the band. At the moment, we were a band with no name and not enough musicians. I told Mike and Aram I needed to work and I needed to do it soon. We started auditioning all kinds of players. After we found our full rhythm section, everyone got excited. We began looking for horn players. We wanted the Breckers, but they were busy and couldn't commit to a band situation. (That's what happened back then with a lot of the chart-reading musicians. They were making money playing recording sessions and didn't want to go on the road.) We finally got a great horn section: Louis Hoff, Dennis Parisi, Jay Silva, Richard Meisterman, and Peter Hyde.

The charts Mike and Aram wrote needed some tweaking, but before long the sound was unbelievable, truly unique. I think Mike and Aram were amazed at themselves and their capabilities as writers and arrangers. Hearing their own music come to life was a revelation for them.

Billy Fields was a close friend of Paul Colby, the owner of The Bitter End on Bleecker Street. Billy asked Paul if we could rehearse at the club in the afternoons; in return, we would do our first gig and our presentation shows there. We were so grateful to Paul that we promised to do a show for him for the same amount of money if we become a popular group. Later on we kept that promise.

One day we were sitting around at rehearsal when Billy said, "We need a name for this group. Let's get a name and stick to it."

We all began coming up with stupid ideas. Aram wanted to call us the Great Train Robbery. After what seemed like a million names, someone said, "Ten Wheel Drive." Now that was big and strong. It had movement. It sounded like us. "That's *it*! That's *it*!" I yelled immediately.

So we had our name. And now I knew we had to move quickly. We were truly a group. We were *Ten Wheel Drive*.

Billy Fields kept coming to the rehearsals and listening to our sound as it grew. I think this may have prompted him to wonder if the band was going to be too much for him to handle alone. It was smart thinking on his part. Eventually he told us he'd come up with a great idea: How would we feel about a friend of his, the promoter and manager Sid Bernstein, coming in to co-manage Ten Wheel Drive? I already knew who Sid was, but the guys didn't. We told them Sid was very well respected, had once promoted the Beatles, had managed the Rascals when they were huge, and had connections to all the right people in the business.

We met with Sid one night after he came down to watch us. He was a good-hearted person, just like Billy Fields. I thought, *Wow, we're surrounded by nice guys for a change.* I mean, after Goldie and the Gingerbreads and being surrounded by "wise guys," nice guys seemed a welcome change.

Sid was not only known and loved by everyone, both personally and in the business, he was the most giving person I ever knew. Every time Aram, Mike, and I got together with him he would take us to Central Park South for ice cream. Sid loved to eat, but he had to watch his diet—he was a little on the heavy side. He would say, "Eat, kids, eat!" with a glowing smile. We used to laugh because he was living vicariously through us.

We did our very first gig at The Bitter End on October 25, 1969, and it was extremely well received. By the time we'd done a few more gigs there, Ten Wheel Drive had become the group everyone was talking about. We soon started to pack the place, even though we didn't yet have a record out—indeed, we didn't yet have so much as a record *deal*. Even the session musicians began to come along to check us out, and one night Miles Davis did the same. We were very quickly making a name and a reputation for ourselves. The news had hit the streets. There was to be no stopping Ten Wheel Drive. Reviewers were using adjectives like "inventive," "impressive," and "powerful," while more than once I was described as "a star"—you can bet I lapped *that* up! We were compared, in that manner the press have of always wanting to make comparisons, with Chicago and with Blood, Sweat and Tears. I drew the inevitable comparisons with Janis Joplin.

After our fourth performance at The Bitter End, Sid brought down Jerry Schoenbaum, the freshly appointed President of Polydor Records, which had just opened up in the U.S.; based in Germany, Polydor was huge in Europe, especially under the guise of Deutsche Grammophon, which was the first Europe-wide label dedicated to classical music. Now Polydor was going to explore rock and blues in the States. Jerry Schoenbaum came down twice to hear us. It was no secret that he loved my singing more than he loved the group—he said that to me and others many times—but he signed us anyway. That advance gave us all a hundred dollars a week. We were thrilled, of course: now we were really on our way.

We went to Jerry's office at Polydor at least once a week. It was a real trip. Jerry had a problem with his left eye—it was stationary—and this sometimes made our meetings difficult. The three of us would be seated in a row across from him, on the other side of his desk. Mike would sit on one side of me, Aram on the other. When Jerry asked a question, we each would think he was talking to one of us individually, so either all three of us would answer at the same time or none of us would answer at all. We just never knew who he was talking to. I would start to laugh—it was embarrassing.

Jerry always thought Aram and Mike were way too uptight and straight, and he didn't like it. The truth was that he didn't know what to make of them—Aram being a lawyer and Mike having an engineering degree. Maybe he thought they were too bright for rock 'n' roll, or something. Me, on the other hand, I liked Mike's and Aram's eccentricities. I used to love making Mike laugh. I told him I could never picture him screwing Jane—that he was just too square to fuck. When Jane got pregnant, I said to him, "I know how you got Jane pregnant. The telephone in your bedroom was on Jane's side of the bed. One night the phone rang, Jane answered it, the call was for you, so you leaned over Jane to get the phone, and then you were told the good news. You were told you got the record deal, and you got so excited you started jumping up and down on her, and *it* accidentally went in. So that's how Jane got pregnant. And you couldn't wait for the second record to come out so you could have sex again. Keep that phone on Jane's side. You might be lucky and get to fuck a third time."

Me with Ten Wheel Drive. No groupies for them either.

We rehearsed like crazy for the upcoming recording. We met for the first time with our producer, Walter Raim, in a West Village coffeehouse. He came highly recommended. He'd done a lot of work producing jingles for Madison Avenue TV commercials; they had a clean, close sound which I liked. The boys weren't so sure, but I pressured them into accepting Walter.

The recording sessions for the album, to be called *Construction #1*, went really well, despite some hair-raising moments. On a cooking take of the song "Eye of the Needle," the bass and bass drum suddenly disappeared—just vanished! We had to overdub the parts. Another time, when we recorded "Tightrope," we found there was a mysterious percussive sound on the playback. We all sat in the control room trying to work out where it had come from, isolating each musician's track in turn to see if we could solve the puzzle. No luck until we tried the last track, mine. We eventually worked out that the mike was so sensitive it was picking up the movement of the silk blouse I was wearing. It sounded pretty okay, so we left it—in fact, we gave the blouse a credit on the album cover.

When *Construction #1* was released, in 1969, it got rave reviews, and it charted. Some of the reviewers made favorable comments on the way I could go from loud, raucous rocking vocals on some of the tracks to softness and sensitivity on others, comparing this ability to Billie Holiday. Wow! They couldn't have said a nicer thing.

• • • • • •

I loved the West Village, especially Bleecker Street, the street The Bitter End was on. There were boutiques (with all kinds of hand-made tie-dyed clothes), leather shops, art stores, stores selling hand-made jewelry—lots of good stuff. The streets in the West Village were alive with an energy that made it feel like a quaint town and not part of a big city. Music blared out of the boutiques.

The coffeehouse next to The Bitter End was the one I always sat in, and it was there I met Tim Hardin. He'd written some of the best songs of the 1960s—"If I Were a Carpenter," "Misty Roses," "Reason to Believe," "Black Sheep Boy," "Hang on to a Dream," and others—but by the time I met him he was pathetic. I felt awful that he was in such bad shape. I guess it was the height of his heroin addiction, which ultimately killed him in 1980, when he was only thirty-nine. I'd wanted to record "Reason to Believe" but Rod Stewart beat me to it and had a hit with it.

(It seems Rod and I have the same musical tastes. I've often heard it said that *Urban Desire* feels like early Faces music.)

Tim liked me and we talked a lot. There was nothing I could do for him—I couldn't even tell him how much I loved his music—although I did wonder if I could kidnap him and put him in a hospital or a rehab clinic. One time I complimented him on the snakeskin jacket he was wearing, and the next thing I knew he was trying to give it to me. Of course, I refused. I knew it was just the drugs talking. Anyway, it was freezing outside; he needed his jacket for himself.

At The Bitter End we played with Richie Havens, Odetta, Janis Ian, Melanie, Taj Mahal, and the comedy group The Ace Trucking Company.

Then one day I got a call from Sid. "When do you think the band will be ready to play a big gig? There's an opening at the Fillmore East in two weeks with Steppenwolf."

I screamed, "We're ready *now*! We'll do it!"

At the next rehearsal I told Aram and Mike about the Fillmore East gig we were going to do. The two partners turned green. When Aram became nervous he'd get this dazed look in his eyes and play with his mustache. He played with that mustache full-time for the next two weeks.

"Do you really think we'll be ready?" Mike asked.

"Of course. Hell, we're ready now," I said.

Aram, worried, chipped in. "I don't know about this gig."

"Hey!" I yelled. "I'm not going to just rehearse until I die! We're doing the Fillmore gig. Period."

We rehearsed as if our lives depended on it. The wives came along to rehearsals, just like a little fan club. I was excited, even though everyone else was primarily just nervous. The band was hot and ready.

It was a wonderful time to be at the Fillmore. You could smell the incense in the streets back in the magical Sixties, all the patchouli and musk. I loved the scents, the attitudes, and the feeling of everything and everybody in those days. The clothes were great, too. The big bellbottoms with rhinestones and sequins, combined with the big hair—what a look. Even greater was that Black was Beautiful. Black was happening. Black had always been beautiful in my eyes. It was the Dawning of the Age of Aquarius.

I was yet again living in Brooklyn at my parents' home. It was hard for me to get to rehearsals and take trains and cabs from Brooklyn to New York City and home again. We were all on a small retainer, about a hundred dollars a week, hardly enough to pay rent and live. Aram and

Mike got an advance for the publishing of their songs, and decided to help me out by paying the rent for a basement studio apartment I found on Thirtieth Street between Second and Third Avenues. The apartment was small, but fine for my purposes: Between rehearsals and gigs, I was never home, so all I needed was a bed and a roof over my head.

I was walking past a clothing store on Thirtieth Street one day when I saw a belt in the window with big studs all around it; it looped down in the front like a chastity belt. I said, "That's me. I want that!" I wore that chastity belt for almost all my performances, and it became my emblem. I still have it.

• • • • • •

Summer 1969. And so to the night of the Fillmore gig.

I bought a black see-through jacket and a tie-dye teeshirt, and wore my hip-hugging jeans with a big butterfly on the ass and rhinestones that I'd applied myself on one leg—and, of course, I had on my chastity belt. I spotted this guy backstage painting flowers on people's faces and I got an idea. I called him into my dressing room, took off my top, stood naked from the waist up, and said, "Paint big stars on these. I'm going out on stage without a blouse."

He looked at my boobs and, without a blink, said, "Cool." He painted two huge stars on my boobs—red stars with blue outlines, the left star higher than the right star. It looked good. I knew I had a great body. (People always thought I had my breasts augmented and I used to tell 'em, "Nope, they're mine, all mine.")

The group almost choked when they saw me. The horn section looked like they were going to start drooling.

Just keep blowin' your horns, boys, I thought. Mike had a dirty-old-man smile on and I swear Aram got a hard-on. Aram himself looked pretty hot; he had on his leather chaps and a long leather coat with a slit up the back.

I wanted a big reaction from everyone, and that's what I got. As someone said to me back stage, "You not only look good enough to eat, you smell good enough to bathe with"—this compliment from a hippie-looking guy who looked like he hadn't had a bath in a month. I reeked of patchouli oil.

When we went out on stage I was wearing the see-through jacket. We started the set with a song called "Tightrope" to which I'd written the

Creating chaos at the Fillmore East (may Mom rest in peace).

first couple of songs and then, as we moved into the third, took it off. The audience charged toward the stage. People weren't sure what they were seeing, or what they thought they were seeing. The lighting guy put the red spotlights on me so the blue outlines of the stars disappeared and I looked totally naked right down to my belly button.

Even though my breasts were a shock factor, the audience eventually got past it, and loved us for our music. We did an encore—pretty good when the main attraction, still to come, was Steppenwolf.

A few of our record-company executives were in the audience that night, and after the show they came back stage. One of them grabbed me. "Genya, I've never seen anything like this before—both the guys *and* the girls are nuts over you. The girls looked like they would have died for a night in bed with you. I saw little girls creaming themselves over you! The boys went nuts! You've got this androgynous stage presence."

I said, "Yeah, it's that 'bi' thing. It's what's happening."

The late 1960s were such heady days. For me and lots of others it was a time of peace, love, drugs, sex, organic veggies, and fresh fruit! (The only problem was most of the vegetarians I knew looked like they'd swallowed a hand grenade, their skin was so bad.) It was the time of "Make Love Not War." And it was a great time to be in California and New York City.

• • • • • •

One thing going on in the 1970s that really bothered the fuck out of me was the whole astrology scene. The "What's your sign?" line.

Come 1970 and we were doing a gig at the Fillmore West in San Francisco with Sha Na Na and The Steve Miller Band when, during a break, a girl came over to me back stage and said, "I've done lots of stars' charts. Let me do your chart. What sign are you?"

Despite my dislike of astrology I went ahead and talked to her. "Aries," I said.

"What time were you born?" She was as bald as an eagle, wore at least four layers of skirts, and had a scorpion painted on her face. She had a notepad and pens in her hand.

"I don't know."

"Was it night? Day?"

"I don't know. So, will I ever know where my moon is?" I asked her, half-kidding.

"What do you mean, you don't know?" she persisted.

"You can't do my chart. I don't know what time I was born, or the real date I was born."

"Oh," she said. "Were you adopted? We could research . . ."

I explained it to her. "Due to the confusion of the war in Poland, I never had a birth certificate. I was born in a cellar and quickly given away so my life could be saved. I have no way of finding out what time I was born, or what town I was born in." Of course it bothered me that I could never have my chart done, but that was the least of it. It has always been awful not knowing the details of my birth.

She got tears in her eyes and told me to make up my own birth time and date.

I told her, "Take more acid. Maybe my moon is up somebody's ass."

• • • • • •

When we got back to New York City we were booked into an up-and-coming club on the East Side, on St. Marks Place between Second Avenue and Third Avenues. The club was called the Electric Circus, and it sure was happening there. It was *the* club for rock and jazz. We played there more than once. Every band worked The Electric Circus. All the black guys there looked like Jimi Hendrix, or maybe it was really that Jimi looked like all the black guys at the Electric Circus. Fringed jackets and vests, head bandannas—they looked very colorful and alive.

Ten Wheel Drive performed frequently opposite the Tony Williams Lifetime, and we also worked often with the Chambers Brothers. One of the times we toured with the Chambers Brothers, I told my roadies to never hand me a jug of water when I was performing, but instead always to pop open a fresh bottle of water for me. The Chambers Brothers were known to spike their drinks with LSD and not warn the other musicians.

One particular night I was standing behind the curtain, getting ready to go on to perform. The guys had already taken their positions on-stage for our opening number. A roadie from the Chambers Brothers stood there smoking a joint. He turned to me and said, "Have just one toke, Genya."

I said, "Okay. But only one." I took a long drag. I had no idea the joint was laced with angel dust until I went out onto the stage and the band started up for our song "Eye of the Needle." The intro to this song was particularly hard on the trumpet players because of the high register of the notes. The joint kicked in and I was so stoned I forgot the opening line, and the horns kept repeating the same intro for what seemed like twenty minutes while I stayed silent. I looked at the horn section. Red in the face and with their veins popping in their necks, they were staring back at me with pleading eyes—at least, I think they were pleading; maybe they were just wishing I was dead. Aram gracefully slid across the stage and mouthed to me, "Sharp-edged summer time . . ."

"Oh, yeah," I said, then started to sing. What a relieved look from the horn section! It seemed the audience knew what was happening and liked it.

The horn section always played from a platform behind me. During a gig at some college auditorium we were playing the song "Brief Replies" when I heard a really foul, screeching high note coming from the horn section. I noticed some people in the audience were laughing. I turned around to see what was so funny and saw that our trumpet player, Steve Satten, leaning back to play his part, had leaned too far and fallen off the platform. He was so stoned that he just kept on playing flat on his back, like a bug with its legs flailing.

• • • • • •

I loved working at Steve Paul's Scene, an intimate little New York club not unlike The Bitter End. I enjoyed working up a sweat, and the place was always hot. It had a bigger stage than The Bitter End, and the audience was all in front of you. (At The Bitter End the stage was in the middle of a long, narrow room with tables and chairs on both sides of the stage as well as in front.)

One night we were playing Steve Paul's when I got a note from one of my roadies that Janis Joplin and singer/keyboard player Chris Farlowe, an old friend from England, were in the audience.

Aha! A good opportunity! I thought. Finally I can show the world that Janis and I don't sound alike! I was so sick and tired of people comparing us—in the press, interviews, and articles. I imagine she was as weary of it as I was. I couldn't even drink my favorite drink, Southern Comfort, without the comparison being made. Boy, that got to me. It was my drink, and had been since way back when I'd had Goldie and the Gingerbreads. I had nothing against Janis herself, of course: I liked her (we'd met some while earlier) and I liked the way she sang. It was just that I felt she and I sounded totally different—I believed I was smoother, more R&B.

I called Janis up on-stage. At first she didn't want to come up—she needed coaxing; Ten Wheel Drive songs weren't easy to jam to. Towards the end of our song "Tightrope" I got the band to stay between two chords and set up a groove. I got Chris Farlowe on-stage first, and then I called, "Janis, get up here and sing with me!"

The audience yelled, "Come on, Janis!"

At first she shook her head "No." But I insisted. The band sounded safe enough playing—we caught great grooves. I finally got her up beside me and we started to jam on "Tightrope." I took the song outside of the chart. The band had to watch me like a hawk; I had hand signals for them. I made them go really soft, then loud, with drum breaks, and then I'd get a R&B thing happening. For anyone to be able to sit in with us, I had to get a tag going, a simple two-chord rhythmic groove. We had one of these really going up there on "Tightrope" when Janis joined us. It was a great jam session. Too bad no one recorded it. Needless to say, we brought the house down.

Free-style jamming was hard with Ten Wheel Drive. The players worked from charts. I was not that thrilled with the practice because sometimes it felt too confining, too structured. I was a singer who came from a background of people jumping up on-stage and jamming to cover songs—"You play and I'll make up the lyrics"-type performances. As the band would play, the song would change, and everyone would go with the song and the flow. The strict adherence to charts was one of my biggest problems in Ten Wheel Drive.

The horn players would get a horrified look on their faces when I randomly pointed at one of them to do an impromptu solo. Then I would put my hand down for the solo to end. (Mind you, they were all great soloists in Ten Wheel Drive—we always had super horn sections. David Liebman went on to play with Miles Davis, and some of our players, like Tom Malone and Dean Pratt, became part of the house band for *Saturday Night Live*.)

The horn players got belligerent about my habit of picking the soloist right on the spot. I also think they were chauvinistic. I'd heard that in the days of the big band era the female singer would sit on the side of the stage waiting to come up in front to sing her song. I think our horn players would have loved it if we'd played in that kind of set-up.

I used to tell them, "Listen, I'm the one who *feels* the audience. I can sense what they want. I'm the one *with* the audience. You read your charts and think about playing your parts. You're not staring at the audience . . . you don't see them eye-to-eye. You're behind your horns and your music stands." (I hated those black music stands. Eventually I made everyone memorize their music charts.)

Even so, they resented the fact that it was me who called the shots as to who went solo when. It's one of the reasons Ten Wheel Drive wound up with three different horn sections on the three albums. There was always a fight between the rhythm section and the horn section, so Aram and Mike and I had to fire them all five at once. They would try to form a sort of union between them and get one spokesperson to do all the complaining. It got out of hand. Once any one player in the horn section became dissatisfied, they would all stick together. Very childish. One time after I'd fired the horn section *en masse,* two of the players wrote me personal letters saying it wasn't them who'd started it all.

And they were always thinking first and foremost about money. Ten Wheel Drive was supposed to play Woodstock, but the horn players didn't want to do it because there was no money involved and our managers weren't strong enough to make them. Bad choice on the horn players' part . . .

When that kind of discontent got a grip, the whole section had to go. As I said, we had three different horn sections in two and a half years—that's fifteen horn players. For once the charts that Ten Wheel Drive relied on came in useful: We had the horn arrangements written on charts and, as all good horn players read music, it was easy enough for a new horn section to slot in. Getting a new rhythm section, on the other hand—that would have been a different story. Thankfully, we kept our rhythm section long enough to satisfy me.

• • • • • •

The Atlanta Pop Festival in July 1969 has to be one of the highlights of my career, and this was definitely one of my most memorable concerts. I had never performed in front of so many people before, not even with the Stones or Chubby Checker. At the Middle Georgia Raceway, Ten Wheel Drive played before over 350,000 people. Wow! One of the hottest days of the year gave us one of the best gigs we ever did. What a great experience! The place was packed to the rafters with screaming, tie-dyed, painted people wanting to hear music by their favorite groups.

Everyone was colorful, everyone was high. The audience ate and slept at the festival. As I was singing I watched this massive audience from the stage, and it gave me a rush I've never felt before or after. That audience loved us.

The other bands at the festival were amazing: Led Zeppelin, Pink Floyd, Sly & the Family Stone, Canned Heat, Janis Joplin, Blood, Sweat and Tears, Creedence Clearwater Revival, Grand Funk Railroad—just about everyone who was anyone. It was so hot that at one point while performing I had to pour a jug of water on myself and just *hope* I didn't get electrocuted!

It was at the end of this festival that I actually talked to Janis Joplin for the first time. At the end of the three glorious days and nights of pure magic, music, and heat, we all boarded a plane for home. Janis sat down with me. She poured herself a drink from a flask and asked if I wanted any. "It's too early," I said; it was about two in the afternoon. (This was before I myself crossed the line into alcoholism.)

I asked her, "Why are you drinking so early? What the hell is wrong with you?"

"It's a party," she said.

We talked a while and she got real quiet.

I said, "What's the matter? Why do you look so down?"

"I'm upset at an asshole."

"What happened?" I asked, because she looked really sad.

She told me that the night before she and David Clayton-Thomas of Blood, Sweat and Tears had got it on together. She'd really liked him. When they were through having sex, he'd said he had to run; he abruptly dressed and left the room.

What David hadn't realized was that the room she was in faced the pool area. She was watching him as he went over to the pool—where everyone was hanging, including the rest of Blood, Sweat and Tears—and she could hear him say to them, "Hey, guess who I just fucked? Janis!"

So she was upset. I kinda got upset for her. *That schmuck*, I thought.

I said, "C'mon, Janis. Why you gonna let him get to you?"

She told me she felt alone. "I just want someone to love and love me back in my life."

I said, "Hey, that's the life we choose. It's the road—the business we're in." Then I told her I could relate to her lonesomeness. Five to ten thousand people in love with you one minute, and then you're alone—the theater gets empty. So is the life. We have to learn how to live with it. The audience's love is so massive, and it's very personal. Performers really feel it. But off-stage you'd do just about anything to find comfort. You might start fucking a guy in your band—I'd done that, I told her. Some artists, Janis included, went on to die too young or even to kill themselves outright because of drugs and booze. Substance abuse was just another way to comfort yourself, to help you forget your solitude. Sometimes you did so permanently.

On the road there was always a party in somebody's room, especially at the Hospital Inn (as I called the endless succession of Holiday Inns we stayed in). There were fans and groupies with drugs, everyone with lots of booze—but eventually you had to go to your own room and there you found yourself very much alone. The fans, if they were lucky, went home to their loved ones, their families.

On-stage, I got to live and love for forty-five minutes at a time. That forty-five minutes gave me a feeling like no other feeling in the world. It became bigger than life—nothing can ever compare to that kind of passion. It's bigger than any one person. It's difficult to describe the state of euphoria that exists when you're up on-stage while your band, your song, and your audience become one pulsing beat. You feel loved by so many people at one time. It's pure ecstasy. The hair on my body would stand up, my nipples would harden, and I would get chills. The feeling was beyond orgasmic. On-stage, your life becomes a public private moment. My microphone was my power, my strength. I ate it, I fucked it, I breathed it.

Goldie the Dancer, on-stage Goldie could not be a shy, secretive Genyusha. I had to reinvent myself, create a new persona. This person could not feel pain. She had to "eat nails for breakfast and kick ass and take names." The tough rock 'n' roll chick, the exterior me, had to become the caretaker for control. The real person, inside, had endured so much pain as a child that she was a walking contradiction to the public Goldie. The sensitive Genya had to take a backseat to the loud, powerful, exhibitionist Goldie, the Stage Goldie. It was a defense mechanism, and it would ultimately cause me great pain.

※ ※ ※ ※ ※ ※

We did a free live concert in Central Park in 1970 for the radio station WNEW. People packed the park—on the ground, hanging from tree limbs, everywhere. What a rush it was to sing my song "House in Central

Park" in a situation like this! Scott Muni and a few other jocks attended. It was a great gig, and very successful for us. WNEW, a very powerful FM station, loved Ten Wheel Drive. It was also the sister station to Boston's WBCN, a huge station that carried lots of weight.

It was at this concert that I met the Nightbird—the DJ Alison Steele. Whenever she played my records on air, she would call me "The Big G." She was hosting the concert dressed in a Native American costume, right down to the feather in the hair, and she looked great. After the show, we got on well enough that she became my best friend for a while.

• • • • • •

On April 19, 1970, my birthday, Ten Wheel Drive played Carnegie Hall. The other act was a band called Rhinoceros. If playing Carnegie Hall on your birthday's not thrilling enough, add the audience singing "Happy Birthday to You"—how cool is *that*?

In the middle of one of my songs I saw this chubby little woman running down the aisle, throwing kisses. I realized the woman was my mother! I was mortified. I'd known my parents were in the audience, but I'd not expected this . . . well, exhibitionism. She finally sat down only when my father grabbed her. Mom and Dad came to the dressing room after the performance. They were glowing and I was sweating. I'd had to wear a shirt that went all the way up to my neck; I wasn't used to performing with that many clothes on. The reason was my tattoo.

Tattoos are forbidden for Jews. Mom once told me that if I ever got a tattoo—God forbid—I could not be buried in a Jewish cemetery. Jewish people could not have anything artificial done to their skin. I asked her if that included Jewish nose jobs, boob jobs, face lifts, or pierced earrings. "If I die, you could take my body to the Veterinary Office," I told her.

Tattoos were also illegal in the States in the late 1960s and early 1970s, but that didn't mean you couldn't get one. I went to Spider Webb's tattoo parlor in Yonkers; he had a great reputation. Of course, I got totally ripped beforehand, but it still hurt. It was worth it. I had him do a line of stars running across the front of my left shoulder to the back. I still love my tattoo.

My mother could not be allowed to know I'd gotten a tattoo. Once she came back stage at a performance of ours at the Bottom Line in

New York. When she saw my tattoo, she rubbed my stars and said, "Vat's dis?"

I told her, "Oh, don't worry, it washes off."

She found out much later that it never washed off.

We played Carnegie Hall a second time in 1971. Polydor Records made a huge mistake in not recording Ten Wheel Drive that night. Aram had been doing a lot of reading and research on the subject of Native Americans, and he and Mike had written a masterpiece rock opera titled *Little Big Horn*. We were backed by the American Symphony Orchestra, conducted by Stephen Simon, and a sixteen-voice choir.

This performance was timely, because Native Americans were (rightly) much in the public spotlight at the time. Programs about Native American history had started at a number of universities throughout the U.S. during the late 1960s. The following year the movie *The Godfather* was released; when Marlon Brando won an Oscar for his part in it he sent Native American rights activist Sacheen Littlefeather to pick up his award, rather than accepting it in person, as a protest about the treatment of Native Americans in Hollywood movies.

Our musical piece, recounting the story of Custer's Last Stand, predated other rock operas like the Who's *Tommy* and Pink Floyd's *The Wall*.

Once again, being pioneers did not work in our favor. We wanted to record the whole performance, but Jerry Schoenbaum didn't want to spend the money on this "Indian Opera" piece, even though it was going to be a one-time event. I swear to this day that, if that performance had been recorded, Ten Wheel Drive would have gone down in music history. The concert was absolutely incredible.

· · · · · ·

For the most part, the 1970s produced music like glam rock—the New York Dolls, Gary Glitter, David Bowie, and so on. (I'll always love Bowie's music.) Disco had its day, too. And Ten Wheel Drive was extremely popular.

Walter Raim asked me to sing on some of his commercials, and I did. Pepsi Cola, Jell-O, Reese's Peanut Butter Cups, Maclean's Toothpaste... Ten Wheel Drive as a whole did a very silly on-camera Delco Battery commercial showing the band playing under Niagara Falls, plugged into a Delco Battery. It was pretty scary—we had to climb down a steep hillside for some of the shots, and in order to get me back up again they had to put a rope round me. We also did a commercial for Fabergé's new scent, "Music," for which we played a cool melody.

Lots of radio stations in the States were still very uptight, though. For our second album, *Brief Replies,* we recorded a sort-of-country song, "Morning Much Better," and it was released as a single. The song had the line "I usually like it in the morning much better, yeah!" and that was enough, believe it or not, to get it banned by radio stations all over the place.

As Ten Wheel Drive progressed, I was often invited to the home of Aram and Ettie. One night Ettie went to bed while we were discussing a song. Then something happened. It was the way Aram looked at me. I thought, *This straight married lawyer musician guy is coming on to me—he's flirting with me.* Boy, that turned me on! I wasn't thinking about Ettie right then—I was just thinking about Aram. We didn't take it any further that night, but I'd been alerted, as it were.

We spent a lot of time together, rehearsing and gigging. I guess it's the old saying: "Shit happens." One night Aram came over to my apartment on Thirtieth Street to drop off some lyrics. We were at the door saying goodbye when we reached passionately for each other and started kissing. I was so hot for him, but this time I did think about Ettie.

"Leave," I said, and he did.

But he was so good-looking! I thought about it. *Oh well, a onenighter with a married guy couldn't hurt, could it?* The next day at rehearsal, though, I made myself not look at him.

Aram and I continued to have the hots for each other. At every rehearsal and gig, you could have cut the sexual tension with a knife. I was turned on by his intellect; he was turned on by my earthiness. It seemed inevitable that we were going to have some sort of relationship.

When it did finally happen that we fucked, I said, "We can't tell anyone in the band about this." I remembered too well my experiences with Goldie and the Gingerbreads and then again with the Les DeMerle Quintet. Musicians get jealous. I'd had no idea how unhappy Aram and Ettie were. They had had problems way before I came into the picture. We talked about their relationship in between having sex ourselves.

Trying to keep our affair a secret was a joke, though. We were always sneaking into each other's hotel rooms in the middle of the night—a reprise of the Goldie and the Gingerbreads and the Rolling Stones days. Maybe I was put on this earth to sneak into men's hotel rooms?

Right after a gig, we'd hang with the band members in someone's hotel room. All the guys would be smoking dope, taking acid or whatever was available—whatever the fans had brought. It was well known that I didn't like pot, so while they carried on getting stoned I would yawn and say goodnight. Three minutes later Aram would start yawning, too, and leave the room . . . to take himself as fast as his legs would carry him to the room I was in. Subtle, sophisticated subterfuge, hm?

The guys in the band didn't like it that I wouldn't get high with them. They became paranoid about the fact that I just drank and took Quaaludes.

• • • • • •

Ten Wheel Drive worked every weekend for two years. We were, naturally, pretty pleased about that. We did the college circuit, but also some fairly unexpected venues like the Miami Beach Convention Hall, where we performed with Rare Earth. We did the Felt Forum in Madison Square Garden many times with Sly & the Family Stone, also with the Chambers Brothers.

When we played the Whiskey a GoGo in Los Angeles with the Allman Brothers, I got up to sing the blues with them. Man, that felt good—singing real blues with a real blues band. I sang "Stormy Monday Blues" with Gregg Allman joining in on the vocals. And I got a crush on the band's Dickey Betts. He called me when he came to New York City the next month and I met him back at the Chelsea Hotel that night. Everything seemed fine until I saw a cat-o'-nine-tails by his bed. Just then there was a knock on the door and I thought, *Good timing! I can get out of here.* I said my goodnights to Gregg Allman and Dickey "No Way" Betts and left.

Another memorable summer weekend in 1970 we performed at the outdoor Powder Ridge Festival, in the ski area in Middlefield, Connecticut. We appeared with Van Morrison, Chuck Berry, the Savoy Brown Blues Band, Ten Years After, Chicago, Janis Joplin, Jethro Tull, Cactus, The Allman Brothers, Mountain, Joe Cocker, James Taylor, Fleetwood Mac, Sly & the Family Stone, John Sebastian, and many more.

This whole time, Aram and I were keeping "us" a secret. We thought that, if the others knew the singer was getting banged by one of the leaders of the band, some sort of dissent would be inevitable. Of course, because of the way it gets lonely on the road, all the guys in Ten Wheel Drive used to flirt with me. Aram finally told Mike in Boston, when we were there doing the Boston Tea Party. From what Aram told me, Mike flipped out, getting really mad. I suppose he, too, reckoned our affair wouldn't be good for the band.

I knew the fling with Aram couldn't last, and I'd never intended it otherwise. I was just horny for him and got carried away. When Ettie found out what was going on, she and Aram split up. He moved out from their home and we got an apartment together on West Twenty-second Street. Now, of course, the band couldn't help but know.

During Ettie's and Aram's break-up, Ettie's mother called and yelled at me, saying, "In the old days, a woman like you would get stoned to death." I just said, "Lady, I'm already stoned." But in fact I did feel guilty, because I liked Ettie a lot. I didn't love Aram, and his leaving Ettie put a sort of burden of responsibility on me that I resented.

Our relationship went downhill fast. I couldn't communicate with him. His quiet, intense demeanor frustrated me. He was happy just reading his books and keeping his thoughts to himself. I needed to express myself and to talk about things. All in all, it was an impossible situation. My song "Love Me" pretty much explains my feelings.

We never used protection—no condoms, and I wasn't on any pills. In 1970, New York State passed the first abortion-on-demand legislation, so guess what? In 1971 I found out through a home test that I was pregnant. I had such mixed emotions about it. I remember lying in my bed, rubbing my belly, and thinking, *This is the first time in my life that I don't feel alone or scared.*

I heard a voice inside me say: *Genya, you will never be alone again.* What a great thought it was.

I told Aram the news. For days he didn't mention anything about it. I was shocked and surprised at that reaction from him.

Then I asked him: "Well, what do you think? What should we do?"

It was my big question. I knew what I wanted to hear. This was going to be the answer that could change the whole course of my life.

Aram said, "Whatever you want."

I thought, *Whatever I want? Did I get pregnant alone here?*

I knew then that it was over for us. I was upset and hurt, but Aram didn't seem to notice. I just wanted him to say something about how he felt—even if it was negative. Deep down inside, of course, what I really wanted to hear from him was: "Yes, let's have it! I love you!" I would have stayed with him if he'd said that. And I'd probably have fallen in love with him.

Now I was faced with an important decision. When I think about that time, I realize I could have had that child by myself. I often wonder how that would have changed the rest of my life. I'm sorry now that I didn't have the courage to bring up that baby on my own. There was so much happening in those days. We did three albums in two and a half years; we traveled and gigged almost every weekend; the guys kept writing more songs, which had to be learned; we rehearsed during each and every week. When would I have had the time to care for a baby? How could I have raised it by myself? I'd been making only a hundred dollars a week for two years. I couldn't afford a child.

So I talked myself into having an abortion. And I broke it off with Aram.

* * * * * *

Our second album, *Brief Replies*, was released in 1970. For this we had a new horn section, a new producer—Guy Draper. Our engineer was Tony May, who was also the engineer on, among others, Van Morrison's album *Moondance*. Although I'd been the one to insist on Walter Raim as our producer for *Construction #1*, I found I actually felt more at home working with Guy. Both he and Tony were African-Americans, which I liked a lot as well—I guess because of how fond I'd been of Uncle Louie, way back. At my request the three background singers we hired were also African-American.

The sessions for this record were very happy ones. I recall going into the control room after putting down the lead vocal on the song "Last of the Line"—a ballad that just builds and builds—and finding everyone hopping around with excitement. The three background singers were there, clapping, and one of them paid me one of the finest compliments I've ever been given: "Girl, I'll remember you when we're burning down houses!"

Another major treat for me on *Brief Replies* was that I got the chance to sing one of my favorite songs, "Stay With Me" by Jerry Ragovoy and Chuck Weiss. It was originally recorded by the fabulous, much underrated soul singer Lorraine Ellison, and it was her version I'd listened to back in the Goldie and the Gingerbreads days.

We had one charting single from *Brief Replies*, "Morning Much Better," written by Aram and Mike, but it didn't chart very high because, as I say, a lot of the radio stations were frightened by its lyric.

● ● ● ● ● ●

We continued to work weekends, mainly at colleges. I'd never realized how many colleges there were in the U.S.! In the two and a half years of Ten Wheel Drive we never played any of those colleges twice.

We were starting to get our diehard fans now. One of mine came to every concert. He was very young, so his father used to drive him to my gigs in different towns. He even managed to get backstage most of the time. I thanked the father for allowing his son to be such a devoted fan.

The fan letters were starting to come in from all over the world. We always allowed some of the fans to come into the dressing room; most of them were very well behaved. Some would bring joints, some brought LPs for us to autograph; some brought both. Most were genuine fans; a few were just curious.

One night a couple walked in and the guy said, "Genya, how have you been? Long time no see."

I looked at him and wondered who the hell he was.

With a smirk on his face he continued, "Don't you remember me? We were tight one time." He leered meaningfully at me.

His wife or girlfriend was with him, and she looked really uncomfortable about this. I stared at him and said, "Well, you couldn't have been much good, 'cause I don't remember you at all."

From the corner of my eye I saw his girl get a nice smile on her face. I winked at her as I walked away.

I loved teasing the horn players and their "holier than thou" attitudes. I would say things like, "You're the only musicians who get ugly groupies. Learn to rock. Maybe you'll get laid one day."

● ● ● ● ● ●

The third and last album I did with Ten Wheel Drive was *Peculiar Friends* (peculiar friends being better than no friends at all, you see!), which was released in 1972. By now Jerry and Polydor trusted us enough to let us handle our own production, and so Aram and Mike co-produced. The engineer was one of my favorites, Jay Messina, still a dear friend. Jay has done—and still does—a lot of work with Aerosmith. By now Mike and Aram had learned how to write songs tailor-made for me as the vocalist, and I think it shows. One of them, "Shootin' the Breeze," got a lot of airplay, but the song I like best on the album is "No Next Time."

Although you might get the impression reading that paragraph that all was well, in fact things were becoming pretty bad between me and the band and I really wanted out. In a way, I suppose, "No Next Time," with its lyric of "there ain't gonna be no next time," was prescient: there wasn't going to be a next time. I'd gone through the break-up with Aram. I'd had all the trauma of the abortion. I was making no money. The atmosphere was kind of new and very uncomfortable.

By now I had my own apartment on Seventy-first Street, between Columbus Avenue and Central Park West, and had to pay the rent on it. I got together with Mike and Aram and told them I would stay with the band on one condition, that I received three hundred dollars for each performance. At first Mike said the band couldn't afford it, but somehow they found a way to pay me. As you can imagine, they were resentful about it, though. That's when the band really felt like it was breaking up, and the mood showed. In addition, we had already fired Billy Fields and Sid Bernstein (Hal Ray had taken his place), so we had no management.

Jerry Schoenbaum visited me at my apartment one day and asked me if I wanted a solo career; I'd expressed my unhappiness to him about the way things were going with the band. Jerry would have done anything for me. He had always thought the group was holding me back. When I replied to him that, yes, I'd like to go solo, he said I was going to be a star. He was very excited.

I told him I needed to find a manager. (Ten Wheel Drive continued for some years without me, recruiting as a replacement singer Annie Sutton, who'd sung with the Rascals for a while before that band folded. They released the album Ten Wheel Drive in 1974, and oddly enough I made a contribution to it. One of the tracks on the album—"Why Am I So Easy to Leave Behind?"—is a Schefrin/Ravan composition, having lyrics that Aram and I wrote together while I was still with the band.)

CHAPTER NINE

Solo, Then So Low

JERRY CALLED ME the next week and told me about a woman who was planning to leave the company that managed Sly & the Family Stone to go on her own. Her name was Barbara Baccus, and Jerry said she would be a perfect manager for me.

Barbara came to visit me and I liked her well enough. She seemed a bit dykish but that didn't matter—I was used to butch-looking women. Who cared what she looked like or about her private life so long as she was knowledgeable enough and had connections.

She asked me a great question, "What do you want from a manager?" My answer must have been a real bummer for her to hear. "I want to get out of the Polydor Records contract. I want to go to Clive Davis at CBS."

I could see she felt badly about this—after all, it had been Jerry Schoenbaum of Polydor who'd introduced us. But, after shaking her head and falling silent for a few minutes, she responded, "I'll do what I can."

And then she went out and did it. Clive Davis came to one of my rehearsals. At the time I was piecing together a new band and gathering some material for possible recording.

When Jerry Schoenbaum heard about my wanting to leave his label he was very hurt, and that soon turned to anger. CBS Records asked Polydor what they wanted for my contract, and Jerry picked a high number—$100,000. I'm sure he didn't think CBS would go for it, but Clive must have really liked what he heard at our rehearsal because he agreed to that sum and signed me up.

After CBS had bought out my Polydor contract I told Barbara I would sign with her as my manager. The news of the deal made it to the Wall Street Journal. Barbara, joking, said, "Genya Ravan, you're going public."

Sadly, though, Barbara wasn't so good at looking out for my future. I received an advance from CBS and she insisted I use it to buy all the equipment for the band and put the musicians on some sort of retainer. I wanted to invest some of the money in real estate, but she said, "You have to invest in *yourself*. Any good businessperson knows that you never invest with your own money, especially when it's a guessing game. The music business is always a guessing game."

She was wrong. But she was my manager and I wanted to believe she knew what she was doing. So the musicians went on a retainer, as did a roadie. I bought the equipment for the whole band, even a fucking Moog Synthesizer. What I got out of this whole big money deal was a bright yellow Karman Ghia.

Clive tried to get me some good producers, but I nixed them all until Larry Fallon came along. He'd produced for artists like Van Morrison, Jimmy Cliff, and Traffic. I worked with him on a few songs but, even though I liked Larry, something didn't feel right to me on a musical level, so I let him go.

Next Clive suggested Richard Perry as a possible producer, but I told him Richie had once been my boyfriend and I'd be very uncomfortable having him the one calling the shots. I wound up going back to Aram and Mike from Ten Wheel Drive. I thought that with them I'd be safe and could control everything—and that's exactly what I did.

Clive, though, became very concerned about the way my first recording for CBS, *Genya Ravan*, was turning out. Actually, everything about it was as I wanted it to be (except the mixes, which were weak)—so much so that I call it my masturbation record. For the first time I had absolute freedom to sing whatever I wanted to, so I went wild with my choices. Clive thought the production had no real direction and that the songs didn't form a cohesive set: There was no image, no particular style. They were just songs I wanted to sing.

He was right, of course—the album *didn't* have a direction. But it sure was musical. He said my music was too diverse—one track was soul, the next was country, the next one jazz. But that was the way I wanted it. I'm a diverse singer, after all. I loved the diversity. Jazz stations started playing "Moody's Mood for Love" and rock stations started playing "Flying." I even had master percussionist Olatunji and his African Tribe play on one of the tracks, "Takuta Kalaba" ("Turn on Your Love Lights"); about nine different members played assorted drums. I'd invited saxophonist James Moody to play on the song he was famous for, and he contributed a brilliant solo to the ending of "Moody's Mood for Love." What an absolute high that was for me! Unfortunately, the producers cut the solo off halfway through—the only thing that still really bothers me about the *Genya Ravan* album. Maybe one day I'll get to remix that song.

My choice of using Mike and Aram backfired on me, however. I didn't really hit it off with them in the studio. I think they were somewhat happy about being involved, but at the same time jealous of my deal with CBS. Under the circumstances I think they did the best they could, but nevertheless the atmosphere was not the best for me. The net result was that Clive didn't get what he saw at the first rehearsal—the sound that had made him sign me in the first place.

Finally we started to tour. I'd assembled a kickass band. Among them were Tony Levin and Steve Gadd. Tony, who had played with many great artists, like Joan Armatrading, Tracy Chapman, and Cher (and would go on to perform with Peter Gabriel and King Crimson) was on bass. Drummer Steve Gadd had played with Chuck Mangioni. Later Steve became one of the most recorded drummers of our time, playing with Paul Simon, Paul McCartney, Frank Sinatra, and Chick Corea, to mention just a few. In 1971 I kept telling people, "Watch this drummer. He's a star." I was right.

Barbara Baccus was still tight with Sly's organization, and she got us on a tour with Sly & the Family Stone.

During that tour I was arrested for obscenity. We were at the Cherry Hill Arena in New Jersey, playing to a packed house. All was going grand. I was in the middle of a ballad when I heard someone scream something out—I thought they'd yelled, "Sly!" I raised my arm to the band to stop the music.

To the audience I said, "If you don't want to listen to my music, I will get the fuck off. If you *do* want to listen to more of my music, then shut the fuck up." I didn't think twice about the word "fuck"; I used it all the time, and so did many of the others around me.

The audience applauded my statement and I continued with the show—and got an encore. Afterwards I went into my dressing room, sweaty and happy; it had been a great show. Then there was a knock at the door. Three cops, two male and one female, walked in.

"What the fuck?" I said.

The woman cop said to me, "I wouldn't use that word so much if I were you."

I had no idea why they were there. Having read me my rights they arrested me. I asked what the charges were.

"Obscenity and obstruction of justice . . ."

On the way to the police station one of the cops muttered to his partner: "This is a stupid fuckin' arrest."

When I got there I was allowed one phone call. It was late, so I called Barbara. Meanwhile, my musicians were trying, unsuccessfully, to get Sly's attention on-stage to let him know I was in jail.

Barbara told my roadie she'd get the money for my bail. I found out later that it was the promoter—who'd previously worked with Barbara—who had called the police. He said Muhammad Ali was in the audience with his family and had gotten upset by my language, which he felt was lewd and obscene, so I was arrested.

It wasn't just me who thought this was a stupid arrest: The police at the station house thought so, too.

I asked the woman cop, "What happens if they don't post bail?" She replied, "You spend the night in a holding cell, and if I were you I wouldn't close my eyes for one second." That made me as nervous as you can imagine. As usual I was wearing a see-through blouse without a bra. The cops had fun just staring and staring at me before finally one of them handed me his jacket.

Barbara managed to post bail and I got home about six o'clock the next morning. She and Hal Ray, my agent from the William Morris Agency, were thrilled about the whole thing. They couldn't wait until the press got hold of the story, which did indeed make it to the papers the next day.

Later, my trial date was, of course, in the newspapers too, and many of my fans showed up to support me. My lawyer begged me to wear a bra in court, but I wouldn't. He was good, though, and managed to get me off without a hitch. He had researched the word "fuck" and found that it was an acronym originated many years ago meaning "For Unlawful Carnal Knowledge." The law said that, if you used words to incite a riot, it could be an offense, but my lawyer pointed out that I'd used the offending word in my successful effort to calm a situation down. (That got a hand from the fans in the courtroom.) The charge was dropped. I had a special gold ring made up for my lawyer with a big "Fuck" inscribed on it.

* * * * * *

Barbara Baccus sure didn't know how to manage a rocker with a mind of her own. Barbara was strong in some areas and weak in others, and couldn't give me the guidance I needed. I wasn't blameless in this faltering relationship. I did things without thinking. This was a no-win situation, because I was being allowed to call too many shots in situations where I didn't know enough to be the one doing the calling. I had a name, I had some money, and I had the freedom to fuck up my own career. Barbara let me.

While I'd been in the middle of recording my *Genya Ravan* album I'd had a call from CBS's jazz record division. An A&R man asked if I'd ever heard of Ornette Coleman.

I said, "Of course." I was a big Ornette Coleman fan.

He said that Ornette wondered whether I'd like to sing a song on his new record. I immediately agreed. Excited, I went to the rehearsal. The song I was supposed to sing on had not been completely composed; Ornette had written the lyrics for what was to be a free-flowing, improvisational song—meaning that I was to make up the melody as we went along. Ordinarily that would have been fine (I did that with songs all the time), but this particular song I couldn't understand. I just couldn't get into it. It was *too* free. I couldn't find the "one" in the beat. It felt to me like the drummer was soloing throughout the piece. I could tell I was totally out of my element.

Sadly, I took Ornette aside and said, "I'm not right for this song. I can't feel it the way it deserves to be felt." He said he understood. At a table in his spacious loft we spoke for a while. I told him about coming from Poland and how I hadn't been able to speak a word of English until I'd learned the language from R&B and gospel music. He told me, "That's why you've got such great ears, and so much soul. Your ears became like sponges as a child."

* * * * * *

In 1972 I got an offer to appear on *The Tonight Show*—generally known as the Johnny Carson Show. Like millions of others, I'd watched his show forever. Now I was going to be performing on the show live. Very exciting!

First I did a few interviews with the show's producer. The show's staff needed enough information about me to prep Johnny thoroughly. As a result of these preliminary interviews they realized what an outgoing personality I had, and how many funny stories I could tell, and so they decided to have Johnny speak with me on the show as well. The guy interviewing me even declared that I'd be good as a future host!

While I was in the dressing room before the show, Tony Randall came in; he was there to do a taping for the next Carson show, and we shared the Green Room. When we talked about acting he said to me, "Don't go to acting classes. They'll spoil any acting talent you might have." I was nervous about being on the show, and his conversation calmed me down. He was so funny; it was a treat to meet him.

Just before I was due to go on an usher came into the Green Room. "Miss Ravan, you have a phone call." This seemed odd. Perhaps it was a good-luck call. I went out to the hall to answer the phone. A man's voice said, "Is this Genya Ravan?"

"Yes," I answered.

"You're going to die tonight."

The voice sounded familiar, but I hung up too quickly to be sure. I didn't tell anyone about the call, and nothing ever came of it. I've often wondered if other artists on the show got similar nerve-racking calls, or if it was just me. Was the caller someone I knew?

Genya on *The Tonight Show* with Johnny Carson, 1971.

Even though the call had obviously been intended to shake me up, I forgot about it the minute I got in front of the cameras. I thought the show went excellently. I thought I looked funky for it. I was wearing a plain black halter-sheath long dress and a necklace made of pigeon feathers. Dom DeLuise, Professor Irwin Cory, and Richard Roundtree—star of the hottest movie at the time, *Shaft*, were scheduled to be on the show, too.

I had the audience laughing, and Johnny Carson seemed to like me. I sang a blues song with Doc Severinsen's band; some of the horn players in the band had been in Ten Wheel Drive. After the song, I walked back to take a seat next to Johnny.

I hadn't met him before the show, but of course the questions he asked on camera had been pre-written for him by the writers who'd interviewed me.

"What was it like working with five women?" he asked, and then shook his head like "God forbid." The audience laughed. "Great," I said, "if you can stand your pregnant bass player throwing up every time you sing." He made his "Carson face" and the audience laughed again. And so it went on.

I told funny stories about Goldie and the Gingerbreads. We also talked about my being an information operator before entering show business. Carson was the straight man, I was the comic, and I never shut up. It was one story after another, and the audience got off on it. At the end of the interview he said, "The way I see it is that you have just one problem. You're too shy and introverted." The audience roared.

Richard Roundtree never made it on the show that night because it ran over time. When I saw him afterwards I said, "Sorry you got shafted." I thought it was funny and luckily so did he.

Hal Ray and I had made plans to see the Johnny Carson Show (which was taped) in his apartment along with his girlfriend and Barbara. We watched the show, drank champagne, and laughed a lot. We thought it was all very good, although I was naturally very critical of my own part in it.

The next day I got a call from Barbara. "Clive Davis is very upset." All of a sudden, Barbara didn't think my being on Johnny Carson had been a very good idea—the same went for Hal. According to Barbara, Clive thought the appearance on Carson had hurt my image, and a few months later Clive dropped my contract. I was devastated.

I believe now that what Clive really wanted was a replacement for the late Janis Joplin (Janis had died in 1970). That clearly wasn't what *I* wanted and it wasn't what he got. It had never dawned on me that I was expected to be the "replacement Janis." He said I came off too much like a comedian and too legit for rock 'n' roll.

I was so broken up, defeated, and depressed. I thought my career was over. No one had ever dropped a contract with me before. I just wanted to run away. Maybe to California, except I didn't know anyone in California.

When Clive was fired from CBS in 1973 he wrote a book (*Clive: Inside the Record Business*, with James Willwerth). In it he described me as initially "a funky, earthy singer" who, he said, had changed a lot of her musical thinking and had an identity crisis. "She appeared on the Johnny Carson Show wearing an evening gown . . . it was ridiculous because she is a singer in the Joplin tradition with a throaty powerful voice." He said I had diffused my image (this could be true) by telling Johnny Carson I might be playing at the Persian Room in New York City. Clive was particularly unhappy about that remark, because the Persian Room had a reputation for cabaret. What Clive didn't know at the time was that the Persian Room was about to go rock, and the people there had contacted me to bring rock music into their club. He just assumed something.

■ ■ ■ ■ ■ ■

Despite no one less than Tony Randall having advised me against acting classes, I went to the American Place Theatre to study with top acting coach Wynn Handman. One of the lesser known highlights of my career came when Wynn saw me audition for the lead part in a play called *Big Mother*. After the audition he came up to me and told me this was one of the best cold readings he'd ever seen. Wow! What a compliment! And from the best! I got the part, and the play ran for two weeks at Wynn's American Place Theatre. I seemed to have a good sense of timing with comedy as well as music.

So, yes, Clive was right. I wanted to act, I wanted to sing, I wanted to dance. I didn't want to be just one thing. I wanted to be "diffuse."

The word for someone like that is "entertainer."

My appearance on *The Tonight Show* with Johnny Carson was, whatever Clive thought, a complete success. A few weeks afterwards that same show was rerun on television. Joey Bishop, who had seen it, was going to sub for Johnny Carson a week later, and he requested that I be his guest. But my manager, Barbara Baccus, refused the invitation without consulting me. I guess she didn't want Clive to get upset again. I was, naturally, livid when I found out. I seemed to be reliving what John Fenton had done to me in England when Peter Sellers had requested me for that movie.

CHAPTER TEN
Hollyweird

I'D GONE FROM the highest mountaintop to the deepest pit in a very short period of time. One moment I'd been signed by Clive Davis in a deal so big it was featured in the *Wall Street Journal*, the next I'd been dumped from CBS. I'd rented a very expensive duplex apartment on beautiful tree-lined West Seventy-first Street in Manhattan, and I'd bought myself a brand new car. I'd been a hit on Johnny Carson's show. Now I felt like a total failure—humiliated, embarrassed, frightened, completely alone. I thought no one would want me anymore. I couldn't even think what I was going to do next. And I hadn't a clue about how I was going to survive financially.

When someone told me about Robert Fitzpatrick it was like I was being given a straw to clutch. Robert was a supposedly wealthy and respected manager/lawyer from California who was on the lookout for talent to take on; he'd already signed up the hard-rocking, pre-punk punk Hollywood band Shady Lady. I figured, the way my career seemed to go, I could always do with a lawyer as my manager, so I contacted him. He was coming to New York in a week's time, so we set up a meeting at my apartment.

He arrived in a long black limousine accompanied by a Native American named Max whom he introduced as his associate. All very impressive. I found out soon enough that he wasn't actually wealthy and that the limo had just been hired for the day to look good. If he'd only known that I'd have signed with *anyone* who wanted me after my CBS humiliation he could have saved himself the trouble.

We talked about my future for a few hours. His idea was that I should stay in New York with him managing me from Los Angeles, but I convinced him that it'd be better if I moved to California—that it'd be a good career move, that I wanted to broaden my horizons, all that sort of bullshit. I could hardly tell him that the real reason I wanted to move to the West Coast was to run away from where I was now. I probably should have guessed from the ease with which I persuaded him of this that he wasn't all he was made out to be: He was neither wealthy nor respected, he knew nothing about the music business, and he had no connections in it. All this I discovered later. He didn't even pay his rental bill for the limo: the company had to chase him for the money.

Even so, my big priority was getting out of New York City, so I ignored my every instinct and in September 1972 fled to Hollywood.

The first place I lived was on the 12th floor of a high-rise apartment block, the Sunset Towers. It was right on Sunset Boulevard, and I liked the feeling of security that living in a high-rise gave me. Ideal. Well, ideal until one early morning, three months after I'd got there, I woke up to find dishes flying, the TV falling over, and my cats Zulu and Tanya howling like banshees on my bed. I wasn't much better than the cats, to be honest: My bed was jumping around so much with me in it that I was doing a fair impersonation of Linda Blair in *The Exorcist*.

So this was what it was like to be on the twelfth story when a medium-sized earthquake hit. Nothing really to worry about. Yeah, right. I grabbed the cats and was out of there. After that I took an apartment on Santa Monica Boulevard. On the ground floor.

• • • • • •

My first week in Hollywood I went to a party I'd been invited to by a stunning gay black woman I'd met back in New York. It seemed like it'd be a good entrée for me to the West Coast social scene. There was a wild mixture of people there. Some were conservatively dressed, some were chicly dressed, some were half-dressed, and some weren't dressed at all. I'd arrived in the half-dressed category; any nerves I might have had about this vanished when I saw that the pool was filled

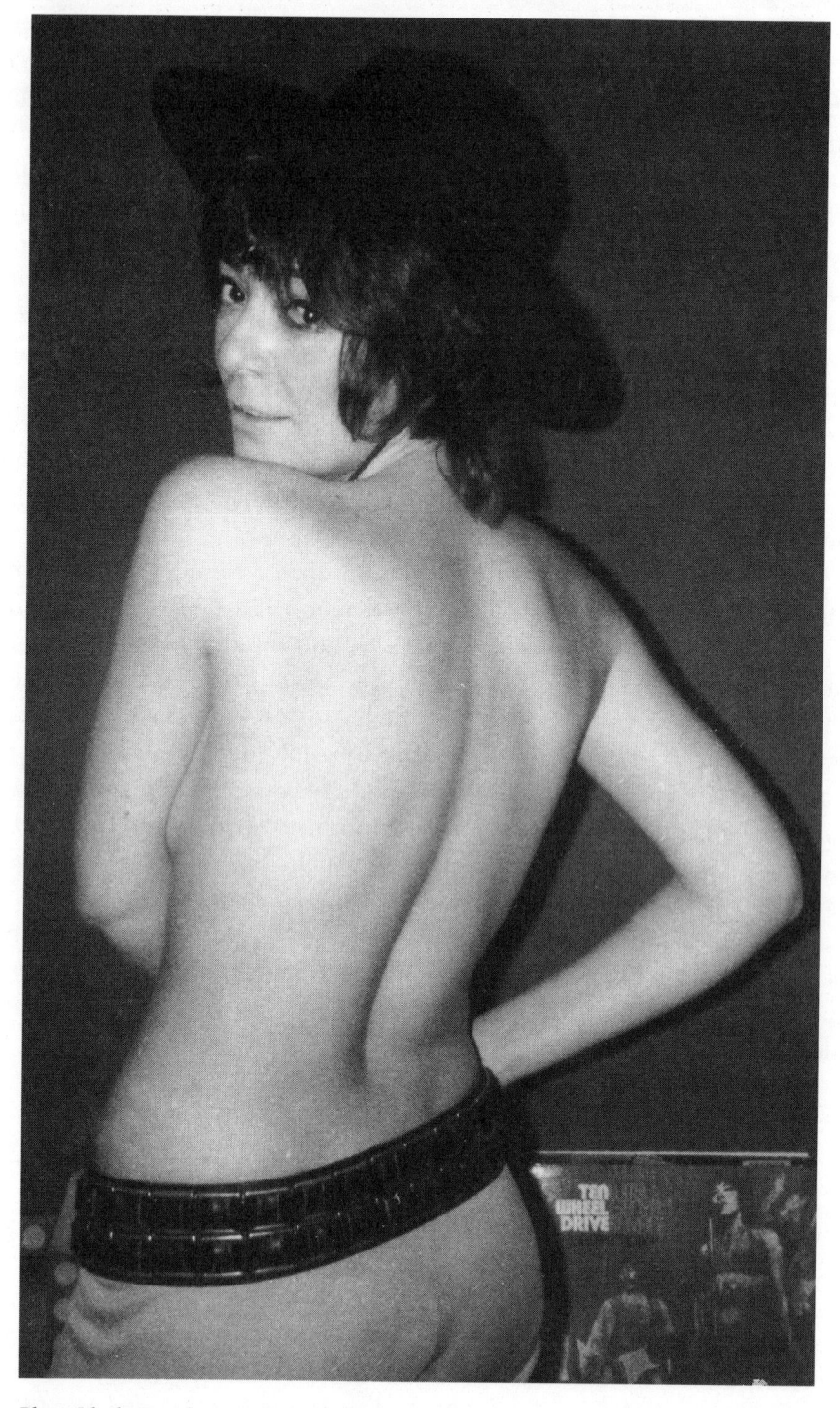

Photo I had printed on my personal checks.

with people wearing nothing at all except maybe their hair dye, purple or green.

I pretty soon noticed that a very handsome man was looking at me. There was something familiar about his appearance, and it didn't take me long to work out that he was the Rat Pack actor Peter Lawford. Our eyes locked and we gravitated towards each other. We danced together a few times and talked. I told him the for-public-consumption reasons—i.e., the lies—for my move to the West Coast. After a while he asked me if I'd like to go back to his place for a drink—oh yeah?—and I agreed immediately.

He had a modest little apartment in town that he told me he used when he had business in Hollywood. My theory was and is that it was his secret hideaway pad, but I didn't ask questions. We played pool for a while on the table he had there, and I had a few more drinks and a Quaalude. Totally whacked, I ended up spending the night with him, but that had been fairly inevitable from the start.

I visited that apartment often when Peter was in Hollywood. The place was always crowded with "the beautiful people"—partying, playing pool, hanging out, drinking. I was drinking a lot by then.

One evening we were hanging out at the apartment when the phone rang. Peter, looking a bit shifty, asked me to answer it. "If it's Liz," he said, "tell her I'm not here." I picked up the phone and, sure enough, it was Liz—Elizabeth Taylor. I'd have recognized the voice anywhere. Hiding my confusion as best I could, I told her Peter wasn't there.

"Who's this?" she said.

"Genya," I replied in a very small voice.

"Tell him he better call me." She hung up.

Peter explained to me that Liz Taylor wanted him to do one of her benefit shows with her and he was trying to get out of it.

He'd hardly finished telling me this when the phone rang again. More or less the same non-conversation ensued.

About the third time it happened she changed her tack. "I want to talk to Peter! Don't keep fucking telling me he's not at home! I know that motherfucker's there! You tell that sonofabitch he better fucking call me back tonight!" And so on for quite a while. I'd never really imagined what Liz Taylor's voice would sound like when she was cursing like a truck driver. Now I knew.

The same pattern repeated the rest of the night—me answering the phone, telling Liz Taylor that Peter wasn't there, me getting sworn at. Finally I told Peter I couldn't take it any longer. "You've made me upset Elizabeth Taylor for *hours* now. I *love* Elizabeth Taylor!"

Except when he was being phoned by Elizabeth Taylor, Peter was always lots of fun to be with. Unfortunately, this was the time when drinking was starting to take precedence over everything else for me—my career, my life. I'd use any excuse to get smashed. A few months later he had to go to Africa to do some volunteer thing, and by the time he got back I wasn't around any longer.

● ● ● ● ● ●

One night I went with some friends to one of Hollywood's "in" restaurants on Sunset Boulevard. I went there quite often because I was new in town: I needed to be seen and the place was always packed. A wide diversity of music people hung out there—John Travolta one day, B.B. King the next—and the food was reasonable. Every evening there'd be good bands performing upstairs. It was while I was having dinner there one time that I heard a familiar voice behind me and realized Cher was sitting at the next table. She was saying to her dinner companion, "He doesn't care about my feelings at all." It was the first I knew of difficulties between her and Sonny.

On this particular evening, when I looked around the room, I saw Richard Perry sitting in a booth with three other people. Richie had been out here on the West Coast for a while, and I'd gotten in touch with him when I'd made my move to Hollywood; we'd sort of experimented with being lovers again, but the old spark we'd had in our youth had been missing. Richie came over to my table and told me one of the guys he was with was this huge manager, George Greif, who wanted to meet me. I said, "Yeah, sure" and excused myself from my friends.

You could tell George Greif was dripping with cash just by looking at him—cash and class. With his expensive clothes, graying hair, and conservative mustache, he was one impressive-looking gentleman. He stood up as we approached the table and said, "Wow! Genya Ravan! Pleasure to meet ya!" After the way I'd been feeling ever since Clive Davis had dropped my CBS contract, this was a direct route to my heart, you bet.

George might have been classy-looking, but a moment later he started shouting, "Richie, this girl sings from her cunt! Did you ever hear her? She sings from her cunt!"

Richie and I looked around the room at all the people staring at us, especially at me, the most unusual singer in a town full of singers. "Oh, ah, yes," said Richie. "I've heard her. Ah, sit down, Goldie"—as if my sitting down with them would be like a sort of volume control for George. Oddly enough, it worked. He stopped speaking so loudly.

George asked me what I was doing with my career these days, and I gave him a sanitized version. I'd left CBS and Clive Davis because Clive couldn't get over his obsession that I was a substitute Janis Joplin, and I hadn't wanted to be a Janis clone. "That's so stupid of him," said George. "You two are nothing like each other." This was just what I wanted to hear. George went on to tell me that he'd just signed this incredible production deal between Jimmy Miller Productions (whom he represented) and ABC Dunhill Records. The Rolling Stones were involved in helping get things off the ground. Jimmy Miller Productions was building a sort of "musicians' family," and George would love me to be a part of it. All the musicians who'd played with the Stones would be a part of it.

Of course, I didn't need that much convincing. This could be the way to save my career, and certainly it'd help me get over the pain of Clive having dumped me.

"And I've got a great idea for who should produce you," said George. "Jim Price! He's producing Joe Cocker's new album, and you know he plays with the Stones."

The name didn't mean a whole lot to me, but I assumed George knew what he was talking about. Richie seemed happy about the whole thing. I shook hands with George and told him to set up a meeting between Jimmy Miller Productions and my lawyers once they'd got the contract ready. I kissed both men goodbye and went back to apologize to my friends for having left them for an hour.

The next day I got a call from the secretary at Jimmy Miller Productions to tell me they were drawing up the papers and I should meet them at ABC Dunhill in a week's time. I called Robert Fitzpatrick and told him the news. "That's great," he said, which it obviously was for him: he was getting twenty-five percent for just sitting back and letting me make the Miller/Greif connection.

Jim Price happened to be in town that week—he'd just got in from London, where he'd been producing Joe Cocker—and George set me up for a meeting with him. When I arrived at Jim's hotel room for this meeting I discovered he'd really set the stage for me: wine on the table, wine in his glass, a glass of wine already filled for me. I don't know what else he'd been ingesting before I got there, but it was obvious from the get-go that he wanted to fuck me as soon as possible. I thought, *Okay, let's get the lust part out of the way so we can get down to business.* I began drinking hard and fast to loosen up, and soon enough we fucked. I'm sure it was a control-fuck so far as he was concerned; it certainly was for me.

Afterwards, I began to get an idea of his personality. He wasn't what you might call a pleasant guy: a complete egomaniac who had no respect for women at all—they were just fucks to him. He was the most controlling sonofabitch I ever met, and I've met a few. I truly disliked him. I mean, I've forgiven just about everybody who's ever hurt or damaged me, but I still can't find it in myself not to dislike Jim Price.

We were lying on his bed when he started grilling me for information. "What kind of music do you want to sing?"

Kind of an odd question. Surely he knew the kind of music I sang? "Have you heard any of my records?" I asked him.

"No," he said, as if that was perfectly okay.

Asshole, I thought. *He hasn't even done his homework...*

"I sing R&B and jazz," getting up and starting to put my clothes on. I couldn't wait to get out of there.

Even as I was leaving his hotel room I knew this was going to be the nightmare of all nightmares. I wish I'd had the balls to stop it right then, but I was in a vulnerable state of mind.

The set-up turned out to be that I was going to be produced by Jim and a guy called Joe Zagarino. I discovered that the production money Jimmy Miller was getting from ABC Dunhill wasn't going to be used for a professional studio; instead, Joe used a fraction of it to build a recording studio in the basement of the house he and his family lived in. I guess the Jimmy Miller people thought they'd save a lot of money this way; heavy-duty kickbacks all round. As a professional I knew this was a totally absurd idea. The arrangement was a recipe for chaos and disaster. Imagine trying to record with Joe's wife and kids around.

In fact, Joe's wife and kids didn't prove to be the problem at all. Instead it was the completely unprofessional atmosphere. We wasted endless time just sitting around for musicians who turned up late for rehearsals. Some of them arrived drugged-out and useless. The whole dungeon, as I came to call it, reeked of drugs. Rather than rehearsals, most of what we had were hanging-out sessions. I even brought a few friends of my own along on occasion—if nothing else, I wanted witnesses to what was going on.

I wanted Jim to let me record a song I had heard, "When You Got Trouble," which had been a minor hit single for the Native American band Redbone. They were having a major hit at the time with "Come and Get Your Love." I contacted them and became friends with them. I brought the song's writer, Lolly Vegas, into the studio, but Price and Zagarino made him so uncomfortable that he didn't stay long. As we were saying our goodbyes he told me he couldn't believe the atmosphere there. "How the hell are you putting up with this, Genya?"

It wasn't just himself Jim Price was pushing on me, it was his material, his musicians, his arrangements, his everything. Every time I objected he'd tell me that he knew best, that I was the only person standing in the way of my own success. That didn't stop me fighting him every inch of the way, and I guess you can hear it in the songs on that record. It was called *They Love Me, They Love Me Not*, which seems appropriate enough in a way. As far as I was concerned, the fuckers were jerking off and I was paying for it with my money, my talent, my name, and my reputation.

One thing I knew about record production even then was that you needed to keep a sharp eye on the budget . . . If you didn't, things got out of hand and all the available money—which meant any royalties I might ever hope to see from the record's sales—would be frittered away. I hated sitting around in recording studios doing nothing. Time was money. I didn't know then that the budget was soon going to fly even more out of control.

About a month into this fiasco I got a call from someone at the Jimmy Miller office to tell me that Jim Price had some personal business to attend to in England, and that the production would be moved there.

I said, "I'm going too, right?"

"No."

I screamed, "It's *my* fuckin' record! If I don't go, nobody goes!"

An hour later George Greif phoned. "You know, Genya, you're getting a bad reputation. They're saying you're hard to work with."

"Bad reputation?" I said. "Wait'll you see the bad reputation Jimmy Miller Productions gets when I start telling people what's happening on my sessions."

A few hours later I got another call to tell me I was going to England after all.

When I got to London I discovered they'd at least put me up in a decent hotel in the center of town. I arrived at the recording studio to find there was more dope just lying on the console than there was in the whole of Hollywood—mountains of coke. The whole time I was there people kept shoving it in my face, wanting me to do some with them. I kept refusing: I was here to do a record production, not to snort coke. All the time they went on telling me I didn't know what I was missing. But I did. I was missing a good record production.

The sessions went on and on and, of course, the spending got bigger and bigger. The record they were making was supposed to pay for all this—the zoo they'd built in Joe Zagarino's basement, the traveling, the hotels, the studio time here in London, all the bullshit expense accounts. The record was paying for it? Translation: Genya Ravan was paying for it. Even if *They Love Me, They Love Me Not* was a smash hit #1 album I was never going to see a cent out of it. And, anyway, outside of a miracle there was no way this production was going to be a hit: it had no magic, no soul. The sound just wasn't there.

Something bad hung like a black cloud over the whole production. The sessions spun right out of control. Joe Zagarino's mental state was doing likewise: He got nasty and paranoid, and finally he overdosed and killed himself. That sort of brought a stop to things.

Back in Los Angeles, George Greif called and asked me if I'd sing at Joe's funeral. I agreed. I sang Leon Russell's "A Song for You," cried a bit, then left. I didn't stick around for the rest of the funeral. There was nothing good I could say about Joe, and the last thing I wanted to do was bump into Jim Price, who as far as I was concerned had run this entire production right into the ground alongside Joe.

A little while afterwards I phoned the head honcho, Jimmy Miller himself. "Jimmy, this record isn't me. It's all about Jim Price and his fucking ego. He picked the songs, he picked the players. Before we started he'd never heard me sing, and he didn't think it mattered. I know what I should sing and I know what I should sound like, and it's not this."

To my astonishment he said, "Okay. I agree."

The deal was that I could add a few more songs to this already over-budget record.

The first thing I did was contact my friend Bobby Whitlock, a guitar player who'd played with Delaney & Bonnie and Eric Clapton and written with Clapton on the Derek and the Dominos album *Layla and Other Assorted Love Songs*. Bobby came to the studio with me and we recorded a duet of his song "You Got to Keep on Growing." It was great. At that point I began to feel there was maybe some hope for the record after all, although I was still deeply unhappy about all the Jim Price crap there was going to be on it. Bobby hung out with me while I finished the last few songs, and then the record at last came out.

I didn't like it. ABC Dunhill didn't like it much either. When I went to their offices for interviews, photo sessions and the like, I got no sense of excitement from them. They knew all about the problems within Jimmy Miller Productions, and I think they wished they'd never signed the production deal with Jimmy Miller—not because of me, but because of Jimmy Miller's company. Still, *They Love Me, They Love Me Not* was released, for better or for worse. It didn't exactly sink without trace, but it didn't exactly swim, either.

And where, you may ask, was my manager, Robert Fitzpatrick, throughout all this? Nowhere to be seen. I might as well have been on my own in Los Angeles so far as my professional interests were concerned. I complained to him about this on numerous occasions, but all he said was, "Just go on making the record and maybe things will change."

The last week of production, things came to a head with him.

It started when he said, "You know, Genya, you're not easy to work with."

"Really?" I replied. "Okay, I want out of our contract."

And that was that. It seemed I was running my own career again. I was the one who could stop it from continuing its seemingly terminal downward spiral.

I didn't waste any time. I went looking for another record deal.

• • • • • •

Back in the 1960s, when I'd been with Goldie and the Gingerbreads, I'd met a guy called Marvin Schlacter. He was now Head of A&R for Chess Janus, the new label that the blues label Chess had spun off. It was still a pretty small set-up in 1972, and normally I'd have never looked at it twice, but I loved Marvin and besides I seemed to have no other options at the time. I wanted to carry on singing, but it seemed my career had ended in failure: who else would want me? So I called Marvin and told him I was free of all contracts and was looking for a record deal. We met shortly after and he told me Chess Janus was keen—further, that he had a great production duo for me: Gabriel Mekler and Trevor Lawrence.

He added that Gabriel and Trevor wrote songs as well, and at that point the alarm bells should have gone off. It's always in the financial interest of a record producer to push her or his own songs on an artist. That way they get points not just for the production but also for the real score: publishing and writing royalties.

My first meeting with Gabriel Mekler was in my apartment. It was odd meeting a producer who was from Israel, rather than from the U.S. or U.K. He'd never heard me sing, so I played him some of my old stuff. One of the songs I played him was one I'd been holding onto for a year or so that I believed could be a hit: "You're no Good." Gabriel said it was okay, but that he could write a better one for me. I was trying to be the easy-to-work-with artist everyone told me I should be, so I didn't argue with him. A little while later Linda Ronstadt released "You're No Good" and it brought her career back from the dead. Thanks, Gabriel.

As I started working with Gabriel and Trevor, Gabriel kept coming on to me; as he wasn't at all bad looking, I eventually succumbed. There was no emotional attachment on my part: I was using booze to smother my feelings by then. Drinking had become my way of burying my feelings. It seemed that a good drink was the only comfort I could depend on. I often thought that I'd kill anyone who did to me what I was doing to myself with drink.

We recorded the new album at the Sound Factory in Hollywood. From the outset it was as if I was under Jim Price's thumb again. Gabriel and Trevor took over all control: music, musicians, you name it. One day I had a well known musician friend drop by the studio because I wanted him to guest on one of the tracks. Gabriel and Trevor nixed the idea immediately, so away he went. They didn't really want anyone else in the studio during my recording.

They'd just finished producing an Etta James record there, and one day she walked in while I was recording a set of lead vocals. She watched from the control room until I'd finished the song ("Breadline"). When I got to the control room myself I had happy thoughts of *duet* swimming around in my head; even if she wasn't interested in singing with me, it was still going to be a hell of a thrill to meet her. However, as soon as we'd been introduced she started yelling at me, "Why do you sing like that? You're not black! You've got a nerve singing like that!"

I just stared back at her in shock. Before I had a chance to lash back at her, Gabriel and Trevor ushered her out. Talk about being disappointed in a person. I'd looked up to Etta James since I'd been a kid. I'd wanted to tell her how Uncle Louie had bought me her records, how much she'd inspired me, how much I loved her music. As it was, all that had happened was that she'd screamed her prejudices at me.

● ● ● ● ● ●

While we were recording the album my dad took ill. I knew it was serious when my sister Helen phoned me from Brooklyn to say he'd been taken into hospital—my family *never* phoned me. I took the next flight to New York, and when I got there I found that Ta Ta was in hospital with tubes sticking out all over his body. Apparently he hadn't urinated for a week, but hadn't told my mother he was having a problem. That problem had turned to be kidney stones. If his body couldn't be induced to pass them, he was going to need surgery.

While I was visiting him he begged me to get him some booze, and the doctor told my mother that it was okay to let him have one. I thought it was odd—both that Ta Ta should be so desperate and that the doctor should say it was all right for him to have a drink. It hadn't occurred to me back then that alcohol addiction was a disease, not just a personal failing. Dad also had cigarettes in his bedside drawer, and I knew that despite the tubes he dragged himself out of bed from time to time to get one. Of course, I had both of these habits myself—booze and cigarettes—and I knew what it felt like to be denied them, however bad they were for your health.

Ta Ta hated hospitals and didn't trust doctors. Now he was absolutely at their mercy. That wasn't the only reason he hated being there. He'd always thought of himself as the tough guy, the family's pillar of strength. He'd been a boxer in his youth. He'd saved the surviving members of his family from the Holocaust. Now he was like an invalid, a weakling.

During one of my visits he handed me his wedding ring and his watch. "Goldala, I vant you should keep these."

"Don't be so dramatic, Ta Ta." It seemed strange, but to keep him happy I kissed him and took the ring and the watch.

Then he said: "Go back to California and finish your record."

I couldn't tell if he didn't want me around, seeing him like this, or if he was putting my career first. Either way, I did what he said: I headed back to Los Angeles to finish off the recording sessions for the new album.

I was seeing someone there I really liked for once, a talented artist from Japan. Our relationship lasted only about two months, but that was long enough for me to get pregnant—as usual I'd taken no precautions. As soon as I found out the truth, I had to stop seeing him. There was no point in telling him about the pregnancy: As a polite Japanese gentleman he might have pressed me to marry him if he'd realized I was carrying his child, and I certainly wasn't interested in marriage. He kept calling me for at least three months and never cottoned on to why I kept telling him I was "busy." I also didn't want to have a baby on my own, so I fixed up an appointment at Planned Parenthood in Los Angeles for an abortion. The appointment was four weeks away, and during the intervening time I couldn't even smoke or drink alcohol. Morning sickness kicked in. I was surely one miserable singer.

Then Helen called me again. "Dad's still in hospital and he's gotten worse."

I asked her how bad that was.

"He's in a coma."

I cried the entire flight back to New York. All the time I kept repeating, "Please, God, no, no."

By the time I got to Brooklyn there'd been no change in his condition. He was still in a coma, lying there on a respirator with a tube down his throat. A doctor came in and told us Dad had pneumonia and emphysema: his lungs were filling up with water. I could tell the doctor was being cautious in what he said in front of my mother, who was obviously in a fragile state, so I took him to one side and asked for the truth about Ta Ta's prognosis.

"Will my father make it?"

"He doesn't have a chance," the doctor replied. In the same breath he asked me if maybe I liked tennis, hm? I could have slapped him.

This time I didn't go back to Los Angeles.

One night in November we got a call from the hospital in the small hours. "You'd better come down here. He's in cardiac arrest, and he's not going to make it to the morning."

We got there as quickly as we could, but it wasn't soon enough. A nurse said to Mom, "Your husband has expired." For a moment none of us—my mother, my sister, me—knew what she meant. I remember thinking, *Expired? Licenses expire, meters expire, but not my Ta Ta! What the hell is she talking about.*

My mother said, "Vat do you mean? He is dead?"

I started crying, "No! No!" to Mom. I was in full denial, and I wanted to protect her. She began wailing that she wanted to see Dad. The staff gave her a shot to sedate her so she'd not disturb all the other patients, then took her to his room. My sister and I didn't want to see the body, but we heard her scream when she did.

Later Helen told me Ta Ta went into a coma because of an allergic reaction to some medication the hospital gave him. Helen and I still think that's what killed him, but of course we'd never have been able to prove it. Looks like Dad was right not to trust doctors and hospitals.

The whole time we were sitting shiva for Dad I was nauseated by my pregnancy. Just about anything made me feel like puking up: smells, cigarette smoke, the sight of food, even the perfumes people wore. All these visitors were coming to see us and I was the color of a lettuce. In the end I told Helen the problem, and she was wonderful. Every time I'd have to leave the room to throw up she'd have a fresh excuse ready. She told me she'd take the baby if I'd like, but I told her I really didn't want to have it at all. No one could ask for a better sister than mine.

• • • • • •

After the funeral I went back to Los Angeles and straight into the studio to finish recording the album. The work was cathartic. I decided to call the record *Goldie Zelkowitz* as a way of preserving my father's name. Because of World War II, he was the last of his line.

I never really mourned Dad's death. Instead, I used booze to numb the pain. Drinking was the way I'd come to rely on to deal with anything difficult or painful.

I still had the pregnancy to deal with. I wanted the abortion as quickly as possible now. A friend drove me to the clinic. When I woke up from the anesthetic I found myself in a hospital hallway. I told a passing nurse, "My father just died."

She probably heard a lot of crazy comments from people who were recovering from anesthesia. "No," she corrected, "you've just had an abortion."

Genya, Robert Klein, and Frank Zappa at RCA studios.

My friend drove me home again as soon as they'd release me. The moment I got there I said thanks and goodbye, then grabbed a smoke and a drink. Drink blotted out the grief I had for my father.

● ● ● ● ● ●

Not everything about my time in Hollywood was bad, of course. One of the highlights was getting to know Frank Zappa.

I first ran into him during a break at the studio. I was just roaming around, checking out the studio's facilities, when I wandered by accident into another recording room and found him there. I apologized and was just about to leave when he stopped me.

"Are you Genya Ravan?"

The fact that he knew who I was broke the ice immediately. We talked for a while, and he asked what I was up to. He was pleasantly surprised to discover I was Jewish. I told him about how much I was missing New York and how I hated living in California, where there weren't any proper seasons and not even any good bagels. When I started bitching about missing the Stage Deli in New York City he said, "I know a great place here in Hollywood. It'll remind you of the Stage Deli. I'll take you there for lunch one day."

The place was Kanter's, on Fairfax Avenue. We went there to have lunch together about a week later; he insisted that this was on him and that I should have whatever I wanted. I had a great big overstuffed deli sandwich: pastrami and corned beef on rye with a sour pickle. I could have been back in New York, just like he'd said. We did a lot of laughing together—each of us loved the other's sense of humor. Jewish guilt was one of the things we laughed about. There was a vinyl shortage going on at the time, and I told him it was all my fault: "I've had so many records out I must have caused it."

He told me he was working on a new project, a musical that he hoped might become a stage rock opera. He asked me if I'd like to take part in it, singing a particular song he had in mind for me. I said yes immediately; I respected the guy's music so much—and the guy himself—that there was no way I was going to refuse. He offered to give me just a written music sheet, but I told him I'd prefer a cassette of the song as well. The song was called "Time is Money," and it was very fast, complicated, and in general Zappa-esque.

Two days later I went to the rehearsal. Frank put a music stand in front of me but I told him I didn't need it. "I've learned the song."

He looked startled. "You know it already?"

He looked even more startled when I explained to him I couldn't read music; he must have assumed that, since I'd had a big band like Ten Wheel Drive, I must be able to. I'd brought along two giant-sized plastic ears from home, and I threw these at him. "I have good ears," I said.

With players like Aynsley Dunbar, George Duke, Charles Owens, and John Bergamo, the band was impeccable, of course. So was my performance of the song. For one reason or another Frank's project never got off the ground, but even so it's been a great source of pleasure to me that I'm lucky enough to have worked with one of the very best in the business, and that he respected me so much. A big difference from working with Gabriel Mekler and Trevor Lawrence, of course.

The album *Goldie Zelkowitz* was released and did nothing. Yeah, like that was a real surprise to me.

• • • • • •

I made some other good friends while I was in Hollywood. In particular there were the JFLs.

Back in New York, Barbara Baccus, my old manager, had introduced me to Jessica, a friend of hers. When I arrived in Los Angeles, Jessica looked me up and invited me to a friend's house for dinner. That's where I got to know the rest of what came to be the JFLs. They were almost all gay except me, but I adored them. They loved music and shooting pool, and we all did a lot of hanging out in each other's homes—great relaxation for me in between gigs and my dreary recording sessions.

We decided to make it a rule that all six of us women would get together at this outdoor café we knew at least once a week no matter how busy any of us became. It was me, with my gang/group mentality, who first said the bunch of us needed a name, and that's when we became the JFLs—"Just For Licks." Then there was the matter of determining a theme for our meetings; I can't remember quite why I thought this was important. We chewed this around for a while, and out of the group mind emerged the notion that, since we all came from very different backgrounds, we must all have very different fantasies. So our theme for the meetings became that we'd help each other live out our individual fantasies.

I got into the habit of coming to JFL lunches with a tape recorder, or sometimes just a notepad, so I could write the fantasies down. My own fantasy was pretty simple: a female version of something out of *The Wild One*, the Marlon Brando movie. I wanted the six of us to ride into some small Midwest town on big Harley Davidsons, stop into a bar and have a few, then ride in a circle on our bikes around some poor guy, scaring him half to death. One of the girls, Mars, said something about the automatic start-up buttons you can get for big bikes, but I said no way. "Not in *my* fantasy," I cried. "In *my* fantasy we use the kick bars to start the fucking bikes up!"

We played the game for weeks, and had a lot of fun. Mars herself had always fantasized about robbing a supermarket, so we drove around one day, found a suitable supermarket in Venice Beach, cased the joint thoroughly, made detailed plans of how we were going to rob it, and so on. Another girl, Barbara, wanted to be a gypsy fortune-teller catering to the rich, so we worked out how we'd rent space in a wealthy neighborhood, find out from a local dog-sitting parlor—something like that—when the rich people were going to be on their vacations, break into the empty houses and get all the information Barbara needed to "tell fortunes" once the people were back. We never actually did anything about these fantasies, you understand; just worked out how we *could* bring them into being. There were times we laughed so hard we barely made it to the ladies' room.

Everything was going fine until Linda said she wanted somebody killed. That was it. That was when we stopped the JFL fantasy luncheons. Planning fantasy burglaries was one thing. Planning a murder—even a fantasy murder—was another.

CHAPTER ELEVEN
Productions from Hell

FOR SOME TIME I'd been dating the well known actor John Doe. That, of course, is not his real name; for all I know, he's still married to the same woman as he was back in the early 1970s, when I was dating him. John was based in New York at the time, although he'd been in Los Angeles shooting a movie when I'd met him. He was a very heavy drinker; once he got back he phoned me every week, always extremely drunk, begging me to come to New York to live with him and telling me that he'd throw over his wife if I did.

I didn't believe his promises, of course. The truth was, though, that I was getting pretty antsy to go home. I'd been two years on the West Coast, and New York was tugging at me harder than ever. John's pleas added to the pull, as it were. However, making the move back to New York wasn't quite the easy prospect it might sound. I'd been bad about keeping in touch with people there aside from my family, and I felt as if I didn't know anyone there any longer. I had hardly any money. I'd have to start all over again from scratch finding gigs. Where would I live?

By chance, an old friend of mine—the trumpeter John Gatchell—was in Los Angeles on a job and we met for dinner. When I explained my dilemma, he very kindly suggested that I could stay with him, his girlfriend, and her child in their apartment on West Seventy-second Street in Manhattan until I found somewhere of my own. I jumped at the offer. To bankroll myself for the move, I sold all my furniture and all the equipment I'd bought with the CBS money—even my prized yellow Karman Ghia. Farewell, Hollywood.

John and his girlfriend couldn't have been more hospitable to me, but it was immediately apparent that the situation wasn't ideal. I was sharing the child's bedroom, sleeping in the upper bunk, and this was obviously an imposition on all three of them.

Back in Los Angeles an acquaintance had introduced me to the comedienne Liz Torres, and a friendship had grown between us. At lunch one day in New York with her, talking about my plans to put a new band together and start getting some gigs, I groused about my sleeping arrangements, and she proposed that I could move in with her; she had a big apartment and was living in it on her own. I could have my own bedroom. This would definitely be a step up from my current situation! It was great fun sharing with Liz, and she turned me on to *café con leche*, a Spanish coffee made with a cloth sieve and steamed milk. I still make it that way, and love it.

My affair with Jon Doe came to an abrupt end one night when he came to see me at Liz's apartment and arrived so drunk that he threw up all over my bedroom. I've never seen him again. I do hope he's managed to get over his drinking problem. It's been a very long time since he's appeared in a major film role.

Although I enjoyed sharing with Liz, I was obviously keen to have a place of my own. That chance came one day when I was rehearsing at a downtown studio. The owner of the studio told me he also owned an empty apartment in a building called the Parc Vendome, on Fifty-seventh Street. He was willing to rent it to me just so long as I kept the arrangement a secret: The building was in bankruptcy, so it was actually illegal to rent the apartments there, but I didn't care about that. After about six months I discovered there was a huge, empty one-bedroom apartment in the same building; it was ideal for me, so I moved in. (The studio owner wasn't too happy about the loss of his rental income.) For the first five months or so in my new place I was living there illegally; when the building came out of bankruptcy I was able to get a lease and formalize the arrangement.

My ego, which had been so badly damaged by all the disasters of the past few years, was slowly recovering. It was helped by the construction workers on Fifty-seventh Street, there because the Sheffield was being built. They always howled and whistled when I walked by. It got to be pretty irritating as well as flattering. One day one of them—a gorgeous, shirtless, muscular tanned guy—gave me a real stare. Just as I was getting embarrassed, he whistled and yelled in a Midwestern accent: "Anyone that screws that should be horsewhipped! That's eatin' stuff only!"

I stopped dead in my tracks, and then burst out laughing. That was the best line I ever heard.

• • • • • •

Directly across from the Parc Vendome on Fifty-seventh Street was Media Sound Recording Studios, the best recording studio in New York. It had originally been a church, and so it had great acoustics. Studio A was huge. No wonder a lot of the top artists and groups chose to record there.

It was at Media Sound that I first met Harvey Goldberg. He was one of a group of young up-and-coming engineers who worked there; others included Bob Clearmountain, Godfrey Diamond, and Al Varner. During breaks we'd hang out at the diner next door, Café 57. Because my apartment was just across the street, a lot of the staff and musicians often came across there as well, and it became a recognized place to hang out between sessions. Kool and the Gang visited quite frequently, as did Bobby Babbitt, the bass player who, along with James Jamerson, played on almost all the early Motown hits. I still have a rather large memento of those days: a big round wooden table that started life as one of those reels they use for heavy phone cables. I rolled it all the way up from the West Village, and encouraged visitors to carve their names and messages into the wood. I even kept a penknife stuck into the table for that purpose. Today it serves as a record of the decades from the 1960s through the 1990s.

Harvey and I had a thing for a while. Friends thought I was nuts getting involved with this lanky, skinny, plain-looking guy, but something sparked between us. In fact, he was one of the few guys I've ever let get too close to me. I used to take him shopping for decent clothes, because otherwise he dressed so raggedy. He also turned me on to cocaine, after everyone else had failed. That's something I don't thank him for. The first time I agreed to try it, it did nothing for me, but like a fool I kept on trying until I liked it.

The great thing that Harvey gave me, though, was my introduction to record production. I sat in on some of his sessions after he'd okayed this with the musicians concerned (one of the acts was Kool and the Gang). I watched what he did, asked questions, and learned a lot. This was to stand me in very good stead in the years to come.

I eventually stopped working with Harvey for many reasons, few of which had anything to do with the fact that our relationship broke up. The main one was that he applied his own distinctive sound to everything he recorded. This is not at all unusual with engineers: they each have their own way of setting up. Problems arise, though, when the producer has an idea for doing something different and the engineer resists it. You end up with a pushing and pulling match that helps no one. As soon as I started to get my own ideas about how recorded music should sound—that each production should have its *own* sound, not always "the Harvey Goldberg sound"—it was time to move on and find another engineer. I know he'd grown unhappy about working with me, too, so it was the best for both of us. Harvey had his own demons.

• • • • • •

There was a lot of pain inside me at this time, and it was manifesting as constant ups and downs, and major depressions. It was getting uncomfortable to be inside my own skin. I was having terrible dreams. I felt I was living my life through other people's ideas of who I was, as if I were performing according to a script.

Finally things got so bad that I went to see a psychiatrist. I explained to her: "I only feel good when I'm on-stage. As soon as I get off the stage I start feeling lost and unhappy again." She pointed out that this was a control thing. On-stage I could be who I thought I was, and in full control of my life. Off-stage, I hadn't established a role for myself, which was why I was such a mess. Anyone who's read this far in the book will know how important control is for me. I guess it's no surprise I ended up doing record production.

I told her everything I could think of—really spilled my guts. Some of the answers were interesting not just in a personal sense. For example, when I described a recurring vision I experienced when I felt uncomfortable or suffered emotional pain—I would see lots of green, slimy stuff, with some red goo as well—she sat upright in startlement and said: "Oh my God, Genya! You're remembering your birth! Only a handful of people can remember being born." She was thrilled to discover one of that handful was sitting in her office.

I also had a recurring anxiety dream that had haunted me for years. In it, I'd forget something of life-or-death importance. For example, I'd stow away a child or a puppy or some equally helpless creature in a drawer or a trunk, and forget all about it—particularly about feeding it. Only when I'd finally open up the drawer or trunk would the memories come flooding back. The creature would be alive, but only just. The psychiatrist figured out that the helpless creature, whatever the guise it took, was actually *me*. I'd taken to hiding my real self away so securely that even I forgot she was there, starving. Whether her analysis was right or not, I hardly ever have that dream anymore.

• • • • • • •

A few small production jobs started coming may way—really small ones, like demo recordings. Some of the record-company A&R people started calling me with work. I don't know if it was some form of political correctness or if they felt a woman producer would have a better chance of controlling women, but all the productions the A&R people offered me were for female artists, and often difficult female artists at that. I became a baby-sitter in the studios for all kinds of talentless women. One time I was woken up by a knock on my door at seven thirty in the morning. As I hadn't gotten to sleep until five, I was more than just a little pissed by the intrusion.

"Who is it?" I yelled from my bed.

"It's me. Veronica," said a voice I recognized. I'd produced for Veronica the week before.

"Call me later!"

"I don't like my mixes," she said.

"Do you know what time it is? Call me later."

Again: "I don't like my mixes."

"Well, take the fucking tapes and either remix them yourself or shove them up your ass! I don't care."

Finally she took the hint and left.

I needed studio experience, so I never said no to the offer of producing a recording session, even for the Veronicas of this life. It was a learning process. I always chose the best musicians around, and I would ask them lots of questions when I wasn't sure of something. I found a few session musicians I liked and who liked working with me. I would use the same guys over and over again because they understood my thinking and what I was trying to convey. I always listened to my artists when they told me what *they* wanted, too. I remembered the hell I'd gone through myself when being produced by the likes of Jim Price and Gabriel Mekler, who'd tried to stamp every recording with *their* sound, not mine. I earned respect as a producer from some of the best artists and musicians in town because I was one of their number. They knew I had the feel for rock 'n' roll, R&B and soul; the results were always "cookin'." Of course, sometimes I wished I could just erase those not-so-hot singers from the vocal tracks and sing the shit out of the songs myself!

In my spare time I was taking a few more acting lessons—still ignoring Tony Randall's advice! I eventually wound up with a part in a play called *The Cracker Club* that had a run at La Mamma Theater in the Village.

And, of course, I was starting once more to sing some New York gigs myself. A couple of these were at the club called Reno Sweeney in the West Village on Ninth Street. As backing musicians I had the best session guys from Media Sound, with the group Rosie providing the backing vocals. Reno Sweeney was a great place to perform. It had a feeling of real intimacy to it, even though it held about three hundred people. The club featured performers of all kinds, not just music (rock, folk, Broadway) but comedy. Both times I sang there I had lines around the block waiting to get in. I liked that, as you can imagine.

It was at Reno Sweeney that I first met one of my favorite comediennes, Gilda Radner. She was very sweet and friendly. She'd come to the club to watch the performance of a friend of hers, who was opening for me that night. His name was Meat Loaf.

Another artist I met for the first time at the club was John Phillips, of The Mamas and the Papas. He was introduced to me by Harvey Goldberg, who was working in the studio with him on a new album that week. At the time, John was writing for everyone, so of course I was anxious to see if I could get a song out of him. Unfortunately, I was drinking very heavily. Even by the time I got to the club I was as drunk as a skunk, and couldn't really hold a proper conversation with John when Harvey introduced me to him. I just kept saying drunkenly, "I need a song. I have to have a song. It's all about a *song*, I tell ya!"

I was mobile enough that I was able to tag along to a party John was having that night at the brownstone he was staying in. I know we all did a hell of a lot of drugs at the party, but that's all I remember about it. I have no idea how I got home.

All this self-destructiveness—the alcoholism, the drugs—was, of course, born out of the pain I was still feeling inside me. To put it a shorter way, I was totally fucked up. The psychiatrist helped, but even so it was going to take me a long while to get over it. And the worst was yet to come.

• • • • • •

In June 1975 I got a call from Sid Bernstein, the one-time manager of Ten Wheel Drive; we still kept in touch. He told me that among the acts he was now managing was a female duo called Cryer & Ford, who'd just been signed up by RCA, and he was wondering if I'd like to produce them. The person who'd signed them to RCA was Ken Glancy, head of the A&R Division, so this was likely to be a major release. The problem, he explained, was that they currently sounded too clean, too legit; he was looking for a producer who'd "rockify" them. Sid had told the two women about me, and all agreed I could be the right producer for them.

I really wanted to get this production job. With Ken Glancy's involvement, this seemed like the chance at last to get my name as producer on a record that a major label would be pushing hard. Having my name attached to a hit could be the big breakthrough for my fledgling production career. I knew this was something I had to get right. First, though, we agreed I had to meet the people at RCA as well as, obviously, Gretchen Cryer and Nancy Ford themselves.

My meeting with RCA's A&R people went well, and I was introduced to a guy called Mike Berniker, a producer who was already working for them. (He'd won a Grammy Award for his production of Barbra Streisand's 1964 album *People*.) Mike and I hit it off immediately, and it was settled that I could have the Cryer & Ford production job if I wanted it. Before I made my final decision, however, I still had to listen to their music and see how I got on with the singers themselves.

Gretchen and Nancy turned out to be two of the nicest artists I've ever worked with. I went to Gretchen's apartment on the Upper West Side to hear all their songs so I could work which ones should go on the record. After listening, I knew Sid had been absolutely right: the two women had their roots in Broadway, and this came through loud and clear. But the material was great, and I had no hesitation in deciding to

GENYA RAVAN: ROCK'S ONLY WOMAN PRODUCER

1973, the only known female producer.

take on the production. It was obvious to me that the record should go in a mainstream pop direction. This was going to be a bit of a challenge for me, because, of course, all my own experience was in R&B and soul. But I love challenges.

It was also clear to me that the songs needed the best arrangers I could get; in particular, I'd have to supply clever and extensive vocal backing arrangements. In the end I used two incredible arrangers. Ken Ascher had worked with musicians like John Lennon, Harry Nilsson, Paul Williams, and Phoebe Snow, and he was also an amazing pianist. For the other arranger I turned to Mike Zager of Ten Wheel Drive— another first-rate arranger. Between them they did a superb job for me. The musicians I hired were impeccable as well. They included Rick Morotta on drums, Bob Babbitt and Will Lee on bass, and Hugh McCracken on harmonica and guitar.

The project was great fun for me to work on, because Gretchen and Nancy were easy to get along with and had complete trust in my judgement. They took direction well, and were always open to advice and suggestions. I was a whole other breed to them, and made them laugh a lot. Because of their trust in me I was able to relax; I didn't feel I had to keep proving myself the whole time.

The result, called simply *Cryer & Ford*, was a wonderful pop record. Unfortunately, RCA didn't give it the kind of push it deserved—the kind of push I'd assumed from the outset it was going to get. It failed miserably, and I was shocked. Whatever happened to Ken Glancy's original excitement? I began to wonder if maybe the signing had just been done as a favor to someone.

Gretchen and Nancy went on to have a fairly distinguished career writing for the musical stage. Among the shows they've done have been *I'm Getting My Act Together and Taking it on the Road*, *Now is the Time for All Good Men*, and *Shelter*. Meanwhile, although the album *Cryer & Ford* has never been reissued on CD, copies of the original vinyl release have become something of a collectors' item.

• • • • • •

After I'd worked with Cryer & Ford, the flow of small-scale production jobs continued and increased. Various companies sent me artists for demo recordings. In particular, Jobete Music Publishing threw a number of female artists my way. Yes, female artists; people still had this fixed idea that a woman producer should be producing women artists.

In the midst of this I'd met the singer/songwriter David Lasley, who was part of the band Rosie who'd sung with me. He played me some of the music he'd been making with the other two members of Rosie: Lynn Pitney and Lana Maranno. I was floored by it, and resolved to get the band a record deal. This was blue-eyed soul, and it was magnificent—music I could really get my teeth into. I wanted to produce them so bad it hurt.

I got on the phone to Mike Berniker and raved to him about how good Rosie was. He was disposed to believe in my judgement; he'd been much impressed by my work with Cryer & Ford. We set up a meeting so he could hear Rosie for himself. I walked into his office and asked him if he was ready for a real treat. Smiling, he turned on his stereo ready for the tape he thought I was going to play. Instead I called for David, Lynn, Lana, and their pianist to come in, and they pitched straight into a live performance of their song "Roll Me Through the Rushes." At first Mike was open-mouthed, because *nobody* in the record business by then gave a live audition; he was amazed I'd had the balls to spring this on him. But after that he was open-mouthed because he loved what he was hearing. "Unbelievable," he mouthed to me.

The harmonies knocked him out. David's voice has a tremendous range. One moment he was sounding high and light in falsetto; the next he was hitting all the deep notes. Someone once said David's singing was like "a visual vocal ballet," whatever that means. The girls were singing lusciously around David's vocals.

Rosie did three songs for him. I'd promised him a treat and he surely got it: a real live show in his office. Other RCA staffers were gathering outside in the corridor to listen. There was no question but that I'd successfully sold Rosie to Mike—or, really, given them the opportunity to do it.

The next week Mike and I talked about budgets for the project. He said that RCA needed budgets written out in advance. I teased him on this: "You think I'm just going to take the money and run out and buy a fur coat or a washing machine instead?" He laughed and said this was just the way RCA did things. I had no difficulty in complying. All I really cared about was that Mike signed Rosie up, which he did.

One condition imposed on me was that I had to use the RCA studios. In itself this was no problem—the RCA recording facilities were great (although I'd still have preferred to use Media Sound)—but it meant I had to use a union engineer; the union was very strong in RCA. I was worried about this. A lot of the union engineers were old-guard, that sort of thing, whereas this was going to be a very hip R&B record. I was working with Harvey Goldberg on a few demos at Media Sound at the time, so I brought him in as an engineer but called him a joint producer; that way the union would be kept happy while I'd get, I hoped, the sound I wanted. But I was still having problems with Harvey wanting to push his own sound onto me and the group. In the end, the union engineer RCA wanted me to use, Mike Moran, turned out—much to my surprise—to be splendid. I needn't have been concerned.

The album that came out, *Better Late Than Never*, sounded fabulous. I'd used the top session musicians and the best arrangers I could find. However, RCA gave it no promotion whatsoever, so it didn't become the hit it deserved to be. That made twice in a row RCA had done this to me—first with Cryer & Ford, now with Rosie. I had also heard that Lou Reed had complained bitterly to everyone, including the press, about how lousy RCA was as a label, and had moved mountains to get out of his contract there. I should have paid more attention at the time.

Now I made the same vow as he had: Never again with RCA.

CHAPTER TWELVE
On the Bowery

IT WAS THE SUMMER OF 1977, and I was still living in my apartment on 57th Street. I was isolating myself from the rest of the human species, licking my wounds, drowning myself in vodka or whatever else I could find to drink or take. By then, anyone who came to visit me knew to bring booze or drugs. I needed somebody or something to drag me from this dark cavern of the soul.

My friend Hank called and asked me if I'd like to come out to this club he'd found on the Bowery. He warned me that it was a dump—"make sure to pee before you get there"—but said it was a good place to hear some new local bands. I said okay, I'd go, so he picked me up and we took a cab downtown.

As soon as we walked in I fell in love with the place. It had neon bar signs hanging from the ceiling, and the air was rich with the heady aroma of smoke, booze, and disinfectant—and worse. Writer Charles Shaar Murray once theorized that the staff pissed against the walls each night before opening the doors, just so the clientele could get an extra dose of "atmosphere." But I felt comfortable there—at home. On the right was the bar, long and narrow; on the left was a platform with some tables and seats on it; straight ahead, against the wall, was the stage (eventually moved to the right). Everyone called the club CBGBs, although it had been started as Country, Blue Grass, Blues, and Other Music for Urban Gourmets, or, for short, CBGB&OMFUG.

The band on-stage when Hank and I arrived was called Manster. They reminded me of a punk version of the Mothers of Invention. Their music was loud and raucous—the sound system was incredible—and completely unpolished. I realized how much I'd been missing the rawness of live music; after all, that's what my records were all about. I'd been performing in large venues for so long now that I'd forgotten how I loved the intimacy of small ones, where you can have full eye contact with the audience from the stage. Lounges and clubs were my background. I adored not just performing music in bars but listening to it there as well.

Hank introduced me to the club's owner, Hilly Kristal, who was handsome in a rugged sort of a way, like a big burly Russian who chopped wood in the forest for a living. Hilly and I became friends immediately; we had a lot in common, and knew a lot of the same people in the music industry. (We're still good friends. He's another of those few shiningly honest people in the business.) We sat at the bar and drank and talked. He knew about Ten Wheel Drive, so he knew who I was. He'd been around a long time, and had managed a number of clubs before opening CBGBs. A shy guy, he didn't talk to strangers much. I could tell that he liked me, and I felt privileged.

Hanging out with Hilly (second from left) at CBGBs.

Hank had been right to warn me about the club's rest rooms, though. They were the one bit of CBGBs I never did grow to love. After the first time I used them I did my very best never to have to do so again. Your feet half stuck to the floor there. The stalls had no locks. The toilet seats were sometimes missing. The graffiti not only covered the walls but, incredibly, went right down into the toilet bowls.

When I asked Hilly how he found the bands who played at CBGBs, he told me that he didn't need to: they found him. Each Monday night he'd hold auditions at which anyone could try out. It hadn't been his intention for the club to establish itself as a rock venue—he'd been shooting for country—but rock was what the local bands played. There were no good rock clubs to speak of in New York City then; CBGBs was the first hot club in a long time where new bands could go to perform. Hilly has managed to keep CBGBs going while other clubs have opened and closed again. (The low rent he must pay could be a help here. Who else would think of opening a bar in the Bowery in the 1970s?) The groups made money from the cover charge at the door—the bigger their following, the more money they made—but plenty of the groups weren't worried about earning anything: they played just for the exposure, or for the pleasure of performing. All the bands wanted to play CBGBs—still do.

I told Hilly I very much wanted to produce some good rock bands, and asked him to keep an eye out for anything special. He said he'd do so—and he did. Thereafter Hilly would come every now and then to my apartment bearing cassettes of bands he liked; we'd listen to the music and talk about it.

The first band Hilly was really eager I should come and hear live was called the Shirts, or sometimes Annie Golden and the Shirts. To be honest, I was never really all that crazy about them: They were good, but I wasn't too keen on the songs they wrote. Their music was too dramatic for my liking. At one point I did start working with them in the studio, but I tangled with the lead singer, Annie Golden. I liked her as a person, but not to work with; her "I'm the star" attitude really got to me. At the time, I could do without negative influences on my life, so I walked away from the project.

That was good for me, and it turned out to be good for the Shirts, too, because instead they were produced by my very good friend Mike Thorne, a producer I really admire. With him as their producer, the Shirts went on to do well in the Netherlands, although they never really made much of a noise in the States. Later Annie began a solo career as a singer and actor; she was in the Broadway production of *The Full Monty*.

* * * * * *

As a record producer, I sometimes found myself being placed in defensive situations because of my other roles as singer and band leader. Some of the singers I produced loved the fact that I was a singer too, because I could understand them better; but others were intimidated by it. Even this early in my career I had learned to maintain a tough demeanor and a thick skin the whole time; it was hard work keeping that up, but essential.

The producing end of the music business was still male-dominated. As a woman, I had to be loud in order to be heard, tough in order to be "understood." It hurt a lot, hiding my feelings, stuffing them away like this. That psychiatrist had been only too accurate in her interpretation of my recurring anxiety dream. In the 1960s and 1970s it was a struggle all the way for women in the music industry. It was tiring having to prove myself the whole time—not just to the suits but also to the other musicians. I'm sure they thought I ate nails for breakfast. All the while I tried to act as if I knew everything, whereas in reality I was still trying to learn everything. I always had guys questioning me, feeling me out—musicians, engineers, agents, managers, accountants, none of them knowing if they wanted to work with me or fuck me. I began to forget the sensitive person I really was. This clash between my inner and my outer selves caused me a lot of pain. No wonder I tended to isolate myself.

I often get asked: "What does a producer do?" I always reply that a record producer is to music what a movie director is to a film. You work closely with the group the whole way through. You mastermind the arrangements of the songs at rehearsals. You pick the material. You choose the studio to record in. You hire the sound engineer. You decide which take to work with. You do the mixes.

Just as often as I'd hear "Genya's hard to work with" I'd be told, "Thanks, Genya. I learned a lot from working with you." It was usually the engineers who said the latter, the musicians the former! Most musicians are never satisfied with the end results of a recording session. They're always saying that just one more take and they'd have done it better. The vocalist says the vocals should be more prominent, or the guitarist says the guitar part is too low. The drummer *always* says the drums should be louder. As I said, some singers would find it intimidating to be produced by a singer, but many of them loved it: they felt they could trust another artist.

Trust. It's one of the most important things in the relationship between artists and their producer, and it makes for the best end results. I was in touch with the singers' needs. In a way I was on both sides of the glass. I was also an educated audience, giving them the kind of atmosphere they needed; a good rock artist always wants the right atmosphere. Sometimes I wasn't just audience but also mother, father, girlfriend, or—the worst—baby-sitter.

Everyone had to give the artists the right atmosphere in the studio, the feeling that they were wanted, that people were eager to hear what they were doing. I once found that an engineer had fallen asleep on a couch in the control room during a break; he was startled when I bawled him out for it, telling him that if he ever did that kind of thing again I'd fire him from the project. I explained to him that the artists needed to believe everyone was excited by their music. That wasn't the message they'd get if they found an engineer snoring. I always had a smile on my face for the artists, to help them feel secure, as though they were the only ones who mattered, everything was under control. Sometimes, of course, keeping the smile there wasn't easy.

Engineers could be a trial, too. Sometimes I got through two or three of them during the production of an album. Different projects called for different types of sound, and that meant different types of engineer. In some cases the engineers fought me when I tried to get them to produce the sound I wanted. If they really developed an attitude, I had to fire them. I could never let them intimidate me; the control room was still thought of as a man's place. I had to run a tight ship—otherwise it'd sink.

Many sound engineers get the idea that they're really the producers, when in fact they're there to, you know, engineer the sound. I never understood how engineers imagined they could run the board, checking for sound and levels, and listen to the band and the arrangements at the same time. Of course, some engineers do wind up becoming producers. If they're any good, the first thing they do is hire another engineer to run the board while they do the producing.

• • • • • •

I produced a lot of demos for the CBGB groups Hilly Kristal sent me. Most of them were definitely raw garage bands, and Hilly hoped that with my experience I could make them sound more polished. Most of the time I could indeed make them sound better. I started, more formally, to produce for Hilly.

One of the many reasons I respect Hilly Kristal is the sensitivity he displays towards musicians; he's a singer/songwriter himself. As a manager, he could have signed each and every one of the groups that went through his club—they were all desperate to record, to sign a record deal. But he felt that would have been taking advantage of the situation. I've often thought that it's Hilly himself who needs management. He passed up bands like the Ramones, Television, the Clash, Blondie, Talking Heads . . . all because of his ethics. The only problem Hilly has is giving up control; he just can't do it. If he could do that he'd have been much more financially successful in his life.

His tastes in music are eclectic—he can go from grunge to pop in a split second. He has "good ears." I soon learned to pay attention whenever he said an act had something special. It's hard now for me to remember all the groups I worked with for Hilly. The Miamis were a fun band—they wrote very pop. I really liked a glam-punk band called Tuff Darts, too, and was eager to have them into the studio, but one of the bigger labels (Sire) got them before I had a chance. If they'd stayed together their music would have been exactly the type of thing radio stations liked to play.

When I heard Manster again—the band who'd been playing during my first visit to CBGBs—I realized how musical and clever they were. Hilly thought they weren't commercial, and he was right, but I knew I just had to work with them—and one day, much later, I did.

One time Hilly phoned me up sounding really excited. For Hilly to sound excited is so unusual that I was immediately on the edge of my seat. He was calling to tell me about this group from Cleveland he'd just heard, the Dead Boys. "They're punk and very charming," he said.

I thought: *Punk? Charming? Has Hilly flipped?* Out loud, I asked him when they'd next be playing CBGBs.

"Tomorrow."

"I'll be there," I said.

When I arrived the next night the Dead Boys were on-stage. There were four of them in those days. They looked very young and ragged. The lead singer, Stiv Bators, reminded me of someone I'd seen a while back—Iggy

Pop of the Stooges. The thing that bothered me most about the Dead Boys was that they didn't have a bass player.

I turned to Hilly. He was looking back and forth at the band and me with a big grin on his face, like he was a proud new father. The music was pretty loud, even for CBGBs, so I had to lean against his ear as I yelled at him: "The first thing these guys are doing is getting a bass player! There's no rock without bottom."

I went back to watching for a while. Then it was time to scream in Hilly's ear again.

"What kind of guys are they? Nasty?"

"They're real nice!" he bellowed back.

As I listened to their song "Everyone Knows You Were Caught with the Meat in Your Mouth" I thought, *Yeah, right, "nice." They're probably the archetypal snot-nosed kids from Cleveland with an attitude I'll have to spend fucking hours and days dealing with.*

As the set continued, I began to realize what Hilly had been talking about. Yes, they needed work. The songs certainly needed arranging. But the songs actually had hooks. There was potential for radio play. I

(From left): Liz, Genya, Cheetah Crome from the Dead Boys, and Hilly Kristal (owner of CBGBs).

was just hoping they had some songs without the words "fuck" and "suck" in them.

By the time I left CBGBs that night I still wasn't entirely convinced they were good enough for it even to be worth my while meeting them, let alone commit myself to working with them. I came back the next night to hear them again, and this time I asked Hilly to introduce me.

To my surprise, he'd told the truth when he'd described them as nice. Stiv Bators, the lead singer, was a rock 'n' roll junkie, a mine of trivia knowledge: He could reel off the names of band members and the years they recorded individual songs. He not only knew who I was, he knew all about Goldie and the Gingerbreads—he said he'd read about me years ago in the magazine *Teen Trend*. I respected him for his encyclopedic knowledge and he respected me for who I was; this made communication really easy from the start. Johnny Blitz, the drummer, and guitarist Jimmy Zero had no problem with me. Cheetah Chrome, the other guitarist, was, however, clearly dubious. Hilly had told him I was going to be their producer, but Cheetah wasn't sure he trusted me. I knew that, before we got into the studio, I was going to have to work hard to make him comfortable with me.

Standing at the bar with Cheetah, I asked him if his orange hair color was real or if he'd used dye. He claimed it was real. I told him I didn't believe it, that he'd have to prove it.

"What?" he said.

"Drop your pants and show me."

"*What?*"

"Whip it out and prove it to everyone here at the bar."

Next thing I knew, he was pulling down his jeans. That hair was orange.

"You're right, it *is* orange," I said.

Everyone, Cheetah included, roared with laughter. The ice was broken. From then on, we got on fine. Thereafter I called him the Orange Cocktail. Stiv was, of course, Master Bators.

The Dead Boys were sleeping in vans when they first got to New York City from Cleveland. After a few gigs, they were able to sleep in the apartments of various groupies. One time Stiv introduced one of these groupies to me with, "She's so good to all of us." He meant it sincerely. They'd all been in a taxi the night before, looking for somewhere to stay, and they'd been feeling kind of lost and low. To improve their spirits, she'd given them all head in the taxi. "Wasn't that nice of her?" he concluded.

"Yeah," I said. "She sure is a good girl."

For some reason Stiv felt the need to show me every scar on his body. He had a story for each of them. "This one's from a gig in Detroit, and I got this one at a show in Cleveland, and . . ." On and on it went. His body was his journal.

* * * * * *

In the later 1970s the people at CBGBs looked so cool—this was long before the make-believes from Jersey and Long Island discovered the club. Everyone had their own costume. Plenty of "designer rips" in the clothing. Some of the clientele—girls as well as boys—had their heads shaved bald. If people had hair it was likely to be green or hot pink. Some of them, on the other hand, looked like Robert De Niro in *Taxi Driver*. Some of the girls would wear net stockings and short tops; nothing else. Body-piercing was the coming thing. It was still rare, but at CBGBs you could see boys and girls rings and knives in their noses and studs in the bottom of their tongues. As for earrings, there were hatchet earrings, knife earrings, gun earrings . . . There were always some Hell's Angels sitting drinking at the end of the bar—they had a club just round the corner, on Second Street between Avenue C and First Avenue.

Sometimes when I got to CBGBs there'd be people lining up around the block and limos parked outside. This was a weird contrast for a club that had a shelter for the homeless next door and drunks sitting or lying on the sidewalk outside it. Some of the guys lying there looked not so much drunk as dead, but Hilly was able to rouse them when he came out every now and then to yell, in his big, deep voice, "Come on! Get up! Move! Go away!" And around this scene there'd be these glitzy people and punks arriving. All strangely exciting.

As for me, that friend of mine, Hank, had been wise. Now that I was involved in CBGBs and production work, I wasn't drinking the whole time. I was still binge drinking, though. This meant that some nights I'd drink a hell of a lot, and still not get drunk even if I wanted to. But other times I'd be saying, "No, I won't have a drink. I had too much last night." I was also going pretty easy on the coke.

* * * * * *

I managed to secure a deal at the Electric Lady Studios ("Electric Ladyland") for the Dead Boys. As you can imagine, the Boys themselves were thrilled they were going to be recording in a studio Jimi Hendrix had built and where he used to record. I told them I'd rehearse them right in the studio—I didn't want to over-rehearse them for fear of losing the raw quality I liked. I also made it clear that before we went any further we had to get a bass player. They didn't like that at first, but didn't put up too much of a struggle. I called my old friend Bob Clearmountain, one of the engineers at Media Sound who was a fine bass player, and he agreed to take part.

Before we went into the studio for the first session I met up with the boys to show them the room we were going to be recording in. Afterwards we went to a bagel joint, and Johnny Blitz said, "What's a bagel?" I just about fell off my seat.

Then, as we were getting the equipment into Electric Ladyland, I saw the boys had put swastikas all over their cases. I got really mad, and read them the riot act. "Guys, you take those swastikas off your cases or this production stops right here. Do you realize your manager [Hilly] is Jewish, your producer—me—is Jewish, and the owner of this studio, who's doing us all a favor by letting us record at these prices, is Jewish?"

One of the Dead Boys said, "I don't even know what the swastika thing stands for."

I told him. I also told them that the owner of Electric Ladyland had numbers tattooed on his arm in Auschwitz—I had to explain to them what Auschwitz was—and that I'd lost both my brothers and my relatives in Poland to those Nazi fuckers. "So get those fucking things off your equipment."

When they arrived the next week the swastikas had gone. We started the session.

Other than that, the recording sessions for the album—called *Young, Loud and Snotty* —were great. The group was fine throughout the basics and the overdubs. Bob Clearmountain fit in perfectly, as I'd known he would. He pushed like crazy on the bass parts. These were songs he was just learning and he sounded like he'd been playing with the band for years.

It was a pity, in a way, that I couldn't use him as an engineer as well (although I did try him on a few songs, like "Sonic Reducer"), because we had problems with the engineers when it came to the mixing. I knew what I wanted this record to sound like, and I had to have it exact. I went through about three engineers before I found one who'd listen to what I told him and then do it.

I basically arranged the songs as we went. The beginning of the track "Sonic Reducer" I arranged entirely with the mix in mind. I told the boys to give me a very long drum intro at the start of the song because I knew I was going to be putting all this through a heavy harmonizer and a Cooper Time Cube. They let me be as creative as I wanted to be. It was a matter of trusting, and that's why it all worked. For the ending of "Sonic Reducer" I had three very sensitive mikes positioned on the floor of the big studio. When I told the engineer I was planning to drop a big, heavy, metal garbage can on the floor he said, "But it'll blow the mikes . . ."

"Great!" I said. "Record it!"

All the while there was a lot of beer flowing into the studio on direct consignment from CBGBs, but as far as I could tell nobody was doing any form of hard drugs. I'm certain the boys did some speed, and I know I did—it was somewhat essential since we laid down the entire album in twenty-four hours, from one morning right through to the next morning. Then we took a day off before putting on the guitar overdubs.

There were only a couple of bones of contention throughout the whole process.

The Dead Boys were big Hell's Angels fans, and unknown to me they'd invited a bunch of them to the studio for the first night of the recording. I never like anyone in the control room but me during basics—there's too much going on, too much concentration required. These Hell's Angels walked in and started talking to the boys. I told them all to shut up, and they did . . . for about five minutes. When they started talking again I realized I was losing my crucial connection with the artists.

It's at moments like these that my natural diplomacy comes into play. "All the people not recording here tonight, get the fuck out!"

There was a moment's silence, and then they all left. The Dead Boys couldn't believe that I'd just thrown out a bunch of Hell's Angels. Hilly walked them out, and later he called me from CBGBs. "You made a real impression on those guys, Genya. One of them asked for your phone number because he wants to go out with you."

The other point of discord concerned Bob Clearmountain's credit. The Dead Boys had got my message and found a bass player to gig with them, Jeff Magnum. They insisted on putting his name on the record as their bass player. I was mad about that. As I told them, it just wasn't right. Bob had played bass on their record, so Bob should be the one credited. But the matter was out of my control. (Hell, I barely got paid for the production!) Years later, after Bob had gone on to become a well known producer/engineer, they realized how stupid they'd been; they could have done with having his name associated with theirs. In some interviews Stiv lied, claiming Bob had done the mixes on *Young, Loud and Snotty*.

Nope. Bob never touched the mixes. I know. I was there. He played the bass. And they didn't give him the credit for it.

Dead Boys went on to make a second album, *We Have Come for Your Children*, this time getting Felix Pappalardi (the bass player for the band Mountain) to produce it. *We Have Come for Your Children* didn't make as much noise as *Young, Loud and Snotty*. I was always pissed that they didn't come to me when there was finally some money for a production. Cheetah Chrome says he tried to fight for me to be their producer again, but Stiv wanted a bigger name involved in the production. I felt, too, that Hilly Krystal, as their manager, should have fought for me. But, as usual, I didn't have a contract.

Later, singer Stiv Bators formed another band, Lords of the New Church, with Brian James from the Damned and Dave Tregunna from Sham 69. He died in 1990 in Paris after being hit by a car.

CHAPTER THIRTEEN
Original Punk

ONE DAY IN 1977 I was sitting in the diner next to Media Sound Studios having lunch with a friend when I noticed a strange-seeming guy in the next booth staring at me—he looked like Pugsley from the *Addams Family*. In due course he came over, explained to me that he'd overheard me talking about music, and started picking my brains. Of all the questions he asked the one I remember best was: "Is it hard to get into the music business?" I burst out laughing.

He introduced himself as Mike Hektoen. He told me he was very successful in marketing, and was keen to apply his marketing knowledge to the music industry. The more he talked, the more interested I became. I told him about my own career; when I mentioned that I was currently producing at Media Sound Studios next door, he asked if he might sit in on one of my sessions one day to see what went on. I said okay, and gave him my phone number.

Soon after, he phoned. I invited him to my apartment and played him some of the music I'd produced as well as some of my own recordings. He asked the obvious question: Why wasn't I cutting records of my own anymore? I described the bad experiences I'd had with the various labels I'd recorded for—how they always wanted all the production control—but said that, if I could ever raise the money to do an independent production, where I wouldn't be at the mercies of the wrong producers, I'd be more than happy to record again.

He still seemed dubious as to why I wouldn't want simply to take the money the major labels offered, so I explained that you could actually get more money from them if you went to them with an album that had already been made. That way they didn't have to think too hard: they could hear exactly what they were buying. Inevitably, he asked how much it would cost to produce a full album, and I told him that about $15,000 would probably cover it. (I was assuming I'd be able to beg some favors from friendly musicians and from Media Sound. I was nervous about borrowing too much.) That sum didn't faze him at all; he said he could find investors for me, that some of his business contacts were music freaks and would be willing to put up the money.

To be honest, I thought he was a bit dorky and that it was unlikely anything would ever come of this, but I liked him and there was always the chance that he really could come up with the investors. So I went along with his ideas, still wanting to believe. What did I have to lose?

Around this same time, the owners of Media Sound—John Roberts and Joel Rosenberg—were starting a production company of their own, Media Productions, and we talked about my being one of their artists. This was really thrilling for me. And Mike Hektoen came through with the investors, just like he'd said he would: three guys I'd never met were each willing to put up five thousand dollars. I was very impressed with Mike for doing this, and started getting tighter with him. The upshot was that I brought him into the Media Productions deal with me; I told him he could be my business manager—that he could speak for me but that I'd be the one making the decisions. Basically he'd be my mouthpiece and at the same time he'd get an education.

As soon as I'd signed up with John and Joel I started looking around for suitable songs to sing. I came across an excellent songwriter called Joe Droukas. There was also the exciting development that at last I'd found the confidence to start writing my own material. Between Joe's songs and my own, there was more than enough that I wanted to record for the new album. And, of course, I'd be producing myself. At last I was going to make a Genya Ravan record that really *was* a Genya Ravan record.

I also needed to find musicians. I didn't want to use the session men for my rock group: I wanted fresh young energy. I already knew the guitarist Conrad Taylor: He was a very good player and I could write songs with him. Unfortunately, he lived in Riverhead, Long Island, so getting to and from rehearsals and gigs was a bit of a drag for him; however, he promised that'd be no problem, and it wasn't. (He also looked pretty square when I first met him, but I soon changed that.) For a keyboard player I put an ad in the *Village Voice*, asking for a '50s-style Jerry Lee Lewis–style bang-out pianist, and started listening to the hundreds of tapes I was sent. I could usually tell within moments of putting on a tape if the pianist was likely to have what I was looking for, and one grabbed me immediately: the pianist was playing those funky 16th notes right from the start. The player proved to be a kid from Brooklyn called Charlie Giordano, so I auditioned him live, then brought him on board. The drummer—and the backbone of the group I was assembling—was Bobby Chen, who'd been recommended to me by my good friend Mick Ronson, the original guitarist for David Bowie's backup band the Spiders from Mars, and later a solo artist. Bobby was a solid, no-nonsense drummer with as much rock 'n' roll in him as rock 'n' roll begged for!

While I was rehearsing and auditioning musicians, Mike announced that he was joining forces with a guy called Jerry Delet who had a money-management firm for major sports stars, TWM Management. This company shared offices with Martin Bregman, Al Pacino's manager and a producer on the movies *Serpico* and *Dog Day Afternoon*, among others. It was pretty fascinating sitting in their reception area, because you never knew which sports or media personality might suddenly appear. What Mike and Jerry set up was a music arm for TWM, and it wasn't long before a lot of the top acts were seeking them out. Me, I promoted them like crazy. The more big artists and groups they were handling, the better it would be for me—my reputation would benefit through being associated with a successful management company. I also liked the fact that Jerry was a musician himself—a lounge-type piano player.

Working with John Roberts and Joel Rosenberg at Media Sound was always a pleasure. There are relatively few people I've met in the music business who're completely honest—no backstabbing, no strings attached. John and Joel were like that, as was the third member of the Media Sound "family," Susan Planer. John and Susan are alas no longer alive; may they rest in peace. Another excellent friend I made in association with them around this time was a young producer who'd not long arrived in town from London, Mike Thorne. Even today I love hanging out with Mike and his wife Lila.

Alison Steele—the Nightbird from WNEW—had an actor friend who'd rented a two-bedroomed summer cottage in East Hampton. Because he'd gotten a film part, he wasn't going to be around to use it, and had asked her if she'd like to take it over. She wondered if I'd like to share it with her. The cottage was small, but plenty big enough for the pair of us, and it had a lovely situation right on the water at Gardner's Bay. It was called Salter's Cottages. We had such tremendous fun there that summer that we rented the place ourselves for the following summers.

Alison and I were invited to all the "in" parties in the Hamptons, and it was at one of these that I was introduced to a guy called Roy Radin. He was very wealthy, was involved in movies, and was just getting into the music business. He knew my name at once, and was keen to talk to me professionally. Although he lived in the Hamptons, he also had a permanent suite at the Sherry Netherland Hotel on Fifth Avenue in Manhattan, where he spent a few days each week. We had several lunchtime meetings in the restaurant at the Sherry Netherland—mainly liquid lunches on my part. The meetings were constantly being disrupted

(From left): Alison Steele, Scott Muni, Genya, Lars Hansen, Charlie Giordano.

by him getting phone calls from his wife upstairs in their suite; she was very pregnant and often felt lousy. Although I'd initially thought Roy was full of shit, I talked myself into thinking he was a nice guy. I should have followed my first instincts.

He told me he had a friend, Harvey Cooper, who had just become head of A&R for 20th Century-Fox Records. He said he'd already whetted Cooper's appetite about me, and was certain he could get me a record deal there; for that he'd want to be my manager and have a few points of income from record sales. I explained that I was already signed up with Mike Hektoen and TWM, and Roy's face fell. However, I proposed to introduce him to Mike to see if they could work something out together, and he jumped at that—probably on the basis that something was better than nothing. They went ahead and organized a points deal for him.

A few weeks later Roy called to say he needed a demo to present to Harvey Cooper. Charlie Giordano and I went into the studio at Media Sound and did a quick version—just vocals and piano—of a song called "Shadowboxing in the Rain." Roy gave the tape to Harvey, and the next we heard was that Harvey loved it; he was prepared to release it as a record the way it was.

"No way," I said. I had an arrangement for "Shadowboxing in the Rain" in my head, and I knew it would sound better with the full band I was rehearsing with: Conrad Taylor and Richie Fliegler on guitars, Charlie Giordano on keyboards, Bobby Chen on drums, and Donny Nossov on bass. This band was really hot. We were planning to call ourselves Taxi, but I was eventually talked out of that: I would have better control of my life as a solo singer than as the singer for a group.

Mike Hektoen and I made the trip to Los Angeles together to meet Harvey Cooper; we were also invited to his house. I liked Harvey a lot, and felt I could relax with him—just let myself be me. We worked out the contract for 20th Century-Fox Records, and the deal was signed. It was agreed that I should be the one in control of what the record sounded like. There were to be no more compromises, no more outside interference. What I wanted to produce was a kind of music that wasn't being played on the radio—that wasn't really being made anywhere, in fact. A loud, raucous street sound. Rock 'n' roll, yes, but more than that: *hard* rock. The album was to be called, appropriately, *Urban Desire*. It's been called a "seminal album of the New Wave." I can live with that description.

Genya takes the reins.

* * * * * *

The recording sessions for *Urban Desire* went well. I worked everyone very hard. We had lots of rehearsals, and sometimes we'd do last-minute rearranging and rewriting right there in the studio. I wanted to capture the feeling of live music.

One of my guitarists, Richie Fliegler, was working with Lou Reed at the time, and he suggested Lou might sing a duet with me on one of the songs. I thought this was a great idea, and proposed a song I'd just written about my first, Puerto Rican boyfriend, "Aye, Co'Lorado." Richie thought the song might appeal to Lou, and about a week later brought Lou to the studio.

The first thing Lou said to me after we'd been introduced was: "My grandmother bought your records years ago."

There was a deathly silence in the studio.

I looked him in the eye and said, "Yeah, well at least someone in your family had good taste in music. What happened to you?"

He laughed, the tension eased, and we quickly became friends. He immediately accepted that I was the one in charge here, that I called all the shots.

I gave him the handwritten lyric of "Aye, Co'Lorado" and we went into Studio A. The mikes were already on, ready to go, and we stood facing each other. We ran the song down to the track. It was great!

"Okay," said Lou. "I think I got it now."

I grinned. I'd let him believe we were just rehearsing, but in fact I'd signaled to the engineer to get the tape rolling. It was a deliberate deception on my part, one I often practiced with singers when I wanted to get a "live" feel. The first take is almost always the best, because it's the most honest. After an artist has done more than three takes, she or he has had too much time to think about it and all the spontaneity has gone. Even if a later take is technically more perfect, it's usually lost that true live rock 'n' roll feel, and sounds phony and pretentious. All the engineers I worked with knew this; as soon as I walked into the recording room I wanted the tape to be rolling.

I let Lou do three more takes of the song with me, out of respect for his wishes, but as I'd thought they would they all sounded a bit cold after that, lacking in the real feel. That first take was the one we used. Lou agreed with me after hearing all the takes he'd done.

Some while afterwards Lou called me and asked if I'd like to do background vocals on one of his songs. I said I'd be honored, of course. The recording session was very strange, because there was a dummy head in the middle of the room with two microphones on it, one in each ear. This was my introduction to binaural recording. Normal stereo recording is designed to be played back using loudspeakers in a room to give the illusion of full, 360-degree sound. The illusion isn't quite perfect, because it doesn't take into account the shape of the human head or the physiology of the ear canals. Binaural recording does, although you only get the effect if you listen to the recording on headphones.

The sessions on *Urban Desire* continued to go well. The deal with John and Joel at Media Sound was that I could use the studio whenever it had any down time—that is, when it would otherwise have been empty because no one had booked it or because someone had canceled. This gave me plenty of time there to experiment as much as I wished. I used to put a jacket over the clock on the wall when we arrived so that no one would be aware of the time; there was to be no rush, no cutting of corners on the music. I didn't want there to be the experience I sometimes had when producing for other groups and having to watch the studio budget: settling for a take not because it was really good enough but just because there wasn't time for another. I'm eternally grateful to John and Joel for having given me that freedom when I was making *Urban Desire* and its follow-up, . . . *And I Mean It!*; it was a big contribution to how good the two albums sound. Needless to say, I never abused that freedom.

When I listen to *Urban Desire* today I get the chills. It always make me feel like that tiny blade of grass that grows between the cracks in the concrete in a busy city: the beauty, the tenderness, the strength. Of all the recordings I've made, *Urban Desire* and . . . *And I Mean It!* are my two favorites, the records I'm the proudest of. They're *me*, through and through, and they're me giving my best effort.

● ● ● ● ● ●

Roy Radin was a weird guy. A few years later, in 1983, he was found dead in a car trunk in Hollywood. He'd been shot at least twenty-seven times. He'd been in Hollywood on a trip to secure finances for the film *The Cotton Club*. Apparently the woman they charged with employing a hit man to murder Roy, a Florida drug dealer named Karen DeLayne ("Laney") Jacobs, had been involved in the deal with Roy and the movie producer Robert Evans (*The Godfather, Chinatown*, etc.), and Roy had tried to freeze her out. Guess he messed with the wrong woman this time. Jacobs was also alleged to have later had her husband murdered as well.

That Roy might come to a bad end could have been predicted when I knew him. He had a seventy-two-room mansion on the ocean at Southampton, and one day he invited me there; he even had his driver pick me up. When I arrived he announced that he'd laid on a live S&M show to entertain me. I thought he was kidding until I saw his entourage—he always had an entourage around him to do things for him—started bringing out the whips and the rubber sex-toys. At that point I put my foot down. When he saw I was serious, he had to call the women he'd booked for the show and cancel.

Even after that introduction to his weirdness, I visited him quite often in the Hamptons. By now he was separated from his wife and the baby. He spent most of his time in bed. Visitors were ushered into the presence of this big, heavy man drinking and doing blow while he sat in bed, his lower half under the covers and his top half naked. He was always on the phone there, too, hustling someone or something—he told me plenty of stories about his wheelerdealing on music deals, movie deals, any kind of deals.

One weekend I was out at Roy's house for dinner when I saw Tiny Tim coming down the stairs. He was stoned out of his mind, which on top of his natural state was something to behold. I was pretty mad at Roy for letting Tiny Tim do drugs.

It came as a big surprise to me to discover that Roy was Tiny Tim's manager. As it happened, I had access to an old song called "They're Coming to Take Me Away, Ha-Haaa!" that I had rearranged with a zany disco feel; it had been a hit in 1966 for an artist calling himself Napoleon XIV. A few weeks before I'd had Zacherle, a DJ from WNEW, put a vocal track down on the version I planned, but now I decided Tiny Tim's falsetto might be better for it: he was as quirky as the song. I called him, and we reminisced about when we'd all hung out at the Hip Bagel in Greenwich Village, back in my Goldie and the Gingerbreads days. Then he'd called me Miss Goldie. Now he called me Miss Genya.

He was in a major depression over his divorce from Miss Vicky, the girl he'd married on *The Tonight Show* in 1969; I told him that recording the song would take his mind off things, so in he came to Media Sound to sing over the already recorded backing track. He treated it like it was a love song addressed to Miss Vicky. I told him afterwards the recording had come out great, but I never released it. I still have it, and maybe someday it'll be released—perhaps in Britain, where they better appreciate strangeness.

※ ※ ※ ※ ※ ※

I was not going to let any part of the *Urban Desire* project get out of my hands. It was my car, so to speak, and I was driving it.

While we were still recording I did some photo sessions with a really good photographer generally known to us as Studio Stu. Once Stu had a shot of what I thought should be the cover, I flew out to Los Angeles to make sure the cover artwork was properly put together and the sleeve information was correct. Too many times in the past I'd suffered from having erroneous information, dates, and photos on my records.

While I was there at 20th Century-Fox Records we also talked about the promotional campaign for the record. It had to show street-smarts, I stressed to everyone. It had to show strength. I couldn't supervise the photo shoot for the campaign ads myself—I had to fly back to New York

Genya advertising on Times Square.

LOLLIPOP LOUNGE

Publicity campaign for *Urban Desire*: no more tits and ass.

Record release party for *Urban Desire*. Alison Steele, Genya, Jerry Delet (in back), Harvey Cooper, Michael Hektoen.

to do the final touches on the remixing at Media Sound and to get started on the radio promo—but Harvey Cooper and Mike Hektoen really shone on my behalf, showing real guts and, in Harvey's case, assigning the right sort of funds to back that up. They knew what I wanted and they'd listened to the music enough to know why I wanted it: a badass campaign. And a badass campaign is what they delivered.

It was also perhaps the best campaign in record history. They hired a very hip European photographer to take pictures of a French male porno star posing with my record cover, looking as if he was using it as a shield to hide the fact that he was jerking off. Various slogans ran along the lines of "Everybody's Getting Off on Genya Ravan's *Urban Desire*." They did huge posters like this for the sides of buses, for the subway, and so on. In fact, the MTA banned the posters from the New York subway on the grounds that they were lewd, which I always thought was a bit of a laugh considering the kind of stuff normally on display on the walls in the New York subway. We had a record-release party at the Bottom Line for which the caterers were Erotic Bakery: there were cakes and cookies everywhere in the shape of breasts and penises. It was a smash. Everybody was talking about it.

Some people weren't talking about it favorably, though. I heard from friends that Clive Davis at CBS was phoning around to say how disgusting it was. That suited me just fine. The whole music industry was abuzz about the campaign, and hence about the record. Which was the general idea.

And I was loving it. I was finally having fun again. It seemed it was okay for the guys to use plentiful tits and ass in their publicity campaigns; well, here was a woman doing the equivalent from the other side of the gender divide, and they were getting a chance to see what it looked like. I enjoyed being painted as the Bad Girl, as the Rock 'n' Roll Woman. This was the kind of attention I reveled in.

The single from the album—a hard rock version of the old Supremes hit "Back in My Arms Again"—hit the charts. The reviews of *Urban Desire* could hardly have been better. Plenty of the radio station were playing Genya Ravan music: WBCN and WCOZ in Boston, KSAN in San Francisco, and of course my old friends at WNEW in New York. At the same time, though, the program directors at some of the other, more mainstream stations were refusing to let their disk jockeys play my music: this wasn't what female rock should sound like; it was way too hard. Quite a number of disk jockeys told me their hands were tied. I

Genya Ravan at the Lone Star in New York City.

always replied that this was just the beginning—that there'd be plenty of hard-rocking females coming along behind me. Sure enough, that proved to be the case—Pat Benatar, to name just one. But, as always, it was a fight being the pioneer.

A big part of the promotion was, naturally, taking the band on tour. I got them all to look the badass part. The two guitarists were Conrad Taylor and (now) Lars Hanson; the former looked like an escapee from the movie *The Godfather* and the latter like a misplaced Hollywood trick. Donny Nossov, on bass, had the appearance of someone who'd kill you without a thought. Charlie Giordano, on keyboards, wore nothing but jeans, a leather baseball cap, and red suspenders—no shirt. Bobby Chen looked plenty Latino, and we put a couple of giant dice in front of his drum kit. All the guys were absolute pussy cats, but the impression we gave was of a bunch of real hard guys. Myself, I wore tight jeans, a skimpy teeshirt and a harmonica belt. This tough image extended even to the two roadies I hired, Beast and Batman: they came from Staten Island but they looked as if they came from a different island altogether—Rikers Island. No wonder someone wrote of us: "Genya Ravan and

Genya at Max's Kansas City.

her group, including her roadies, could be Hell's Angels reincarnated into musicians."

Beast had a really heavy Brooklyn accent, so I always had him do our stage introduction for us. He sounded like Sylvester Stallone when he had his hands on the microphone. "All right, you Donny and Marie Osmond

Genya at the Bitter End in New York City.

lovers, move over for some real rock 'n' roll with—Genya Ravan and the Genya Ravan Band!" The audiences would go nuts.

Beast was a real character, and immensely protective of me. One night we were booked into a biker bar. As you'll recall, I have a certain partiality toward bikers. After the show I went into the parking lot with one of them so he could show me his Harley. We'd not been there long when Beast came running out. He grabbed me and told me there was someone inside waiting to talk to me. The biker took exception, but Beast stared him down. I shoved Beast back in through the door before anyone got hurt. Of course, there was no one waiting to speak to me. "I tought I wuz gonna have to break some heads, Genya," Beast explained. "Don't do dat again."

I didn't know whether to laugh or hit him. "Cut this shit out, willya? You're ruining my sex life!"

Another night, this time somewhere in Washington, D.C., I was with the rest of the guys in the dressing room after the show, sweating happily, when Beast came stumbling in clutching a timid-looking kid. The kid was obviously frightened: he wouldn't meet my gaze, and his ears were fire-engine red.

"Go on," said Beast. "Tell her. Go on."

At last the kid said, in a small voice, "I'm sorry."

There was a silence.

"Uh, for what?" I said at last.

The kid didn't answer, so Beast did it for him. "I heard him say, 'Genya Ravan's not such a hot singer,' so I grabbed him so's he could come here and apologize to you."

"Beast," I said, staring at him, "people are *allowed* not to like my stuff."

"No they're not!"

"Yes they are. Now let him go—now!"

The kid fled terrified into the night.

When we played the San Francisco circuit my old friend Van Morrison came to see us. I asked him up onto the stage to sing alongside me, but he's a very shy guy and he wouldn't—instead we went and had coffee after the show. Donna Summer was less diffident when we played the Whiskey a GoGo in Los Angeles; we did a duet. Just as with Janis Joplin (see page 148), I had her sit in on the tag of "Tightrope" and we just improvised and sang the shit out of it. Donna loved rock 'n' roll and really enjoyed the session. Afterwards, in the dressing room, she kept telling me how much she wanted to sing rock. I told her to keep on doing what she does so well and continue making money.

Everywhere we went on the *Urban Desire* tour we got a great reception, a great response. Even so, some of the radio stations were persisting in their refusal to play any of our music. They were afraid of it. Despite that, touring was a real ball. What made it even better was the constant feeling that 20th Century-Fox Records and Harvey Cooper were right behind us, one hundred percent.

• • • • • •

It was time to start planning my second record for 20th Century-Fox, *... And I Mean It!* By now I was a lot more confident about myself as a songwriter, and almost all of the songs on the album are written or co-written by me.

One night while recording in Studio A at Media Sound we got down an incredible track and scratch vocal on the song "Junkman," which I wrote with Joe Droukas. Coming out of Studio A I ran into Ian Hunter and Mick Ronson, who were producing Ellen Foley in Studio D. In addition to performing with Ian and Bowie, Mick had played guitar for Bob Dylan, Roger McGuinn, Rich Kids, and John Cougar Mellencamp; as noted, he'd also recommended my drummer, Bobby Chen, to me. (Tragically, Mick died of liver cancer in 1993 aged only forty-six.) I told him he had to follow me into Studio A and listen to this song I'd just recorded. He loved it, so I asked him if he'd do a guitar solo for it.

The next night he came in and recorded a fabulous solo for the song. This time Ian Hunter came with him. As we listened to the playback Ian turned to Mick and said: "This chick knows what she wants. She's good." It was a lovely spontaneous compliment, and I'll always remember it. I'd told Mick that I wanted Van Morrison to sing the male vocal on "Junkman," but later Mick cornered me and asked me if Ian could be considered for the part. I told him that, even though Van was currently on the road and it'd be three months before he could do the part, it was Van I really wanted. Then, just because Mick had been such a good friend to me, I said that, okay, Ian could try for it.

Immediately I began worrying about how I was going to break it to Ian that I wasn't happy with him singing the male track, that Van's voice was what I wanted. A few days later Ian came to the studio for what I assumed would be a mere formality, the fulfillment of an obligation to Mick. Instead, when Ian sang his part I was blown away—it was wonderful, he was wonderful! "That's the take," I said at once.

The recording sessions for . . . *And I Mean It!* went well, but there were clouds on the horizon. The biggest and the darkest of them I didn't know about until after we'd finished. One of the others was that it was at this time that I started my love affair with cocaine. Harvey Goldberg had introduced me to it a while earlier, but now I was really getting into it. A dealer called Susan would come to the recording sessions at my request with the coke. She really got the hots for Mick Ronson, and eventually made me an offer I could not refuse: if I could get Mick into bed with her she'd give me three grams of coke for free. Mick didn't need much coaxing to earn me my three grams. She's credited on the album: "Thanks to Susan for the Flash and Substance."

. . . *And I Mean It!* was another great album. The production and sound were superb. The songs were great. Some of the rawness of *Urban Desire* had been rubbed off, which strictly speaking was an improvement. However, in retrospect I don't think it was. Of all my recordings, *Urban Desire* is my favorite, and one of the reasons is that trace of rawness it has.

The new album got rave reviews. It was the most picked record in the trade music papers—*Billboard, Cashbox* and *Record World*. I was neck-and-neck with Bruce Springsteen for the most picked and most added records of the week. People in the industry were calling to congratulate me. Genya's record was going to be a smash.

What was really happening was that my world was just about to fall apart. The first thing was that Mike Hektoen—or "Helltone," as I'd started frequently calling him—was beginning not to see eye-to-eye with Harvey Cooper. I've never really known what caused the falling out between them, but one night at a party at the Bottom Line I heard Mike yell at Harvey, "You stay away from my artist!"

Harvey left. I should have asked Mike what that had been all about, but I didn't.

I was at home getting happily wrecked when I got the phone call from Hell. The caller was my head promotions man at 20th Century-Fox Records. While I'd been in the studios recording . . . *And I Mean It!*, 20th Century-Fox had decided that its music division wasn't pulling its financial weight. Apart from me they had acts like Barry

White and Stephanie Mills, but still the money wasn't coming in—in fact, 20th Century-Fox Records was somehow managing to make a loss. The parent company was closing it down; he'd been canned along with the whole of the rest of the music division. Harvey Cooper was gone. "Genya, there's not going to be any more promotion of your record. You might as well forget this one. You're on your own. It's not going to be in the stores. It's not going to be pushed on the radio."

Despite all the rave advance reviews, despite all those radio stations adding the album to their playlists, that was basically the end of . . . *And I Mean It!* The record was released, and died instantly.

A big mess.

* * * * * *

I soon decided I wanted out of my contract with TWM Management. I felt I'd been ripped off by them. They were no help at all to me in the fiasco with 20th Century-Fox. Hell, they hadn't even got me the deal in the first place: it had been Roy Radin who'd set me up for that. And it had been me who'd introduced Helltone to everyone—given him all the contacts he had.

Mike had become an egomaniac. They say that all managers really want to be stars. It's not quite true, but the way Mike behaved you'd have believed it. He'd started acting the part of manager-star quite a while earlier, after the release of *Urban Desire*. As part of the promotion, 20th Century-Fox sent me across to the Netherlands to do some publicity work for Phonogram Records, who were releasing the record in Europe. Helltone insisted he should come along as well, and he set up everything to be first class all the way. At the Amsterdam Hotel, for example, he ran up the phone bill alone to the tune of no less than nine hundred dollars! The people at Phonogram, who loved the record, were outraged. They told me they'd never come across a manager or even an artist who'd taken that much advantage of them.

I called Jerry Delet and explained to him sweetly that, if TWM Management didn't let me out of my contract, I was going to tell all the other artists about the way I believed I'd been ripped off. He agreed to let me go.

Meanwhile, 20th Century-Fox had passed my contract with them on to the one label I'd sworn I'd never touch again: RCA. My bad feelings about this weren't improved when one day, doing a radio show at the RCA Studios, I discovered in conversation with some of the people working there that they didn't even know I was with their label, or had just had a record released. I asked one of the RCA promo men: "Who do I fuck to get off this label?"

A little while ago I'd been on the top of the world. Now I was falling farther and farther into the music abyss. There was no one around me who I now trusted enough that I could just lean on their shoulder and cry. I felt utterly on my own. I felt completely humiliated.

My record was gone—taken from me.

Booze.

Coke.

Now I was gone, too.

CHAPTER FOURTEEN
"Polish" as in Shine

DURING ONE OF THE SESSIONS for . . . *And I Mean It!* I'd mentioned to someone that I was planning to go down to Florida to see my mom. My sister and I had persuaded her to move to Deerfield Beach there after Dad had died. Crime was on the rise in the part of Brooklyn where she was living, and we thought Florida would be safer.

My coke dealer, Susan, had been in the studio when I'd mentioned my plans to visit Mom. "Hey," she said, "I've got to go down to Florida, too, on business. Why don't we go together?" She told me when we got there we could stay the night at the house of a friend of hers and then she'd drop me off at my mother's place the next day. Sounded good to me. With Susan in attendance there'd be plenty of drugs around, so I could be flying both figuratively as well as literally.

We were picked up in style in a long limo at Miami Airport and taken to a beach house. There was more coke than I'd ever seen before—more even than in London when I'd been there for the mixes of *They Love Me, They Love Me Not*. I had a lousy night, though; I took too much speed and was vibrating from it. Earlier in the evening, Susan had introduced me to a sweet-smiling guy from the Midwest named Steve M. He was her coke supplier. She'd spend the rest of the night screwing him while I was tossing and turning, totally unable to sleep because of the speed.

The next morning, as we drove to Mom's place in Deerfield Beach, Steve and I struck up a conversation. He said he liked music and thought that one day he might want to get into it. Starting up my own label had always been a dream of mine. "Steve," I said, "we ought to talk when we get back to New York." I knew there'd be no difficulty running into him there, because Susan was a groupie and he was supplying the drugs she was dealing. Steve had the two most important qualifications to be my partner in creating my own label: He had the money, he had the drugs.

We saw each other many times in New York over the next few months and, in between passing the razor, the mirror, and the straw, we talked about our hypothetical label until the early hours. Steve did a lot less coke than I did, even though he was supplying it. (By now, instead of doing coke just at nights or weekends, I was doing it all the time. I was also drinking very heavily to come down from the coke. I was on a merry-go-round I couldn't get off of.) At my invitation, he came along to a few of the remaining studio sessions for . . . *And I Mean It!* (I was still recording the song "Wired"); he loved the experience.

We agreed how ideal it would be to kick off our label with Ronnie Spector; for reasons I'll explain in a moment, I knew she would sign with us. Steve's eyes lit up. He might not have known much about music, but even he had heard of Ronnie Spector.

Around about this time I got that terrible call from 20th Century-Fox telling me their records division was going down the tubes, taking . . . *And I Mean It!* along on that terminal plunge. My levels of substance abuse increased yet further. This became an added incentive to get this new label off the ground, using Steve's drug money as its capital. Looking back on it all now, I wonder what possessed me to think that a successful label might be built on drug money—that drug money could actually save my life. Maybe the drugs were doing the thinking for me.

For the past few months, even while still assuming I was with 20th Century-Fox Records, I'd been doing the preparations for setting up what I wanted to call Polish Records ("Polish" as in the shine, not as in the nationality). I arranged meetings with lawyers to draw up contracts for a partnership corporation between Steve and myself. I took him to all the New York clubs, introducing him to musicians and club owners; he visited me in the cabin on the water that I shared with Alison Steele out in the Hamptons. Fitting all this in around Steve's schedule was pretty difficult, as he was always shuttling between Florida and New York for his drug-related activities, but I managed it somehow.

As a model for our record label I had my eye on Stiff Records. This company had been started up in London in 1976 by Jake Riviera and Dave Robinson, managers of several pub rock bands there, as a vanguard of punk, and by now, 1980, it was coining money. What characterized the label was its aggressiveness, its audacity, and the creative wit of its marketing campaigns. For example, they made teeshirts with the slogan: "If It Ain't Stiff It Ain't Worth A Fuck!" Brilliant! Stiff attracted lots of attention to itself, and with that came the musicians to match: Nick Lowe, Elvis Costello, the Damned, Richard Hell and the Voidoids, Motorhead . . .

I decided that the marketing campaign for Polish Records was going to be just as strong. We rented a three-room office on Fifty-seventh Street. We hired an ex-girlfriend of Cheetah Chrome's, Gyda Gash, to be our receptionist; not only was she very bright, she had a great punk image. We also stole a promotions guy from RCA, Andy Francis. Later, as an additional aid to promotion, I called around to radio stations, promoting our artists under the assumed name Kitty Litter; alas for my schemes, some of the disk jockeys, knowing Polish Records was my baby, recognized my voice.

Of course, we needed artists as well. I'd kept in touch with Manster, the group I'd heard when I'd first gone to CBGBs. Hilly Kristal hadn't felt the band was commercial enough, but now I signed them up. At last I was able to fulfill my desire to work with them in the studio.

Another early signing was the Puerto Rican band El Futuro. A Puerto Rican punk band? Just the ticket for Polish Records. I signed them as soon as I saw them. Writing about life on the streets from a Puerto Rican viewpoint, they seemed to me the epitome of punk. They also looked great. The drummer was female—in fact, she was married to the leader of the band. When I took them into the studios I insisted we make the record in both English and Spanish, something that, so far as I can establish, no one had ever done before. The record came out great, but then the drummer decided to leave both her husband and the group, so El Futuro couldn't do any gigs because they were auditioning for a replacement. (I was later told they ended up selling drugs for Steve's clandestine half of Polish Records.)

My company marketing campaign was really starting to make noise by now. I had teeshirts made, the slogan on them being the question I'd asked back when I'd realized the true scale of the disaster of being transferred by 20th Century-Fox back to RCA: "Who Do I Fuck To Get Off This Label?" (I could have made a fortune out of selling those teeshirts. They were the talk of the industry; I still have people today asking me where they can get one.) I also found glass holders in the shape of miniature jockstraps, and got them stamped: "Support Polish Records!" Our logo was a maid in a short skirt bending over as she polished something. As a special Christmas card I had this made as a jigsaw puzzle, with the slogan "Polish Is All That Will Shine This Year," and sent the puzzles out to the radio stations with one piece removed; a week later I sent everyone that last piece with the message: "Polish Records Has The Missing Piece!"

And so on.

When we started the company I thought a great idea for the launch would be to make a 45 r.p.m. single with the hole off-center, copies of which could be sent to all the people in the industry. Locating a company that would produce these for us was an unexpected nightmare; most of them just hung up on me when I called and asked about this. Finally I found a small company in New Jersey that would listen. After I'd explained to the guy what I wanted, he roared with laughter. "Listen, lady, for years we been working on getting the holes in the middle. What are you, nuts?" But the job got done, and the disk jockeys and the press loved us for it.

At the same time as running our marketing campaigns I was also having to go into the studios to produce our records. I was working like a dog, but willingly: this was my own label, my own dream that I was bringing into reality. Every time my partner Steve came back from one of his business trips he'd toss on my desk a baggie of white powder and a big wad of money held together with a rubber band. Both of them were, in a way, for office expenses. I was always happy to see him.

● ● ● ● ● ●

And Polish Records had a major star in Ronnie Spector.

I had my first meeting with Ronnie in my apartment on Fifty-seventh Street six months prior to starting the label. I had taken her into the studio and recorded a four-song demo which I'd tried to shop to the record companies, but they didn't want to hear it. Nobody was interested in

Ronnie Spector. As far as the industry was concerned, she had had her day. Even so, I'd been extremely excited about the prospect of working with her. I was a great fan of hers. I'd loved the sound of her voice ever since I'd first heard it, when I'd been little more than a kid. Also, my own career as a singer seemed to be looking bleak—indeed, so far as I was concerned it had ended—so working with Ronnie seemed to offer an alternative way of permanently stamping my mark on the music industry. And Ronnie herself was so charming at that meeting that I thought it was also going to be a tremendous *pleasure* working with her.

The week after we'd started Polish Records, Ronnie called to say she'd be glad to sign with the label. It was soon decided that I'd produce her next record, which was to be called *Siren*, for Polish. My name was still fresh in everyone's minds from the build-up for *. . . And I Mean It!*, so you can imagine the amount of press coverage once the news got out that Ronnie and I would be working on an album together.

Not long after we'd gotten started into rehearsals, I received a call that took my breath away. The voice at the other end of the line said, "This is Phil Spector." He was calling because he wanted a meeting with me when he was in New York next week.

In the studio with Ronnie Spector at RPM studios in New York City, recording *Siren*.

You'll recall the story of Phil and Ronnie Spector. Ronnie had first come to major public attention as Ronnie Bennett, the lead singer of the Ronettes, the other two Ronettes being her sister and a cousin. Phil Spector had signed them to his Philles label, and given them a massive Wall of Sound hit with "Be My Baby," plus some other hits. Not long afterwards, he started managing them as well. This was really where the problems began, because he became increasingly jealous and possessive about the group, not least of Ronnie, whom he married in 1966. According to Ronnie, Phil had more or less kept her a prisoner in his mansion after that until she finally divorced him in 1973. I had heard countless stories from her about how weird and crazy he was. It seemed obvious to me that his possessiveness towards her was still not at an end, even though they'd been divorced for seven years or so—otherwise why would he be phoning me?

I knew that in agreeing to a meeting with him I was venturing into dangerous quicksand. At the same time, the prospect was so exciting! I don't usually get this way about people, but he was a giant of the music industry, an idol, the king. He was beyond a star. Me and Phil Spector in the same room? Wow! It was an opportunity I most definitely was not going to pass up.

He sent his limo to pick me up and I was taken to the Plaza Hotel, where he'd taken a large suite—Steven Spielberg's suite, in fact. I was left alone for about five minutes in one of its rooms—very dim, hardly any lights on—and then Phil Spector walked in. The first thing I noticed was how short he was.

He gave me a glass of wine and then asked me a few banal questions before coming to the big one: Would I like to co-produce Ronnie with him?

In other circumstances this could have been a highlight of my life, but I realized that what the question really meant was that he was looking for an opening to take control of Ronnie again.

"No," I said immediately.

I explained that I had my own "fix" on what I wanted for this record, and that I consequently wanted to produce it myself. I didn't want any interference, not even from Ronnie herself, because I felt that in many ways she was her own worst enemy.

He agreed that this was the case, and then there was a moment of awkward silence. I drank a little more wine, relaxing, thinking this had all gone a lot easier than it could have.

But then he got mad at me, and shot an angry question my way that I thought was totally out of order. "Are you a singer or a producer?"

"Both," I said. "Both, Phil. I do *both*. Is that so hard to believe? Hey, it's the Eighties, Phil. Wake up and smell the woman producer. Women can sing and produce too."

There wasn't much for us to say after that. I said I had an appointment, and left. His limo took me home. Later he started calling me with weird gibberish messages and sending me cryptic Western Union telegrams, usually the title of an old song. I was supposed to figure out what he was trying to say as if these were components of a puzzle, I guess, but I never bothered. I even asked Steve if he thought I should change my phone number, but he thought that'd be too extreme a response. Ronnie had said that Phil was Out There, but I hadn't appreciated how Out There he truly was.

• • • • • •

At my initial meeting with Ronnie she'd seemed thrilled that anyone was still interested in her. In the years since she'd left Phil her career had been largely in the doldrums, not helped by the fact that she'd emerged from her rotten marriage to him with a severe drinking problem. I'd explained to her that, as her producer, I wanted to get her away from her old "Be My Baby" Phil Spector sound. Even though I still loved and cherished that sound, it was time for her to start thinking "now."

I knew this was going to be a hard production. Ronnie didn't write her own material, and nor did she come with a band. I had to put the whole package together and maintain a theme. It was a challenge.

I was recording some good bands for CBGB at the time, and I wanted to put some of those musicians with her. I started taking her to some of the clubs so she could get an idea of what was going on musically. It didn't take me long to discover that she couldn't stand any of it. Nothing made sense to her. She didn't like the realism of the lyrics—she was still in a 1960s "baby, baby, I don't mean maybe" mental mode. But I persevered. I told her this was going to be a new way, a street way of saying "I love you," and she said she understood.

I recorded Ronnie at Media Sound and Electric Lady. I had rockers and punks in to perform with her on the sessions. In the event, she loved singing the songs I'd picked for her. She was the center of attention, and she loved that as well. In the studio she was The Great Artist, at the same time flirting with all the guys. When anyone complimented her on how great a musician she was she would just lap it up. I soon realized there had to be someone paying attention to her at all times, usually me, but that the effort would be richly rewarded. The energy in the sessions was hot. She was open to all the production decisions I made, which was essential: I needed her to be that open, because I was making a partial U-turn for her, musically. I had to make sure the music had an edge, but at the same time I didn't want to lose Ronnie's 1960s sound entirely. It was like walking a tightrope—a lot of work, a lot of concentration, not easy, wearing on the nerves.

When you produce a recording session, you have to be the one in control. There are all these other people, with far too many egos and far too many opinions, and as a producer you have to learn to shut all of that out; otherwise you wouldn't have space left in your head for a single thought of your own! In her autobiography, *Be My Baby* (1986; with Vince Waldron), Ronnie said that "Genya was a strong producer who knew what she wanted, just like Phil." I'm happy with that professional assessment.

She also claimed in that book that I tried to make her into some kind of a punk singer, but that's nonsense. How could anyone ever hope to make Ronnie Spector sound punk? The thought never entered my head.

My approach to producing her was simple in theory but hard in practice. I wanted her music to sound loose, and that's the effect I got. It worked. I wanted real rockers on her record, and then to introduce her singing into this raw (well, slightly polished) sound. I picked songs that it would never have occurred to her to have done, like the Ramones' "Here Today, Gone Tomorrow." She hated the song when she first heard it and I practically had to force her to sing it, but it turned out to be a perfect Ronnie Spector song. (Here's something weird. I later discovered from Joey Ramone that "Here Today, Gone Tomorrow" had been written with Ronnie in mind.) The Dead Boys were starting to make a name for themselves by now, and I had Cheetah Chrome—the Orange Cocktail—guesting on a few of the tracks. I used all the talented musicians I knew from uptown, downtown, crosstown . . .

But I was getting worried. I began to feel like maybe I couldn't trust her. She bad-rapped everyone around her—not just Phil but her own family. Some of the stories she told me, running down other people, I was finding a little hard to believe. And what was she saying about *me* when my back was turned?

It slowly dawned on me that perhaps, just perhaps, Ronnie Spector was not altogether a nice person.

* * * * * *

Some of the things that Ronnie wrote about me in her book *Be My Baby* really pissed me off. Again and again while reading it I found myself saying, "That's just not the way it happened." Of course, I'm far too dignified to retaliate in kind—I hold myself aloof from all the sordid pettiness of public squabbling. The reader will understand that the following comments are issued solely in the cause of setting the record straight, and are made with complete dispassion. You would hardly expect anything else from someone such as myself.

In other words, payback time.

Ronnie wrote in her book that, during her recording sessions with me, I was doing lines of coke in front of her. That's absurd—a flat lie. Yeah, sure, I was doing way too much coke at the time; I'm not about to start denying that. But I never did it in front of her—and wouldn't have. I was keeping things entirely professional, and working very hard to give her the hit that would relaunch her music career—at the same time giving Polish Records a big launch, which was another reason it was essential to me that I kept everything fully professional.

Ronnie had hoped to get her career back on track in 1977 with the single "Say Goodbye to Hollywood"—it was to be her big comeback record. The song was by Billy Joel and the backing was by the E Street Band, so it had everything going for it, but it didn't chart. It's a great record, but as a comeback it was a flop.

By the time I came along with the Polish Records deal, Ronnie had found she couldn't get a record deal anywhere else. There she was with that wonderful voice, and she was just sitting around. Her drinking problem—and her insistence that she didn't have one—had given her a bad reputation, but that was only part of it. She was considered to be the "old sound" at a time when people were wanting *new* sounds. There was no crime in this—the same was true for Tina Turner before she made *her* big comeback. Ronnie claims in her book that I tried to run her life; the reality is that, by the time I came along, she was desperately in need of some sort of direction. If she was ever going to recapture her former glory she was going to have to change her approach to music. At one and the same time she knew that yet hated it.

I guess that when a male producer exerts strong control over a session it's because he knows what he wants, and is admired for it, but when a woman does the same it's because she's a controlling bitch. I'm very proud of *Siren*, Ronnie's album on Polish Records, and of what I did for her on it. I think it's the best thing she recorded after her glory days with Phil Spector.

Ronnie also wrote in her book about my supposed attempts to run her life. She says that I was always "checking up" on her, as if I were some kind of sadistic military officer. It was obvious even at the time that she didn't know the difference between concern and "checking up," because she'd start sulking and pouting. It was as if she underwent a personality change. And that concern was truly justified. She was walking a narrow line in staving off those predilections that had been partly responsible for getting her career into such difficulties in the first place. At her live performances I was always holding my breath that none of her fans or musician friends would give her drink or drugs in the dressing room. At one gig somebody did give her something—probably a pill—and all hell broke loose. She started falling over, and in an interview she gave her voice was badly slurred. At the end of the evening she had to be carried upstairs to her dressing room.

During our recording sessions it became evident from the start that Ronnie, though possessed of that gorgeous voice, had difficulty holding melody. She would go flat. There were times we would record her vocal track over and over trying to remedy this, but with each take it would actually get worse. The worse it got, the madder she got—presumably at herself. She once admitted that Phil had had the same difficulty with her, and had resorted to tape-tricking (altering the speed of the playback to adjust the pitch).

I had to keep up the momentum of progress on the record but at the same time make sure I didn't embarrass her. Subterfuge was called for. I went into the studio when she wasn't there and dubbed my own voice, mimicking hers, onto some of the vocal tracks. I found that, in my own humble opinion, I could do a better impersonation of Ronnie Spector than Ronnie Spector could do of herself. Ronnie never noticed that I'd done this, so of course I never told her.

Now I can sit listening to *Siren* and think smugly to myself, *Boy, I do love that woman's sound. Her voice sure does have the magic . . .*

• • • • • •

I learned to stop listening to the tales Ronnie told about other people. She could be all huggy and kissy with somebody one moment, then start stabbing them in the back as soon as they turned away. She seemed to be that way with everyone. You could never tell if she really liked a person—yourself included. I wasn't too critical of her for this: I figured it was one of the survival skills she'd developed during the hell of living with Phil Spector.

That year Steve and I went across to the South of France to the Midem Music Expo. Held in Cannes, Midem is an important convention for the music business. The whole record industry—record companies, publishing companies, artists, press, marketing—comes to it. They come from all over the world to hang for a week under a single roof.

Steve and I paid a small fortune to have a Polish Records booth there, but it was worth every last cent. We were there to push our label and get international distribution deals for our acts; by now we had Manster, Mr. Lucky, Metromen, El Futuro, and, of course, Ronnie Spector. Our booth was a hit. People loved our marketing ideas—the "Who Do I Fuck To Get Off This Label?" teeshirts and the "Support Polish Records!" jockstrap glass holders. We were pushing our acts like crazy to the major labels all around the world, and there was considerable interest in distributing our records from many of those countries. (There was a special interest from the Latin countries in El Futuro.) For *Siren* we had, by the end of the convention, deals set up in the U.K., France, and Spain. Steve and I were thrilled that everything was going so well.

And then our bubble burst.

My assistant called me from the office in New York. "Ronnie's starting to bad-rap the company. She's doing it on the radio and in the press."

Holy shit!

I promptly called Ronnie and asked her what the fuck she thought she was up to.

Oh, she said, she had every excuse in the world. The management was no good. The songs were no good. She'd hated her photo sessions (with Annie Leibovitz, no less!). And on and on it went.

I said, "Ronnie, do you realize this whole trip has been spent pushing you and *Siren*? If this kind of talk gets into the music business, we'll all look like assholes." Nobody would invest in the label, and nobody would invest in the artist.

This argument had no effect whatsoever on Ronnie.

There was no sense in my continuing to push the career of this artist, so I stopped right there and then. Ronnie was sabotaging herself—again—and there was nothing I could do to stop her. Steve and I focused our attention at Midem on getting distribution deals for our other artists, which we did.

Siren could have been the big commercial comeback for Ronnie, I'm certain of it. She herself made sure that it wasn't.

Even before I went to Midem I'd become fed up with another of the chores Ronnie expected me to do, which was constantly baby-sit her. That's not my thing. I looked around to find her new management who might be better at it, and I was able to get Cy and Eileen Berlin to take her on. They were great people and great managers, too—they numbered Tom Cruise and Grace Jones among their clients—but Ronnie soon managed to alienate them. Cy was just "an old man." Twice they had to call an ambulance for her when she started to convulse after drinking or drugging or both; no one ever knew what the fuck she was taking. (In her book she admits to smoking a little pot during the recording sessions for *Siren*. When I read that I thought, *Hmmm* . . .) In the end they had to give up on her as well. There's a limit to what you can do for someone who's so determined to fall so much farther.

It was a lesson we all learned with Ronnie.

• • • • • •

It was a lesson I was very lucky people didn't learn with me. My own private life was spinning well out of control with drugs, booze, and sex.

In 1979 I'd been asked to be a Grammy presenter for the New York Chapter of NARAS (National Academy of Recording Arts & Sciences). While the main Grammy ceremony was going on in Los Angeles, we were opening the envelopes at our own, parallel ceremony for the New York people who couldn't make it to California. This was a very prestigious invitation to present at an important black-tie affair. I took Lou Reed as my guest. I got a bit high, but I was okay.

In 1980 NARAS asked me to do the same again. By now, though, I was having real problems with drink and drugs. The stresses of Polish Records and Ronnie Spector were taking their toll, but that wasn't the whole of it; believe me, when you're at the mercy of addictions, *nothing* is ever the whole of it. For the 1980 ceremony I took Lars Hanson, my guitarist from the *Urban Desire* tour, as my guest; poor Lars had to put

Genya and Lou Reed at the Bottom Line in New York City.

up with me getting steadily more shit-faced as the evening wore on. When I was called upon to open the envelope for the Best Rock Group award, my voice was slurring as I read the nominees. I was even worse as I announced the winner: "The Eagles," I said in a disappointed voice, adding an "ugh" for good measure. I thought I was being funny; in truth I was being an embarrassment.

The whole evening was so horrible that even now I just wish I could curl up and die every time I think about what a disaster I was. Steve told me afterwards I was a total asshole; that didn't help. It was true, but after all he'd been the one keeping me supplied with coke all night.

Cy and Eileen Berlin tried to help my sagging career. They booked me on the TV program *Live at Five* for an interview with Pia Lindström. My voice was slurred. Afterwards, Cy broke it to me in his gentle way that I'd been talking bullshit throughout the interview.

Memories like this of myself at the time—and there are many more—are truly painful for me now. I was having blackouts. My ability to do business was getting out of hand. Sex likewise. I'd screw guys and then afterwards have to ask what their name was so at least I'd know what the guy was called before throwing him out. Some mornings I'd wake up to find someone else in bed with me and I'd lie there wondering, *Oh, my*

God, how did he get here? What the fuck did I do last night? I'd swear never to do this again, but a day or two later I would.

I'd wake up with the feeling that there was an empty hole in my chest—it was a feeling I was getting to know very well. I hated not knowing what I'd done the night before.

Yet I still couldn't see that the real problem was my addictions. I couldn't put it together that it was the booze and the drugs that were making my life such a mess. I just thought I was going crazy. I wanted to die but didn't have the courage to kill myself, unless maybe that was what I was trying to do with the drugs and the alcohol.

And I was getting worse.

• • • • • •

In 1981 I had my third abortion, and this time I didn't have a clue who the father was. I was sleeping with three men regularly and countless others casually. I was seeking affection and attention wherever and whenever I could find them.

After a horse race you don't put the horse back in its stall immediately. You walk it around for a while, calming it until the heart and the blood stop churning. It's known as the warm-down. I hadn't had a warm-down after the fiasco with . . . *And I Mean It!* I'd just been brought to a screeching halt. One minute I was the artist in demand; the next I was the artist who didn't have any audiences to sing to. Yes, I had Polish Records, and that was a thrill, but it wasn't the same thrill as performing—it wasn't the thrill I craved.

In a way, the drugs and the booze helped me survive, in the short term. But they were also killing me, especially the coke. When I blew my nose I'd find blood on the tissue because my nasal membranes were being eaten away. I was starting to do a line every ten minutes; my eyes would tear and my nose would run, but I'd shove the coke up there anyway. If I was running low on coke to snort I'd lick the mirrors. I'd find old, empty cocaine bottles and compulsively scrape out the last traces to collect enough to hold me until my next delivery was due. If I dropped any coke on the floor I'd be down there with my straw. (By now I'd lost all interest in keeping the place clean, so you can imagine what all I was sniffing up.) I could leave the apartment only with the greatest of difficulty. All my creativity was gone: I couldn't sing, and you could forget about any ideas of songwriting. My musician friends were disappearing or dying. I got used to calls saying, "Guess who they found dead last night? Overdosed, of course . . ."

Meanwhile, my Polish Records partner Steve was getting sloppy with his own business. He was having large shipments of coke mailed from Miami right to the Polish Records office. He was also trying to screw the kinds of people who take really strong objection to being screwed—like Colombian drug dealers. This was no small-time operation he now had. I was feeling guilty about Polish Records, too: I'd signed up five acts, all produced by me, but all the money for the office rent, the legal expenses, the studio expenses, the publishing advances—it was all coming from a single source: Steve's drug business.

I knew the Polish Records office phones were being tapped, and I was certain my own phones in the apartment were being tapped as well. I started getting very frightened for my own safety.

I phoned my lawyer and explained what was happening. "Get out of it now, Genya," he said. "If Polish Records gets comprehensively busted, it's your name that'll hit the headlines, not your partner's. You're the one who's known in the business. If you've any interest in preserving yourself, get out now while you still can."

I knew he was right, so I did just what he told me. I grabbed what I could, including the *Siren* tapes, which I still have, sitting in a basement. Steve got the El Futuro tapes. I never saw him again, and a while afterwards I heard a rumor that he was dead. I felt really bad when I heard that—I'd *liked* the guy, after all, and we'd been through a lot of things together, having fun much of the time—but now I think that maybe he started the rumors himself to get those Colombian "business associates" off his back, because someone reported spotting him a few years later in Los Angeles.

That was the end of Polish Records, though. So easy to type that. So hard to think it.

※ ※ ※ ※ ※ ※

Lost and lonely, I'd started a relationship with the bass player of Mr. Lucky while I was still producing them for Polish Records. (Mr. Lucky was a great pop group. Pity they weren't on a bigger label.) He told me that he'd once tried to kill his father by choking him to death—that if his mother hadn't been there to stop him he'd have succeeded—and one crazy, very high night he tried to do the same to me. I don't know what made him eventually give up this time; it certainly wasn't me, because I was almost gone by then. Even after that, even with the bruises on my neck, I couldn't get him out of my apartment—he just wouldn't go. I was terrified he was going to kill me. Finally I got rid of him by calling the cops.

Embarrassingly, one of the cops who arrived knew who I was: I was Genya Ravan, the rock star. Except I wasn't, by then. I was Genya Ravan the hopeless addict, totally blown out by coke.

CHAPTER FIFTEEN
Rhythm and Booze

IT WAS 1982. After shutting down Polish Records I'd been left with a huge cocaine habit, and with Steve out of the picture I was no longer getting it for free. I was drinking heavily every day. I was bitterly, bitterly unhappy, but kept trying to tell myself I wasn't. The days I couldn't get any coke I was very sick; it never occurred to me that this was withdrawal, that I was truly hooked on the drug.

In desperation I started dealing coke, both to try to make some money and to have some for myself. I stepped up the coke to ridiculous extremes, using a vitamin powder to make up the bulk—I called it Disco Mix—and justifying the act by telling myself this was better for the buyer. In truth, I was doing virtually all the coke myself. By the time I'd finished mixing there was no coke left to speak of. I was selling people high-priced vitamin powder.

People kept asking me why I didn't start doing gigs again to get a little money for myself. I did still want to sing, but I was so tired of constantly re-inventing myself. What I was really getting tired of was acting as if I was fine when I wasn't fine at all. When people asked me what I was doing I would always tell them I was so, so busy, when often the truth was I was doing nothing at all. I was calling record companies to set up meetings while they still knew who I was, and having to act bright and cheery for them about all the nonexistent great things that were happening for me, when really I was feeling so low. God, but the effort of pretending to be up when I was down took so much effort—it totally drained me. It was around this time I took to oil painting. I had to get my rocks off somewhere in Creativity Land or I'd have gone totally nuts.

As a singer I'd always felt the need to prove myself. Even when audiences loved me I worried about what some lamebrain reviewer might think. The same went for the production side of my business. The whole music industry sucked, I'd decided: It had drained me near unto death, it was trying to kill me. I was in desperate need of a rest from it. Booze helped (or so I thought), but it gave me only a brief respite each time.

I was months behind with my rent, 620 dollars per month, and I couldn't think of how I was going to raise the money. If anyone had suggested to me I take up hooking, I think I'd have done it.

I was getting crazier by the day. One night I was sitting on my living-room couch when I saw someone walking past the window. They paused and looked in at me. I was terrified, and ran to hide in the closet. It took me a while to remember that I lived on the seventh floor.

There were days I forgot to eat. I was getting skeletally thin. I even lost my hips, and I've *always* had hips. One night, when Mr. Lucky's bass player was still on the scene—this being after he'd tried to kill me but before the cops finally ejected him from my life—my sister Helen and her husband Doc came over to the apartment at four in the morning in response to a panicked phone call from me. (They gave him money for a hotel room to get rid of him for the rest of the night.) Much later Helen told me she'd been so appalled by how skinny and terrible I looked that what she really wanted to do was get me to a hospital. I wish she'd gone ahead and done it: she'd have saved me eight further years of misery. I had no idea about intervention, detoxing, rehab. As is so often the case when someone goes off the rails due to drugs or mental illness, no one wished to spell it out to me that I had a problem—a problem that could be fixed, if I wanted it to be.

Blackouts were happening to me with increasing frequency. During one of them I took a lipstick and wrote things like "Die, Motherfucker!" and "Fuck yourself! I hate you!" all over my white kitchen cabinets; when I woke up the next morning I hadn't a clue how they'd got there. During another blackout I wrote myself a letter that was so threatening and scary that, if it had been in anyone else's handwriting, I'd have fled and gone into hiding; it was full of things like "You're nothing" and "You're dead anyway" and "Die, Bitch!" Although I now understand that these messages to myself were attempts to reach out for help, at the time there didn't seem to be anybody I could reach out *to*.

At night I went to bed with my apartment door unlocked—not the safest of practices in New York City. I wasn't worried about people coming in; I was terrified there might be someone or something *already* inside my apartment, and was leaving the door unlocked in case I needed to get out in a hurry. Often I'd ask the Parc Vendome's doorman to come up in the elevator with me when I got home so there'd be the safety of having another human being with me while I checked the closets and under the bed. I was sure there was an intruder hiding in the apartment. Of course, the "intruder" I was so frightened of was myself, but I didn't know that then.

I was on a cocaine-alcohol merry-go-round. I couldn't go out during daylight; I had to wait until nightfall to do my shopping. My dealer came from Harlem every other night to play backgammon with me and feed me drugs, but aside from that I was alone. For me, to be alone meant I was in very bad company.

One night in 1983, about three or four in the morning, I was in the apartment isolating myself as usual: the windows were shut, the drapes were drawn. I had the TV on for company, though I wasn't watching it. Then something on the TV caught my eye, a commercial showing two eggs frying with a voice-over that said: "This is your brain on drugs." The image really hit home. I grabbed a pen and scribbled down the phone number. Before I passed out for the night, I called it and got a recorded message asking me to leave my name and number.

I was still asleep the next morning when I got a return call.

Half awake, I picked up the phone and a voice said: "Hi. This is Ted. Are you Genya?"

"Yes," I said, confused.

"You called us last night. Are you okay?"

"Who's this?"

"This is Ted from Alcoholics Anonymous."

"Oh," I said. "You must have the wrong number."

He persisted. "Is your name Genya?"

I hung up on him.

• • • • • •

Sometime in 1981 I ran into a friend on the street who was so concerned about how bad I looked that he called me later. He'd found out there was a regular Alcoholics Anonymous meeting in my neighborhood, at the Roosevelt Hospital, and he urged me to get myself together enough to go to it. At last someone had put the truth in front of me: I had a problem that could be fixed.

I tried really hard not to have a drink before going to the meeting, because I knew they'd smell it on me. I couldn't manage it. I drank some Campari and soda and hoped for the best. Even so, it didn't stop the shakes. I took a valium, and that helped a bit.

At the meeting I was shaking so much my teeth were chattering. I tried listening to someone giving a talk about how she'd recovered after having lost her family and her business, but I couldn't really take much of it in because I was so nervous—what if anyone there recognized me?—and because the shakes weren't getting any better. There were tears rolling down my face.

One of the recovering alcoholics there came and talked with me. After a while she said, "You need a detox, you know. You might need to go into hospital for it . . ."

That scared me.

I saw a list of the Alcoholics Anonymous Twelve Steps written on a big sheet of paper hanging on the wall. The first of the Twelve Steps is: "We admitted we were powerless over alcohol—that our lives had become unmanageable." I was such a mental mess that I read this as: "We admitted we were powerless over alcohol—that our wives had become unmanageable."

I left the meeting and went straight to a Fifty-ninth Street bar, where I told the barman: "I've just come from an AA meeting where they blame everything on their wives. So why are there so many women going to these meetings?"

He couldn't explain it either.

"Besides," I told him, "I don't have a problem with booze. It's just that I can't drink tequila anymore. Tequila makes me go nuts. So give me a vodka martini, please—easy on the vermouth, and no ice."

He might as well have given me the whole bottle of vodka. For the rest of that evening I sat in a corner of the bar, drinking steadily, worrying myself frantic that I'd get home and find I hadn't any booze left there.

Finally I heard the words I always most dreaded to hear. "Last call," the bartender announced.

• • • • • •

While I was still running Polish Records I'd met a strange and lovable couple, Owen and Lucy Swenson. Owen was a guitarist who'd played the New York club Max's Kansas City many times with a band called the Stilettoes, which had included Chris Stein and Debbie Harry, later both in Blondie. He was also a print artist who'd been recommended to me at Polish Records when I wanted artwork done for some of our acts. Owen and I had struck up an immediate friendship, and I'd begun to see a lot of him and his wife Lucy.

All through my madness, Owen and Lucy kept insisting I visit them in their farmhouse in Palenville in upstate New York; they insisted I'd love it there. I kept putting them off, primarily because I thought that, with them around the whole time, I wouldn't be able to keep drinking as much as I needed to. (As it turned out, they drank pretty heavily as well, so this was no problem.) But they persisted, and finally I gave in. They picked me up in their run-down truck, and off we drove into the country. I thought we must have looked like the Beverly Hillbillies.

That weekend Lucy and I worked in her garden, and I got my hands filthy in the soil, which I loved. I also saw a white house on a hill on a corner lot that had just been put up for sale. I fell in love with it; it looked like a Southern mansion. I said to myself: *This is what I need— a home!*

Like many alcoholics, when I'd decided I wanted something, I was relentless. The fact that I didn't have any money was no deterrent. I was going to buy this house . . . even though I was struggling to pay the rent at the Parc Vendome! Still, I was able to raise the initial cash by raiding all my credit cards. I did have enough sense left not to trust myself for the future, because of the alcohol and drugs, so I persuaded Helen and Doc to co-sign the mortgage papers in case I couldn't make the payments.

Matters were helped when the Parc Vendome announced it was about to go co-op, and offered me $39,000 to move out of my apartment. It was a very big apartment, and anyone in their right mind would have stuck out for a lot more, but I said yes immediately. After all, I now had my upstate home in Palenville to go to.

I really did believe that all the drugging and drinking would stop if I had a proper home life. I thought the root of my problem was that I'd spent so much of my life on the road, staying in lonely, crappy hotel rooms. With a home of my own and living out of the city, I thought I'd be happier and, most important, that I could regain my sense of "self."

Instead, of course, what happened was that I found myself in a big old house, very alone.

I had a friend in New York named Lilly May who didn't have much of a life of her own. She was always crashing out at someone else's apartment. She seemed to live through other people's lives. This made her a great enabler. If I wanted coke, she'd get some for us. At one stage I'd sunk so low I devised a plan to steal from somebody, and Lilly May went along with it and helped me. She'd do anything. So I persuaded her that what she really wanted to do was share my house in Palenville as her second home for the weekends, keeping an apartment in New York City for the weekdays when she worked there.

Lilly May arrived in Palenville every Friday night, and the first thing we'd do was hit the neighborhood bars. The Trailways bus from Manhattan stopped in Palenville right outside one of my favorites, Oh Boys, and I'd wait in there for her to arrive. Oh Boys was the bar where all the local rednecks hung out; the parking lot was full of pickup trucks, and inside there were drunk farmers and drunk countrywomen—and me. Lilly May would find me playing pool or just sitting sloshed at the bar.

I was doing my best to fit in, I guess, though I actually stuck out like a sore thumb. When I got really stoned I'd turn nasty and loud; I had become an angry drunk, just like my father had been. I'd scream things like, "Palenville—where men are men and sheep are nervous!" Sometimes I'd even get into fights—with anyone who happened to be convenient. If anyone said anything derogatory about my New York background, I'd come out with threats like, "I'll go home and get my gun and blow your brains out—*then* you'll see what New York chicks are about!" A catchphrase was: "This town is about suicide. New York is about homicide."

Lilly May would back me all the way. She was the moth to my flame.

During the week, when she wasn't there, I became increasingly a victim of loneliness and isolation. Even the Swensons had stopped coming around to see me. In large part this was self-inflicted. I'd arrived with a sort of aggressive "Do you know who I am?" attitude. It had deteriorated to: "Do you know who I used to be?" The truth was that no one there had ever heard of me. I didn't have even the crutch of my fame to lean on when the rest of myself, the real me, had dissolved away in coke and booze.

Back in the Parc Vendome I'd been paranoid that there were lurkers in my apartment, but at least I hadn't had to cope with the fear that I could be attacked and killed and no one would find me. I'd been in a building full of people, after all. I became afraid to walk out of my house at night, because the trees made their strange sounds as they swayed and rustled in the darkness. Sometimes I left all the lights on all night long. There were even times I left the outside floodlights on during the day when I had to go out in case darkness had fallen by the time I got home. My electric bills were astronomical.

I remember countless occasions when I got home in my car at night and would just sit there for what seemed an eternity, heart pounding, trying to pluck up the courage to climb out and walk the few yards to the front door. Once I finally got inside I'd go through the same old rigmarole that I had back at the Parc Vendome—checking under the beds and in all the closets.

I hadn't been in Palenville more than a few weeks before I was selling drugs again in order to support my own coke and liquor habits. My supplier, a Colombian called Carlos, used to come out from New York in his three-piece suit to deliver the cocaine to me. While he was there he proved, surprisingly, to enjoy some of the more mundane rural activities, like raking the leaves in my yard—which he'd do still wearing his three-piece suit! When he couldn't make it to the mountains to deliver the coke in person he'd mail it to me.

• • • • • •

I finally met a few good musicians in the neighborhood. One of them was Dan Brubeck, Dave Brubeck's son; Dan lived about half a mile from me. We started to put a band together, rehearsing in the studio he'd built in his house. We did a number of gigs together, including one in the town of Woodstock.

Each summer a New York theatrical company, the Bond Street Players, came to Palenville to put on a sort of festival they called Palenville Interarts. In the summer of 1984 they asked myself and Dan Brubeck's band to perform for them. A local bar, the Woodbine Inn, announced that they'd throw an after-the-show party for us—their aim being, of course, to bring in extra business.

The Interarts gig went very well, and afterwards we all headed over to the Woodbine Inn. It was there, that night, that I first met my Palenville coke connection. I hadn't thought there could be any such thing out here among these beautiful mountains, but it seemed that the drug followed me everywhere I went. If I wanted another kind of life—a drug-free life—then it was me who had to change, not the scenery, but I still couldn't get this into my head.

I was at the bar in the Woodbine Inn when a woman came up to me, all wide-eyed, and said, "Ya blew me away . . ."

The accent alone told me she was, like me, from New York. We talked, and she told me she was originally from Hell's Kitchen but had moved to Palenville for the sake of her kids. She thought the country would be a better environment for them.

She suggested we might want to adjourn to the ladies' room to "powder our noses." No prizes for guessing what the powder was. We swiftly became friends, and thereafter I was over at her house all the time. We had so much in common—drugs! It was a great relief to have a supplier right here in Palenville: no more Carlos in his three-piece-suit, no more going through agonies of anxiety as I fetched my packages of coke from the post office.

Around this time I was starting to get really sloppy. I was drunk every night. One time I fell against the wood stove and seriously burned my hands, and I usually had a few ripe bruises from stumbling against things. I was getting equally careless about coke. I used to take a little glass vial of the stuff with me everywhere so that I could snort wherever I wanted to. In bars I'd try selling it to people I'd just met; it was a wonder none of them turned out to be cops.

None of this was helped by the fact that Lilly May was still coming to stay with me at weekends. Sometimes she'd bring a bottle of cocaine as a little house-gift, other times a bottle of booze. One of the guys I met as a customer also sped the process: after he'd bought coke from me he'd share it with me, so we could do it together. I was getting sicker and sicker every day—and broker and broker. I finally managed to get on welfare, but that didn't help my financial situation much.

By the time 1985 rolled round I could no longer afford to go to the liquor store to buy my own booze, and buying my own cocaine was just a wild impossibility. I had no choice but to start getting friendly with a few guys who'd buy my drinks for me. One of them was Ed, a carpenter whom I met while he was doing some work on Dan Brubeck's house. I asked him to do a few odd jobs around my house too, and soon enough we were sleeping together. Just a few years earlier I'd never have given Ed a second glance, but by now I was very broke and feeling more lonely than ever.

It was indirectly through Ed that I finally got a job, sort of. Unfortunately it was the worst sort of job I could have gotten. One night he took me to a place called Brenda's Bar in Kingston, N.Y. Behind the bar was a beautiful woman, who proved to be the Brenda whose bar it was. Ed and I went back a few times together, and finally I got so friendly with Brenda that I started going there on my own. By this time we were calling each other every day, and she allowed me to drink at the bar for free.

Brenda was a heavy drinker herself, and never woke up without a hangover. Combined with her having two small children, it meant she never managed to get her bar open on time in the morning. I persuaded her that I could help out by opening the bar at least two or three mornings a week; I'd get there at eleven o'clock so she wouldn't have to be there until lunchtime. She thought this would be a great idea; it was, of course, perfect for me. By the time she got in at 1:00 o'clock I'd be smashed out of my skull on free drink—far too drunk to deal with money, so the customers were getting the wrong change or being charged twice. I still can't imagine how I survived driving home afterwards along the winding roads of the Catskills.

I was tending bar one afternoon when a guy came in who caught my eye. With his black hair and mustache, he was handsome enough in a macho, redneck sort of a way. He smiled at me and we began flirting. His name was Dennis. I liked that childlike smile of his. When it came time for me to go home, he asked me where I was going.

"Home," I said. "I'm finished for the day."

"When will I see you again?"

"I'll be working here again this weekend."

"Can I have your phone number?"

As I wrote down my number for him I could see that Brenda was looking upset, shaking her head, but that didn't stop me. I thought maybe she had had her eye on him herself and was jealous.

No sooner had I given him my number than I started to dictate a sort of informal prenuptial contract.

"I'm not into cheating—I don't like liars."

"Same here," he answered seriously.

"I want people to keep the promises they make."

"Me too."

And so on.

I drove home. Not long after I'd got there the phone rang. It was Lilly May, calling from Oh Boys. Oops—I'd forgotten she was coming early this weekend. I went back out to fetch her from Oh Boys, and, of course, we stayed a while to have a few drinks. I told her about this guy I'd just met at Brenda's Bar. She seemed a lot less thrilled than I was.

We fell in through the door at home about eleven that evening, and soon the phone went. It was Brenda. She said she'd called to warn me: "Stay away from Dennis. He's bad news!" Brenda told me was married, with kids, although she thought he might be separated or divorced. "He's a troublemaker. He's started fights in this bar often enough."

I still thought she was just jealous, so I didn't take her warning seriously. Besides, this wasn't the kind of stuff I wanted to hear. I was lonely, and Dennis wanted me. That was enough to make him a knight in shining armor in my eyes.

Dennis and I met a few more times over the next week or two, and then I invited him to the house. He didn't leave. He seemed to be genuinely in love with me. A few weeks later I told him I'd been a singer and played him some of my records. Not long after that he asked me if I'd marry him.

Marry him? Why not? It was as good an excuse as any for another party. Not long after the wedding I had a sober moment for once.

Oh, holy shit, what did I do? I just married a fuckin' redneck. I'm not sure I even like this guy! Now I know I need help!

A few days later I contacted a lawyer and started the divorce proceedings.

Getting rid of Dennis wasn't as easy as all that, though. He kept bursting into tears and telling me he couldn't live without me. Then I'd melt, and let him back into my life. After a little while I'd begin trying to get him back out of it again. I was just so depressed and confused at the time that I couldn't set my mind to anything. It took several years before finally I managed to shake him off, and in the end it was a matter of him walking out on me when, for once, I could actually have done with him being there. After he'd gone I discovered he'd been stealing jewelry from me.

● ● ● ● ● ●

There were Alcoholics Anonymous meetings going on in Palenville, and often enough people had tossed hints my way about them. At the time I'd thought they were just being snide; I now realized they were trying to help me.

I finally began attending some of the Alcoholics Anonymous meetings in town. I really had nowhere else left to go but A.A. I thought life was all over for me. Once again, I wanted to die but I was too chicken to kill myself. It seemed I'd never sing again, never laugh again, never make love again. The party was over. Later on someone told me that when I first walked into a meeting he thought I looked like I needed an exorcist.

Someone at A.A. said, "You get to do it all over again, but this time the right way."

The remark really stuck with me. Could it really be true? Wow, what a great hope that was. Could I truly get the chance to start all over again, this time doing it the right way? There were so many things in my life that would have been great if I'd done them the right way.

A wonderful German woman named Lucy became my interim sponsor. She'd phone me and speak to me in her heavy accent. "I vill be picking you up, *ja*? Vot time shall I there be?" I called her Frau Lucy—affectionately. She helped me get dry and stay dry for weeks and months, but no matter how long I'd manage to stay off the bottle—sometimes two or three months—I'd still slide back again and begin drinking.

One of my fellow A.A. members gave me the clue that finally got me to stop permanently. She said: "Genya, just remember that once you're a pickle you can't become a cucumber again."

I was an alcoholic. That was something that couldn't be undone. I could never not be an alcoholic again. What I could be, though, was an alcoholic who didn't drink. Once I finally got that through to my brain, I would be able to kick the booze for good. There was still a while to go before my brain finally got the message, but the light was showing at the end of this particular tunnel.

• • • • • • •

By the summer of 1990 I had one foot in Alcoholics Anonymous but the other foot was still firmly planted in Hell. I had stopped drinking, again, but I still hadn't been able to give up my coke habit. And, because of the coke, it was becoming increasingly difficult not to pick up that "just one drink." I had to fight against the yearning for a drink with everything I had, minute by minute. One strategy I used that summer was to hang out as much as possible with non-drinkers, and I met a few good friends that way. Among them were Tina and Joe. They were from New York City, like me. Joe was so Italian he made me laugh a lot. Tina and Joe were always home whenever I wanted to stop by and swim in their pool or just hang, because Joe was under house arrest. (He would never tell me what for—something to do with New York City.)

The strangest thing happened that summer. One day in July, I suddenly decided I'd had enough of cigarettes. I looked at the pack of Winston Lights I was halfway through, and said to it: "Fuck you. I'm not going to be your prisoner any longer." I threw the pack in the garbage.

This was huge news. All my life I'd made attempts to give up smoking, but always without success. I'd made New Year's resolutions to stop, but broken them almost at once. I'd had bad colds, but still I'd smoked. A doctor had once told me I smelled like an ashtray, and that I really had to give the habit up, but despite his warning I hadn't been able to. Yet for no apparent reason I managed it this day in July 1990 without any particular difficulty. I thought, *What's the worst thing that could happen to me if I didn't smoke when I wanted to?* And the answer was: *Nothing too bad at all.*

Giving up the addiction was one thing. Giving up the physical aspects of the habit was another. I missed having a cigarette in my hand and my mouth—missed the "prop." I'd heard that Native Americans used to chew on licorice root when they couldn't get any tobacco, so I drove to a health food store and stocked up on some of that.

What I discovered from giving up smoking cigarettes was that I could learn to say "No!" to *me*. That could be applied to all the other things I'd let myself become addicted to—booze, drugs, sex. "No, thanks, I've had enough" was never a part of my vocabulary. I wasn't made that way. It had to be "No."

• • • • • •

Helen called me one night to tell me she couldn't stand living with Mom anymore. About a year earlier she and Doc had become concerned about Mom being all alone and forgetting to take her meds, and so on; all in all, Mom hadn't been doing too well, in the way people don't when they get very old. So Doc had asked his company for a transfer to Florida, and he and Helen had bought a mother-daughter house with Mom. But now Mom was going downhill mentally as well as physically, and Helen couldn't take the stress any longer. Mom had lost one leg to diabetes, and her mental condition was deteriorating by the day. She was starting to hallucinate. She had always been difficult to live with, and Helen had taken the main brunt of this, because I was always too busy, or on the road, or just too plain fucked up.

It sounded to me as though Helen was headed straight for a nervous breakdown if she carried on sharing a house with Mom, so the situation called for a choice: either they both became ill or Mom went into a home. I thought the latter was the better option, and told Helen so.

It was a big decision for us, and hurt us both deeply. There was a lot of guilt for us to deal with. We started looking around for good homes, but locating one wasn't easy: most of them were profoundly depressing, and stank of urine. When at last we found one that seemed fairly decent, we lied to her that she was merely being moved to a rehabilitation center for a while. I still feel badly about that deception, and I know Helen does too. We don't talk about it.

CHAPTER SIXTEEN
Don't Let Me Die

I WAS GETTING A BAD COLD. There was nothing exceptional in that, except my chest was hurting a lot as well—enough that there was no question but that I had to see a doctor. Thanks to being on welfare, I was covered by Medicaid, so I could afford to do so. Thanks to being off alcohol, I was sober enough to set up an appointment for the following week at the Family Medical Center in Woodstock, which had been recommended by a friend.

The doctor who saw me was kind and gentle. She checked my chest with a stethoscope. "I think you might have just a bad respiratory infection, but it could be that you're in the early stages of pneumonia." She gave me a prescription and told me I should go to the Kingston Clinic for a chest X-ray.

Pneumonia, huh? I was glad I'd given up smoking.

After my session in the Kingston X-ray lab, I went back to my unhappy half-sober life. Thanks to Alcoholics Anonymous, I was more or less clear of booze, but I was still doing coke. Sometimes even at the A.A. meetings I'd go out to the bathroom to do some lines . . . and then I'd have the nerve to come back to a room filled with recovering alcoholics and raise my hand to be allowed to share my experiences with them. The friends I was making at A.A. were the only real friends I'd made in a long time. And the process was working; as their slogan has it, "Bring the body and the mind will follow."

A few days passed by. I got home from Tina and Joe's house, where I'd been swimming in their pool, and found a message on my answering machine asking me to call the doctor at the Family Medical Center. My heart skipped a beat. I phoned the Center and within seconds the receptionist had my doctor on the line. She asked me to come in that day.

"What's wrong?"

"The X-ray has shown something on your lung, and they want you to have a C.A.T. scan. We can talk about it when you come in."

She didn't want to get into it on the phone, which should have been a warning to me, but instead I thought maybe the problem was that I was developing asthma or something.

In her office, I offered this theory to the doctor.

"Possibly," she said, "but I think it might be more serious than that."

No, I thought. *It can't be.*

The doctor told me I needed to get a C.A.T. scan. I'm very claustrophobic, so the prospect of being confined in a metal tube was pretty scary. I asked my friend Maureen—whom I'd met a while back while selling her dope—if she'd drive me to the Kingston Clinic the following week so I'd have someone there for support. The scanner proved to be shaped more like a donut than a tube, so the claustrophobia wasn't too bad, but even so I was glad Maureen was there. Afterwards, I was told I should phone my doctor in a week for the results.

This time, when I called her she said she was going to set up an evaluation meeting for me at the Albany Medical Center. By now I was getting very frightened. Maureen came with me again to Albany. I was also accompanied on this visit by Dennis, my ex-husband, who was going through one of his periodic phases of trying to persuade me that I should give "us" another chance.

August 11, 1990. At the Albany Medical Center I was given an injection of dye into my bloodstream and then subjected to another C.A.T. scan. We waited for a while until two doctors came into the office where we were sitting. As gently as they could, they explained to me what they'd discovered. "There's a tumor in your left lung, behind your heart. The prognosis isn't looking good." They were going to have to do a biopsy to find out what sort of a tumor it was, but they didn't have high hopes that it wasn't cancerous.

My eyes welled up with tears. I couldn't control myself. In the past, whatever I'd felt like inside and however I'd acted in private afterwards, I'd usually been able to confront new disasters with a tough public shell, as if I wasn't, you know, really that bothered: "That's okay, I can handle it." Not this time. I was devastated. I was terrified. I can remember that I started to shake all over, crying, "No! No! My life can't be over! I have *plans* . . ."

When the doctors had finished explaining everything to me, I staggered out of the room and into the hospital lobby, where there was a payphone. I called my sister in Florida. "Helen, I've got lung cancer! I'm going to die . . ."

For days I was in a dark nightmare of the soul. I seemed to spend almost all of my time just weeping. My world had fallen apart. My insides felt hollow and empty, but at the same time I wanted to throw up. I kept looking at the sky and the trees, thinking that soon I wouldn't be able to do this anymore. I wanted God to reach down from Heaven and talk to me. Every part of me was weeping: my bones, my heart, my blood.

The weasel voice of my alcoholism made itself heard. "You're going to die anyway, so why not have fun and drink? What the hell difference would it make?"

But then another, firmer voice interrupted it—my angel voice. "Do you want to go out in the light, or do you want to go out in the dark?"

I had been to enough Alcoholics Anonymous meetings to know that I didn't want to spend what little was apparently left of my life in a drunken haze. If I didn't have much time remaining, I needed to live it in the light as much as I could.

I haven't touched either alcohol or drugs since that fateful day, August 11, 1990.

My sister came up from Florida, bless her heart. We cried like babies in each other's arms. Almost the first words we both said were, "We won't let Mom know." In a way I desperately needed my Mommy at the time, but we knew that if we told her she'd start screaming and howling that it was *her* life that was over.

I didn't want anyone else to know apart from Helen. I didn't want to become an object of sympathy. Maureen and Dennis already knew, of course, because they'd been there in Albany. I swore all three of them to secrecy.

Helen and Dennis came with me when I went for the biopsy. I recall lying on the operating table. As a nurse was marking my body in preparation for the incision, she smiled and said, "I love your tattoo." I thought, *Is she only being nice to me because she knows I'm dying?* But, just as I slid under the anesthetics, I looked up at her and smiled back. "Thank you." Another performance.

I was in agony when I awoke. They'd cut away a piece of my rib cage to get at the lung. I heard screaming and for a moment thought it must be me, before realizing I was in the same room as a girl who'd been injured in a car wreck, and that it was her. She kept screaming that her hair was dirty and she wanted someone to wash it, or that she wanted more painkillers; she wouldn't shut up for a second. Even with all the sedatives they gave me, I couldn't go to sleep because of her screaming. I wished they'd move her out of the room, or me out of the room—I didn't care which. All I could think was: *I have cancer. How could they sentence me to being in the same room as an accident victim? I'm going to die. How could they . . .*

A few hours later Helen and Dennis were by my bedside. They'd both been crying.

The oncology doctor came in.

"How long do I have?" I could hardly breathe because of the pain. My voice came out as barely more than a whisper.

"You're in the third stage," he answered nonchalantly.

"What does that mean?"

"There are four stages of lung cancer. With treatment, you probably have about three to six months left to live. There's not much we can do. Sorry."

I fixed my gaze on his and whispered as loud as I could: "You're not God. You can't tell me when I'll die."

And then the tears came again. Helen and Dennis were sobbing along with me.

After the oncologist had left I pulled Dennis close to me and told him that I had some live tapes of me singing at the Bottom Line. I was sure these would be worth something after I died, I told him, just like all the other rock idols who'd made it big after their deaths. I was entrusting him with the task of selling them to a record company and sharing the royalties with my family. He promised he would do that.

※ ※ ※ ※ ※ ※

My brother-in-law, Doc Kirson, Helen's husband, was let in on the secret that I had lung cancer. He was a fundraiser for the Anti-Defamation

League. They'd recently had a major event honoring some bigwig from the Memorial Sloan-Kettering Cancer Center in New York. He made a few phone calls to find out who was the best thoracic surgeon there. The person recommended to him was Dr. Michael Burt.

Another person I had to tell about my cancer was Dawn Roberts. I'd met her in the summer of 1989 when Ginger (of the Gingerbreads) had come upstate to visit me. Dawn, Ginger's roommate, had come along as well, and we'd become friendly; she'd been a big fan of mine for many years. Dawn had kept in touch, and had come to visit me a few times on her own. She was always able to make me laugh. I knew she had a habit of chattering—she wasn't normally the sort of person it was wise to trust with a secret—but I had to tell her because my sister couldn't drive, and I needed someone to ferry me around. Also, to be honest, I think Helen was having difficulty coping with everything on her own, and I couldn't rely on Dennis. I had no one else.

Dawn came upstate to help us out. She drove me to and from my medical appointments in New York City. More or less from the moment they saw each other, Dawn and Dennis were at each other's throats. This was the last thing I wanted to deal with while I was sick, but the problem soon resolved itself because this was the moment Dennis chose to walk out on me.

Hilly Kristal was another person I told about the cancer. He was an old and good friend, and I trusted him completely.

I met Dr. Burt at Sloan-Kettering. I sat a long time in the waiting room, tormented by the sight of all these people in obvious pain, or with their heads bald and their skin yellow. Was this what I was going to look like in a few weeks' time? When I finally met my doctor I really liked him. He was young, and his attitude toward cancer was positive and aggressive. He did all sorts of tests and, while he couldn't promise I was going to survive, at least he had a plan of attack—at least he didn't just tell me I had three to six months to live and there was nothing that could be done.

The first thing they needed to establish was whether or not the cancer had spread. I had brain scans and body scans. There were traces of cancer in my lymph nodes. The doctors didn't like the way one of my adrenal glands looked, so they decided to do a biopsy of it. The results of the biopsy were unsuccessful, so the next step was that I'd have to have the gland removed before any further treatment could be initiated. This operation was even more painful than the lung biopsy had been, but the good news was that the adrenal didn't show any cancer.

The plan was that I would undergo intensive chemotherapy for four months to see if that would shrink the tumor. If it did, they'd operate on me to remove my left lung. This was the first time I'd ever thought of having one of my lungs removed as being good news, but if it was going to keep me alive . . .

I was getting worried about the amount of stress Helen was under. She was worrying herself sick about me, and she had the strain of traveling back and forward between Florida and New York the whole time. I knew that she and Doc had tickets to go on a vacation to Israel; it was a trip they'd been planning for a long time. I knew that if I told her I was going to plunge immediately into chemotherapy she'd cancel their trip to be with me. So I lied to her. I told her the chemo wasn't going to start for at least another four weeks. So off they went.

My veins were bad. During my first chemo session I ended up with seven holes in my arms! Later on they put a port in my chest, with an I.V. running from my neck vein to it. They were worried that otherwise a vein might collapse in the middle of a session, leaking chemicals that could burn my skin.

I was given a combination of three different chemicals: Cisplatin, Velban, and Mitomycin. The treatment made me very sick. But the real agony of chemotherapy was that, for the full four months it was going on, no one could tell if it was being successful or not—whether I was likely to live or die. Only after the complete course of treatment would they be able to X-ray my chest to see what improvement, if any, there had been.

The chemo was so treacherous that, during the four months, I had to have a three-day stay in hospital every third week. Most food made me feel sick, but each time I came out of hospital I'd get weird food yearnings. I'd ask for things like blintzes. My wonderful chemotherapist, Dr. Katherine Pisters, asked if maybe I was pregnant; she was joking.

When I had the port put in I had to stay in the hospital overnight. By the end of that time I was starving—I'd had nothing to eat for twenty-four hours. As at any other hospital, at the Sloan-Kettering you have to have a form signed by your doctor before they can release you. But there was some foul up, and no one could find my form. I couldn't wait any longer. Dawn was there with her car, so I just grabbed my clothes in a bundle and fled, still in my hospital gown and all. She drove me straight to a supermarket. She wanted me to wait in the car while she went and bought something for me to eat, but I couldn't sit still another moment. I *needed* to see the deli counter for myself, to wallow in the sight. Of course, I forgot that

I had a shaved head (from the one chemo session they'd given me before putting the port in), a big Band-Aid hanging off my neck, a hospital band on my wrist, and blood on my neck and the hospital gown I was still wearing. The woman serving at the counter looked on in absolute horror as I stood there joyously, smacking my lips, saying in a loud voice, "I want bagels with lox, and . . . and, yes, I'll have olives too."

"Miss, are you all right?"

"I just got out of hospital—I've got cancer, you see. Boy, am I hungry! Mmmm, make those *black* olives . . ."

I was losing a lot of weight, and looked awful. But the worst part was when my hair started falling out. I'd get out of bed and take a shower, and there'd be big clumps of hair all over the sheets and in the shower drain. It was a horrendous sight; it made me feel as if the whole of me was just disintegrating away. Dawn took me to stores to buy scarves and wigs, but having anything on my head for long gave me headaches. Dawn, my sister, and another friend, Pat, contributed five hundred dollars each to buy me a beautiful real-hair wig, but I couldn't wear it; I still have it in my closet.

Each time we drove into Manhattan I'd see all the people walking around, shopping, talking, laughing—just going about their lives—and I'd get so sad and consumed with jealousy. I'd think, *I used to own Manhattan! I lived here once. I was so popular my name was in lights, on buses, on billboards. Now look at me! I'm getting treatments that make me throw up, make my hair fall out, make my skin turn yellow . . .*

I tried to cling onto my sense of humor. I had to go every week to the blood lab at the Sloan-Kettering so they could draw a sample. The nurses who drew the blood would always say, "Let's check your platelets." Eventually I asked them why they were never interested in my knifelets or forklets. It wasn't the world's greatest joke, but it made them laugh. More importantly, it made *me* laugh. Humor kept my spirits up, and that could help me fight the cancer.

I was told to avoid public places as much as possible, for fear of infection. The chemotherapy knocks out the immune system, so catching even so much as a cold can be fatally dangerous, as it can develop into pneumonia. As if I wanted to go out in public much, the way I looked. My Alcoholics Anonymous group in Palenville came to my house to hold meetings for me. There was much talk at these meetings about the Higher Power: I needed to believe, I needed to know there was more to life after death. This was when I first gained the spiritual strand that is still very much a part of me.

I later found out that the local A.A. group was closing their regular meetings with: "Let's say a prayer for Genya." My sober friends were so good to me.

Someone recommended that I should listen to the meditation tapes made by Dr. Bernie Segal. I so desperately wanted to live that I'd anything anyone recommended to me! The tapes were wonderfully calming. Dr. Segal is totally understanding of cancer patients, and has theories that make sense. He talks about the negativity that surrounds most cancer patients, and how to counter it. The tapes helped me tremendously.

The effects of chemotherapy are cumulative. With each new session I felt much worse. After my second round I called Dr. Pisters, and we talked about the third session. I said I wasn't planning to come in for it. I had no real hope in my heart. "I'm getting very sick," I told her. "I've got no feeling left in my fingertips or the soles of my feet. Besides, I know I'm dying, so what's the sense of going on?"

"Gee, Genya," she said, "I'm sorry to hear that. I really believed you could make your reunion."

"'Reunion'? What's that?"

She explained that cancer patients who survived five years had a reunion. What she was saying was that she thought I had at least another five years. This was the most positive thing I'd heard about my lung cancer since that dreadful day when I'd been told I had it. Maybe I could defeat it altogether!

"Please go for that last round of chemo," she continued. "If you can beat alcohol, you can do this, too. You're strong."

I couldn't believe she was comparing beating cancer to beating alcoholism.

Yes, okay. I'd go in for my next round of chemo.

One of the things Bernie Segal's tapes taught me was that I should learn to think of chemotherapy as my ally, not my enemy. I'd been warned that it was dangerous—that it could damage some healthy organs while attacking the tumor—so each time the I.V. tube was put into my port I made myself visualize the chemicals as a kind of miniature SWAT team going through my body. They might break a few things along the way, but they'd get the main job done as efficiently as possible.

I also used the meditative technique known as White Light Imagery. I would lie down and concentrate on imagining a white light coming in through my head and down into my body until it got to the cancer. I found this exercise difficult, but I made myself do it every day anyway.

There were times I so very much wanted to be alone. I grew tired of hearing Dawn's endless talking, and got into arguments with her about it, telling her I didn't want to hear this shit, that she was sicker than I was. I guess I wasn't the easiest person for her to live with.

● ● ● ● ● ●

The day came when I was going to get the big news. Had the chemotherapy worked? Would they go on to the next stage, the operation?

Dr. Burt came into my room with three other doctors. His handsome face—he looks like a marine—broke into a smile.

"Your tumor has shrunk. We can operate!"

I burst into tears of gladness.

As soon as I could I phoned my sister Helen, who was staying in Long Island with her daughter, Cherie. She, too, wept with relief. Her prayers had been answered she told me.

My prayers too.

● ● ● ● ● ●

During one of the examinations I was given preparatory to the operation by Katherine Pisters I asked if I could talk to someone who'd survived the operation. Then I added, shyly, "*Are* there any survivors?" I still wasn't totally convinced I was going to make it.

Yes, she said. Indeed, one of the survivors, Carole Kramer, had been suffering from the exact same form of cancer that I was (non-small cell cancer). Dr. Pisters said she'd ask Carole if she wanted to get in touch with me.

One day during the two weeks I spent in my Palenville house preparing myself mentally for the operation, Carole Kramer phoned me.

"Dr. Pisters and Dr. Houlihan gave me your number," she said, introducing herself. She was so sweet and comforting.

I began asking her all the questions I'd been afraid to ask the doctors.

"How bad will it be after the operation?"

"Genya," she said, "you just went through the worst part. The operation is nothing compared to the chemo."

"Oh, thank God!" I cried. "And thank *you*!"

Now I couldn't wait to have the cancer cut out of me. I wanted to get the operation over with so that I could carry on with a life that I knew had already changed for the better.

The operation was scheduled for January 11, 1991. Preparing for it was a nightmare.

I saw in the New Year with John Cougar Mellencamp. I was sitting in my living room in Palenville with a scarf on my head, watching television. He was performing on a stage somewhere in the Midwest.

As I watched him and his guests, I wondered, *Will I ever be able to sing again?* I missed it so much. I was done with isolating myself. I was going to go back to New York City and this time try to lead my life there the right way. No drugs. No smoking. No drinking.

But first I would take my car and drive down to Florida. I wanted to see my mom. I wanted to hold her in my arms. I needed her. I would recuperate in Florida, where it was warm. No more wood stoves. No more Palenville.

Things like money and material possessions didn't mean anything to me any longer. The search for riches, fame, and glory was over. When you've been told you're going to die, your perspective shifts. Things that were once so important to you, you now recognize as completely trivial and irrelevant. What are important are family, love, and support.

And, above all, breathing.

• • • • • •

January 11, and I'm in New York City preparing to enter a theater once more. Where are the limos? Where are the champagne, the people with love in their eyes for me, the men who want to devour me? Where are the chants of "Genya . . . Genya . . . Genya . . ."?

I'm lying on my back on a hard gurney. Fluorescent lights are whizzing by. I'm very woozy, very stoned—a state I know very well, but this isn't the warm stonedness of Southern Comfort. There's an I.V. pumping something wonderful into my arm. I'm scared, but I don't care that I'm scared.

"Genya, just a few more minutes. You're next."

The nurse says it like I'm the next act up on-stage. I guess in a way I am.

• • • • • •

They let my sister Helen into the holding room to see me before I was wheeled off to the operating theater. She was wearing a mask. She must have begged them to let her in.

I said to her, "Helen, I have to pee but they won't let me off this gurney."

She ran for a nurse. They wouldn't let me up, but they gave me a small pan to pee in. It tipped over and spilled urine all over me. Now I was lying in my own pee. I was freezing.

They wheeled me into the theater, and I was still freezing. I was shaking so much I was nearly jumping out of my skin. Nine or ten doctors were working all round me, getting things ready for my six-hour operation. I told them I was wet, lying in my own urine, and I was cold, and I pleaded with them to give me a cover. They gave me a small heated blanket; they apologized for the fact that they had only one of these. Then they went back to preparing me for the operation.

I saw one of the doctors carrying a big shiny metal device that I realized was the lung spreader. I started screaming.

"Where's Dr. Burt?" I yelled.

"I'm here, Genya," said a calm voice from behind one of the masks.

I closed my eyes. Tears were running down the sides of my face.

They stuck needles into me that were bigger than anything I saw back on Ellis Island. The one they stuck into the side of my neck really hurt.

I was terrified of falling asleep in case I never woke up again—*this might be it*—and at the same time I was begging them to put me under.

And finally they did.

• • • • • •

I woke up in the intensive care unit twelve hours after the operation. I was going to be in there for another twenty-four hours.

My mouth was so dry I could hardly part my lips. I begged a passing nurse in a whisper to give me something to drink. She told me she couldn't do that, but she put something moist and sweet on my lips.

I was afraid to breathe. What had they done to my lung? Had they managed to cut the whole cancer out? Had they cut the whole *lung* out? Where was my doctor?

Too many questions scurrying through my mind. No way to answer them.

• • • • • •

Dr. Burt came into the I.C.U. a few hours later. He smiled that handsome smile of his at me and said, "It was very successful."

He told me the tumor had been small—he used his fingers to show me how small—so that when they'd opened me up on the operating table they hadn't at first been able to see anything. They'd called Dr. Pisters to the operating room and told her the cancer seemed to have gone, but she told them to take out the upper left lobe and part of the lung anyway, just to be on the safe side. It was a good thing they did; they told me later they'd found some little cancer colonies in the material they took out.

I spent the next two weeks in Sloan-Kettering, and my sister came to visit me every day. The nurses taught her how to clean the various tubes that were sticking out of my side; one of them led straight into my lung. She coped with it perfectly. Here I'd thought that Helen was the weak one, yet I don't know if I could have done what she did.

What lingers in my head the most is the time when Helen was sitting by my bedside, stroking my head gently, and she said, "Look at my poor baby sister."

I think it was the first time I'd ever felt like her baby sister. Lying there helpless, I was so vulnerable.

I finally allowed the feelings to start kicking in. My sister was protecting me! I was so sorry I'd put her through all this. I'd never wanted to be a burden on anyone. That had been one of the first things I'd learned as a child: Don't be a burden.

* * * * * *

While I was recuperating from the operation back home in Palenville, Margo called. Margo from the Gingerbreads. As soon as she heard about my cancer, and the operation, she came upstate to see me, bringing Ginger with her. Dawn hadn't even told Ginger about my cancer. They couldn't believe that Dawn had managed to keep something a secret for once.

I was getting stronger by the day. I told Helen to go back home to her family in Florida. I'd be joining her there soon.

* * * * * *

The soles of my feet still tingle today from the chemotherapy. It's a very small price to pay.

CHAPTER SEVENTEEN
Doing It the Right Way

THERE'S NO REAL END to my story as yet, of course, although I've a few times come close to giving it one. But this chapter gives you the end of The Story So Far. For what happens next, what you've gotta do is—you guessed it—Stay Tuned.

* * * * * *

A month after the operation, still weak but mentally stronger, I made the long drive down to Florida—just me and my beloved Yorkshire terrier, Yoyo. Finally I had a chance to think: no one chattering at me the whole time, no one looking at me like they thought I was about to faint at any moment. I'd come off the pain medication far faster then the doctors had anticipated; they kept telling me that I was strong, that it was my attitude that had seen me through.

I drove south on Route 95 for three days. I felt free for the first time in so long. Even though I was driving on standard highway the whole time, I was drinking in the scenery. Just a few months ago I'd been looking at the sky and trees as if I might never see them again.

Now I was looking at them because I appreciated life so much that I wanted to live every experience to the fullest.

When I got to Fort Lauderdale I stayed with Helen and Doc for a while, then found my own place by the beach there. As I walked the beach daily I thanked my Higher Power for sparing me to enjoy the beauty of life.

But deep inside I was still thinking I didn't have long to live. I can remember at one point wanting to buy a coffee table and then thinking, *Why bother? I'm not going to be around that long to enjoy it.* I shared that experience at one of the cancer support meetings I'd started attending, and found that some of the others there were thinking the same way. It was sort of depressing going to those meetings. Some of the people there were indeed destined to die soon.

It wasn't long before I got a job in Florida. A label called Saturn Records asked me to join their A&R Department. I knew this wasn't going to last long. The owner of Saturn was so jive, and the company president might have been better off working in the garment industry. I started to feel guilty that groups were signing up to this crummy little label because they trusted me and my reputation, so I quit. One of the groups I found, Angel of the Odd, was really good; if they'd been with a better label they might have had the success they deserved.

While living in Florida, I visited my mom as often as I could in the home where Helen and I had talked her into living. I still felt guilty about the fact that she was there, no matter how much I told myself there had been no other choice.

※ ※ ※ ※ ※ ※

The stronger I got, both physically and mentally, the more I yearned to return to New York City. But how could I? I had nowhere to live and very little money. The money I got from welfare was hardly anything and, while I was getting a certain amount of income from renting out my house in Palenville, that income was unreliable: most of the tenants were awful, and missed rent or just didn't pay it at all before skipping out in the middle of the night. The house and property were beginning to look run-down. It came to me that what I really needed to do was sell the house. That would bring me a lump of cash, and it'd also be a way of getting rid of all the memories associated with it: my failed marriage to Dennis, my crazy, degrading addictions to booze and drugs, and, of course, my experience with cancer.

Back in the days when I'd been recording *Urban Desire,* I'd become friends with a guy named Steven Knee; he and his partner Joe had a beauty salon. They'd been busted, and I'd been one of a bunch of artists who'd put on a benefit concert at Max's Kansas City to help pay their legal bills. We'd kept in touch over the years, and though we'd never been lovers we were still very close. While in Florida, I'd asked him to keep an eye out for an apartment for me. Now, a few months later, he called to say that I could have his apartment on East Seventy-third Street at a low rent because he was planning to live for a while on his houseboat at the Seventy-ninth Street Boat Basin.

It sounded like a great idea, so I took him up on it. In the middle of 1995 I packed up my belongings and my life in Florida and headed back to New York with Yoyo and a new member of my immediate family, a Siamese cat called Clawdius; Clawdius mewed for nine hours a day on the drive home, and Yoyo and I got tired of it!

I lived in Steven's apartment for four months. The arrangement wasn't ideal, because Steven came and went any time he wanted to; I was both fond of him and grateful to him, but I needed my privacy. I looked around for an apartment I could afford, and eventually I found one on West Thirty-first Street. It was small but it was mine.

● ● ● ● ● ●

Around this time I started to do a little producing again. Among the groups I produced was one called Betty Ford that I thought was pretty good. I enjoyed working with them, and liked the writing of their lead singer, a girl named Elin Hunter. Her songs were punky and musical. I also produced six songs for a girl singer Steven recommended to me, named Blue. A pop-punk group called Bring Back Joel got in touch with me by e-mail from the Midwest and asked if I'd like to produce them. I said yes, but only if they came to New York. To my surprise, they did. It was a very interesting group, and I liked them as people. Back in the 1980s I'd produced both Avis Davis and Joy Ryder, who were very popular in Germany. Avis created Fifties-style R&B rock; Joy sang like a white, pint-sized James Brown. Now Avis was living in the States (as in fact was Joy). He tracked me down and asked me to do some production with him, so we went into the studio and recorded four songs. Avis was into sort of "bad boy biker" pop—his music sounded as if it came from the 1960s. He even looked a bit like a dark-haired James Dean.

But I took things slow getting back into production work—I had to. I had to keep my stress levels low; if it looked as if things were about to become stressful, I stopped. I also made it clear to each of these artists at the outset that I wouldn't get involved in securing record deals for them; I was merely their producer. Until I was sure they understood this, we went no farther.

Hilly Kristal and I had always stayed in touch, and after getting back to New York I stopped by CBGBs a few times. Around that time he announced that he was going to start his own production company; he had two young guys ready to back him and get distribution for the label.

One night in 1999 he called me and told me I had to come to the club. He wanted me to listen to an all-woman punk band called the Wives. I did, and fell in love with their music immediately. They were sensational—a trio with the biggest sound I'd heard in a long time. Hilly has always been right on the button when he thinks he's spotted something special, and he was right again.

I went into rehearsal with the Wives and started picking out the songs we'd record, rearranging some of them. I wanted to make their sound just polished enough without making it overproduced or even over-rehearsed. As I've said before, in production you always have to know where to stop, so that the freshness isn't lost. While visiting upstate I'd found a studio in Woodstock that offered a sweet deal; we were able to rent it by the day, and the fees were low enough that we didn't have to worry too much about time. It was the ideal situation: it would be good to be out of town, so we could concentrate without worrying about interruption in the form of the girls getting phone calls or visitors. Producing the Wives was fun, and I'm pleased with the album, *Ripped*, we made for CBGB Records.

Hilly had booked another all-woman band at CBGBs a few times. Called Linda Potatoes, they hailed from Germany. I hadn't been too impressed by them, but Hilly wanted me to produce them anyway. He knew I was professional enough to make a good recording even if I wasn't into the music. (I liked these musicians as people, though; in fact, I'm still in touch with bassist Meike Shy.)

Not long after finishing production with the Wives, I was off to Germany—to Bremen, to be precise—to produce Linda Potatoes. They were very easy to work with; because they wanted so much to be good musically, they worked very hard. The language barrier sometimes made things difficult in the studio. The engineer barely understood any

English at all, so it was sometimes a bit of a struggle with him. We had problems with some of the lyrics as well because, however good they might have been in German, some of the translations into English made no sense at all.

And there was one other, totally unforeseen difficulty. Hans, the owner of the recording studio, used to bring his big dog, Roderick, with him. Roderick would meander into the control room, where the engineer and I sat. There, at least twice a day, Roderick would let out a most indescribably poisonous fart. The room would stink for at least half an hour afterwards. The girls in Linda Potatoes, unaware of what was going on, would look through the glass and see me and the engineer making the most awful faces at each other . . . and they'd assume this was an expression of what we thought of their performance! Finally I told them what was going on, and, after we'd laughed about it, I asked them please to tell the owner in German that, while we really appreciated his studio rates, we'd be grateful if he could keep his dog elsewhere while we were working.

Back in New York City afterwards, I started to do radio promotion for a few acts. I found I was very effective at getting them radio play, especially on college radio stations.

I also kept on producing for Hilly's CBGB Records. One of the groups was, alongside the Dead Boys, probably my favorite of all the acts I've produced: Dripping Goss. It was led by two brothers, Brian and Tommy Goss. Brian, whom I'd known when he was a kid in Palenville, is probably one of the most talented songwriters I've met in the last decade. The record I produced for them, *Blue Collar, Black Future*, is a concept album. We did it in less than a week.

One of the things that's little known about me as a record producer is that I'm kind of like the Alfred Hitchcock of the music industry! I've appeared in some sort of "cameo role" on every record I've produced . . . somewhere.

The two investors who'd been involved in the launching of CBGB Records eventually backed out, leaving Hilly to shoulder the whole financial burden. I knew this was very difficult for him. I was working for him on a fairly generous salary; without that responsibility, his life would be a bit easier. I told him I needed to leave the company because—and this was true—I was finding the constant production work tiring. CBGB Records was a great label while it lasted.

● ● ● ● ● ●

As the years turned by, various things began receding into the past: the operation, for example, and the addictions I'd had for cocaine and booze. There were other habits I got out of, in particular the habit of trying always to run away from my feelings—the habit that had led me to drown myself in drink and drugs in the first place. I began to realize that far more important than all the bad things I'd done in my life were all the really great things I'd done. In about 1996 or 1997 I was able for the first time in years to pull out all my old photos and review clippings and take a good look at them—and be *proud* of them.

Were there still people around who might remember me and my achievements in music? Yes, there probably were. So in 1997 I decided to set up my own Web site, www.genyaravan.com. My dear friend Steven Knee did all the design and technical stuff for me.

Much to my surprise—I'm not kidding about the surprise!—the Web site got a terrific response. I received a ton of e-mail from fans telling me how much they loved my music, asking me where they could buy CDs of *Urban Desire* and *. . . And I Mean It!* to replace their old vinyl copies, and inquiring about whether I had anything new coming out. I had to tell them there were no plans to reissue *Urban Desire* and *. . . And I Mean It!* on CD (there still aren't, alas), but the idea of releasing something new gnawed at the back of my mind.

The idea germinated for a long time before finally, in 2001, it blossomed. I decided to create a new CD called *For Fans Only*, containing material drawn from just about every stage of my career—unreleased songs and out-takes from as early as 1970 all the way through to a couple of new ones: a cover of Trade Martin's "Take Me for a Little While" and a Joe Droukas original, "Reconsider," which I made Joe sing as a duet with me. I had no money for studio time, engineers, or musicians for these two tracks, but my old buddy Bobby Chen—who'd drummed for me way back—stepped in: he got me the studio time and an amazing band, and they all gave their services for nothing. Their kindness blew me away—so much for feeling unloved!

Most of the older tapes had just been moldering away in my attic. Lucy and Owen Swenson played a major part in my bringing them into the light of day, with Owen listening alongside me to hours of tapes, and me and Lucy doing the CD's cover artwork; the album was compiled in their studio, The Turning Mill Studios, Palenville, New York State. Their daughter, Valen, helped me add background vocals to a 1982 recording I'd made of "Fly Me to the Moon." There's a duet I recorded with Long John Baldry in 1978 of "Something's Got a Hold on Me" with Thunder Thighs doing the background vocals. Two of the tracks—"Rattle Snake Shake" and "Two Steps from the Blues"—are rehearsal versions that I like because they have a really great feel to them. And so on. It's a CD full of good memories for me.

• • • • • •

But not every memory has receded: some will stay with me forever. One of those dates from June 1995. Ever since the start of the cancer episode I'd needed to take pills at nights to make me lethargic enough to get off to sleep. At three a.m. one night late in that month I was in a heavy sleep when the phone rang.

It was Helen. She was in tears. "Mom's died."

I answered: "Okay, talk to you tomorrow."

Helen thought I must have gone into shock. In fact, my reaction was partly denial but mainly the influence of the sleeping medication. I went straight back to sleep, and dreamed that the phone had rung and it had been Helen, sobbing, and she'd told me that . . .

When I woke up, I still thought the call had been a dream. And then I slowly realized it hadn't been.

No! It can't be true! Mom hasn't died! She can't *have!*

But it was true.

I could barely get myself out of bed. I just lay there, crying my eyes out. I hadn't known there could be so many tears in a single body. When I finally climbed out of bed I just walked around in circles for an hour.

Helen and Doc phoned again, asking me if I was all right, worried about the way I'd reacted. Still crying hysterically, I explained to them about the medication.

I had to go to Florida. Helen and Doc arranged the airline ticket while I sorted out where Yoyo and Clawdius could be looked after in my absence.

A car service picked me up to take me to the airport. I cried in the car, I cried in the airport, I cried on the plane—I just couldn't stop. I'd lost the woman who'd pushed me into the world at the worst possible time of her life. She'd also been the one to push me onto the stage back in the days of Mr. Levinsky's musicals, and had given me the guts to become somebody even if I hadn't thought I was anybody. She'd been my biggest fan, the one who'd saved all my press clippings, the one who'd put an enormous star on my bedroom door.

Mom had died because, basically, the home Helen and I had put her in didn't keep a watch over her. Gangrene had spread throughout her body, and they'd done nothing about it. By the time they'd called my sister, Mom had been taken to Emergency. She died in the emergency room that night, June 27. How strange that my two parents had survived the horrors of the Nazi death camps only to be killed by the carelessness of the people who were supposed to be looking after them.

I remembered the single roller skate that Mom had given me so that I'd not fall over and hurt myself.

I suddenly forgave her for everything.

Epilogue

I've shared the stage with many great performers, and for that I'll always be grateful. But when I was on the road, I was too drunk on my own perfume to take the time to keep friendships going. I was always too busy to stay in touch. I didn't have time for a family.

It's different now. I cherish my friends and family, and I cherish them dearly. All good relationships require work, communication, commitment. I enjoy being a friend. I will always remember the time when I was alone and friendless because I'd made it that way.

Today, I live life on life's terms. I've been given my life back several times–the life I'd lost to alcohol, to drugs, to cancer. I've joined a race of people I never knew existed: the people who can live through the very highs and the very lows and still feel safe and secure in the knowledge that they're loved and can love in return. I can do that too, now. I've been given the chance to live my life all over again, but this time the right way.

When I go to the Memorial Sloan-Kettering Cancer Center for my six-monthly checkups, I see Dr. Kris looking at me with pride and happiness. He introduces me to all the younger doctors as if I were his own creation. In a way, each six months, I am.

I've taken neither alcohol nor drugs since August 11, 1990. I've been clear of cancer for fourteen years now.

I sing without medications of any kind.
I love without medications of any kind.
I'm Genya Ravan.

EPILOGUE

Genya—very live.

Discography and Production Credits

DISCOGRAPHY

SINGLES

1962

"Somewhere" (Leonard Bernstein) / "Submarine Race Watching" (Zelkowitz/Perry/Berg/Rosenberg). The Escorts with Goldie.

1963

"One Hand, One Heart" (Leonard Bernstein) / (Bobby Lance/Fran Robbins). The Escorts with Goldie.

"Something Has Changed Him" (Bobby Lance/Fran Robins) / "Back Home Again" (Willie Headen). The Escorts with Goldie.

1964

"Skinny Vinnie" (Goldie/Stan Green) / "Chew Chew Fee Fi Fum" (Bobby Lance/Fran Robbins). Goldie and the Gingerbreads.

1965

"That's Why I Love You" (Jones) / "What Kind of Man Are You" (Ray Charles). Goldie and the Gingerbreads.

"Can't You Hear My Heart Beat" (Carter/Lewis) / "Little Boy" (Stillman/Wood) (U.K.) Goldie and the Gingerbreads.

"That's Why I Love You" (Jones) / "The Skip" (Margo Crocitto) (U.K.) Goldie and the Gingerbreads.

1966

"I Do" (Peden/Smith/Peden/Stephenson/Mason) / "Think About the Good Times" (Roe/Jarvis). Goldie and the Gingerbreads.

"Think About the Good Times" (Roe/Jarvis) / "Please Please" (C. MacDonald). Goldie and the Gingerbreads.

"Sailor Boy" (Goffin/Titelman) / "Please Please" (C. MacDonald) (U.K.) Goldie and the Gingerbreads.

"Going Back" (Goffin/King) / "Headlines" (Andrew Loog Oldham). Goldie and the Gingerbreads.

"Disappointed Bride" (Trad.) / "Disappointed Bride" (instrumental). Patsy Cole.

1967

"Walking in Different Circles" (Scott English/Larry Weiss) / "Song of the Moon" (Lenny Stogel/Alan Lorber). Goldie and the Gingerbreads.

1969

"Tightrope" (Genya Ravan/Leon Rix) / "Lapidary" (Aram Schefrin/Mike Zager). Ten Wheel Drive with Genya Ravan.

"Eye of the Needle" (Aram Schefrin/Mike Zager) / "I Am a Want Ad" (Aram Schefrin/Mike Zager). Ten Wheel Drive with Genya Ravan.

1970

"Morning Much Better" (Aram Schefrin/Mike Zager) / "Stay With Me" (Ragovoy/Weiss). Ten Wheel Drive with Genya Ravan.

1971

"Down in the Cold" (Genya Ravan/Aram Schefrin/Mike Zager) / "Last of the Line" (Aram Schefrin/Mike Zager). Ten Wheel Drive with Genya Ravan.

1972

"Mammy Blue" (H. Giraud/P. Trim) / "Groove Me" (Genya Ravan). Genya Ravan.

"Sit Yourself Down" (Stephen Stills) / "I Can't Stand It" (S. MacAllister). Genya Ravan.

"Morning Glory" (Michael Holmes) / "What Kind of Man" (Ray Charles). Genya Ravan.

DISCOGRAPHY AND PRODUCTION CREDITS

1973

"Keep on Growing" (Eric Clapton/Bobby Whitlock) / "Under Control" (Jim Price). Genya Ravan.

1975

"Feel the Need in Me" (A. Tilman) / "Feel the Need in Me" (disco mix). Genya Ravan.

1978

"Back in My Arms Again" (Holland/Dozier/Holland) / "Do It Just for Me" (Wally Liberty). Genya Ravan.

"Jerry's Pigeons" (Genya Ravan/Charlie Giordano/Joey Ribaudo) / "Cornered" (Stuart Daye). Genya Ravan.

1979

"Junkman" (Joe Droukas) / "Love Isn't Love" (Genya Ravan). Genya Ravan.

"Steve . . ." (Genya Ravan/Conrad Taylor) / "It's Me" (Genya Ravan/Lars Hanson). Genya Ravan.

ALBUMS

1969

Construction #1, Ten Wheel Drive with Genya Ravan, Polydor. Produced by Walter Raim.

Credits:
Genya Ravan: vocals, harmonica, tambourine
Aram Schefrin: guitar, percussion
Mike Zager: organ, piano, clarinet
Bill Takas: bass
Leon Rix: drums, cello, percussion
Louis Hoff: flute, tenor sax, baritone sax
Dennis Parisi: trombone
Jay Silva: flute, trumpet, flugelhorn
Richard Meisterman: trumpet, flugelhorn
Peter Hyde: piccolo, trumpet, flugelhorn

Tracks:
Tightrope (Genya Ravan/Leon Rix)
Lapidary (Aram Schefrin/Mike Zager)
Eye of the Needle (Aram Schefrin/Mike Zager)
Candy Man Blues (Louie Hoff/Elizabeth Hoff)
Ain't Gonna Happen (Aram Schefrin/Mike Zager)
Polar Bear Rug (Aram Schefrin/Mike Zager)
House in Central Park (Aram Schefrin/Mike Zager)
I Am a Want Ad (Aram Schefrin/Mike Zager)

1970

Brief Replies, Ten Wheel Drive with Genya Ravan, Polydor. Produced by Guy Draper.

DISCOGRAPHY AND PRODUCTION CREDITS

Credits:
Genya Ravan: vocals, harmonica, percussion
Aram Schefrin: guitar, percussion, vocals, banjo
Mike Zager: keyboards
Allen Herman: drums, percussion, vibes
Bob Piazza: bass
Steve Satten: trumpet, flugelhorn
John Gatchell: trumpet, flugelhorn
Dave Leibman: soprano sax, tenor sax, baritone sax, flute
John Eckert: trumpet, flugelhorn
Dennis Parisi: trombone

Tracks:
Pulse (Genya Ravan/Mike Zager)
Come Live With Me (Genya Ravan/Aram Schefrin)
Morning Much Better (Aram Schefrin/Mike Zager)
Brief Replies (Aram Schefrin/Mike Zager)
Stay With Me (Ragovoy/Weiss)
How Long Before I'm Gone (Aram Schefrin/Mike Zager)
Last of the Line (Aram Schefrin/Mike Zager)
Interlude: A View of Soft (Aram Schefrin/Mike Zager)

1971

Peculiar Friends, Ten Wheel Drive with Genya Ravan, Polydor. Produced by Aram Schefrin and Michael Zager.

Credits:
Genya Ravan: vocals, harmonica
Michael Zager: keyboards
Aram Schefrin: guitar
Blake Hines: bass
David Williams: drums

Alan Gauvin: reeds
Dean Pratt: trumpet
Tom Malone: trombone
Danny Stiles: trumpet
Frank Frint: trumpet

Tracks:
Peculiar Friends (Aram Schefrin/Mike Zager)
The Night I Got Out of Jail (Aram Schefrin/Mike Zager)
Shootin' the Breeze (Aram Schefrin/Mike Zager)
The Pickpocket (Genya Ravan/Aram Schefrin/Mike Zager)
No Next Time (Aram Schefrin/Mike Zager)
Love Me (Aram Schefrin/Mike Zager)
Fourteenth Street (I Can't Get Together) (Aram Schefrin/Mike Zager)
I Had Him Down (Aram Schefrin/Mike Zager)
Down in the Cold (Genya Ravan/Aram Schefrin/Mike Zager)

1972

Genya Ravan, Genya Ravan, Columbia. Produced by Aram Schefrin and Michael Zager, coproduced by Larry Fallorn.

Credits:
Genya Ravan: vocals, harmonica, percussion
Peter Hodgson: bass
Brian Keenan: drums
Nick Oliva: keyboards
John Platania: guitar
Mitch Styles: guitar
Bernard Williams: percussion, conductor
Arnie Lawrence: saxophone
James Moody: saxophone
Michael Olatunji: African drums

Larry Fallorn: string arrangements

Tracks:
What Kind of Man Are You (Ray Charles)
Sit Yourself Down (Stephen Stills)
I Hate Myself (for Loving You) (Doc Pomus/K. Hirsch)
I'm in the Mood for Love (J. McHugh/D. Fields)
Takuta Kalaba/Love Lights (Michael Olatunji/D. Malone/J. Scott)
Lonely, Lonely (Aram Schefrin/Michael Zager)
Flying (Rod Stewart/Ronnie Lane/Ron Wood)
Every Little Bit Hurts (E. Cobb)
Bird on a Wire (Leonard Cohen)
I Can't Stand It (S. MacAllister)

1973

They Love Me, They Love Me Not, Genya Ravan, ABC Dunhill Records, Jimmy Miller Productions. Produced by Jim Price and Joe Zagarino.

Credits:
Genya Ravan: vocals
Jim Price: keyboards, bass
Jay Graydon: acoustic guitar, electric guitar
John Uribe: electric guitar
Dave Farrell: bass
Don Poncher: drums, percussion
Ray Cooper: percussion
Jim Horn: alto sax, baritone sax, flute
Bobby Keys: tenor sax

Tracks:
Gotta Tell Somebody (Van McCoy)

Don't Press Me (Genya Ravan/Jim Price)
Missy (Mister) (Gary Rowles)
I'll Be With You (Genya Ravan/Jim Price)
That Cryin' Rain (Jim Price/Carol Price)
Keep on Growing (Eric Clapton/Bobby Whitlock)
Swan Blues (King Pleasure/Richard Carpenter)
Roll Roll Roll (Jim Price)
Southern Celebration (Paul Goldsmith)
Under Control (Jim Price)
When You Got Trouble (Pat Vagas/Lolly Vagas)

1974

Goldie Zelkowitz, Genya Ravan, Janus Records, GRT Corporation. Produced by Gabriel Mekler and Trevor Lawrence.

Credits:
Genya Ravan: vocals, harmonica
Kenneth Spider Rice: drums
Fred Beckmier: bass
Ken Marco: guitar
Daniel (Kootch) Kortchmar: guitar
Steve Beckmier: guitar
Larry Nash: piano, clarinet
Gabriel Mekler: piano, clarinet, Moog
Trevor Lawrence: piano, clarinet, Moog, horns
Maito Correa: percussion
Steve Madaio: horns
Bobby Keyes: horns

Tracks:
My Oh My My Mama (C.C. Williamson/Trevor Lawrence/Gabriel

Mekler)
Whipping Post (Greg Allman)
Get It Back (Trevor Lawrence/Gabriel Mekler/Genya Ravan)
Hold On, I'm Coming (Isaac Hayes/David Porter)
Little by Little (Gabriel Mekler/Trevor Lawrence/Genya Ravan)
Letter (C.C. Williamson/Trevor Lawrence/Gabriel Mekler)
Breadline (C.C. Williamson/Trevor Lawrence/Gabriel Mekler)
Walkin' Walkin' (C.C. Williamson/Trevor Lawrence/Gabriel Mekler/Genya Ravan)
Need Your Lovin'/Peeping & Hiding (B. Robinson/C. Lewis/D. Gardner/J. McDougal)

1978

Urban Desire, Genya Ravan, 20th Century-Fox Records. Produced by Genya Ravan Productions.

Credits:
Genya Ravan: lead vocals, background vocals, percussion, harmonica
Charlie Giordano: keyboards
Conrad Taylor: electric rhythm, electric lead and acoustic rhythm guitars
Ritchie Fliegler: rhythm, lead, acoustic, slide and mandolin guitars
Don Nosov: bass
John Paul Fetta: bass
Bobby Chen: drums and percussion
Lou Reed: duet vocals ("Aye Colorado")
Joey Cola' Ribaudo: background vocals
Ivan Kral: background vocals
David Lasley: background vocals

Tracks:
Jerry's Pigeons (Genya Ravan/Charlie Giordano/Joey Ribaudo)
The Knight Ain't Long Enough (Joe Droukas)
Do It Just for Me (Wally Liberty)
Shot in the Heart (Stuart Daye)
Aye Colorado (Genya Ravan/Charlie Giordano)
Back in My Arms Again (Holland/Dozier/Holland)
Cornered (Stuart Daye)
The Sweetest One (Joe Droukas)
Darling, I Need You (John Cale)
Messin' Around (Genya Ravan/Conrad Taylor/Paul Opalach)
Shadowboxing (Joe Droukas)

1979

. . . And I Mean It!, Genya Ravan, 20th Century-Fox Records. Produced by Genya Ravan Productions.

Credits:
Genya Ravan: lead vocals, percussion, harmonica, all background vocals
Charlie Giordano: keyboards
Conrad Taylor: electric, acoustic, rhythm and lead guitars
Lars Hanson: electric, acoustic, rhythm and lead guitars, mandolin
Bobby Chen: drums, syndrums
Mike Lombardi: bass
Ian Hunter: duet vocals ("Junkman")
Mick Ronson: guitar solo ("Junkman")

Tracks:
Pedal to the Metal (Genya Ravan/Godfrey Diamond)
I Won't Sleep on the Wet Spot No More (Genya Ravan)
Steve . . . (Genya Ravan/Conrad Taylor)

Stubborn Kinda Girl (Fella) (Gaye/Stevenson/Gordy Jr.)
It's Me (Genya Ravan/Lars Hanson)
Junkman (Joe Droukas)
Love Isn't Love (Genya Ravan)
I'm Wired Wired Wired (Genya Ravan/Conrad Taylor)
Roto Root Her (Genya Ravan/Conrad Taylor)
Night Owl (Tony Allen)

1995

Best of Ten Wheel Drive, Polygram.
(Credits: same as those listed above for individual albums)

Tracks:
Tightrope
Lapidary
Eye of the Needle
Candy Man Blues
Ain't Gonna Happen
House in Central Park
Morning Much Better
Brief Replies
Come Live With Me
Stay With Me
How Long Before I'm Gone
Last of the Line
The Night I Got Out of Jail
Shootin' The Breeze
Love Me
I Had Him Down

2003

For Fans Only!, Genya Ravan, Privately Released.

Genya Ravan: vocals on all tracks

Tracks:
"Fly Me to the Moon" (Bart Howard), 1982. DT: piano; Steve Horton: sax.

"202 Rivington Street" (Genya Ravan). Recorded live at the Bottom Line, 1981.

"Don't Let Me Down" (John Lennon/Paul McCartney), 1989. Uptown Horns: horns; Mike Thorne: everything else.

"Rattle Snake Shake" (Peter Green), 1979. Charlie Giordano: piano; Bobby Chen: drums; Conrad Taylor: guitar.

"To Keep You Satisfied" (Marvin Gaye), 1978.

"Anyway That You Want Me" (Chip Taylor), 1978.

"Something's Got A Hold On Me" (James Cleveland/Etta James/Pearl Woods), 1978. Long John Baldry: duet vocals; Thunder Thighs: background vocals.

"Two Steps From The Blues" (James Brown/Deadric Malon), 1978. Charlie Giordano: piano.

"Easy Evil" (Alan O'Day), 1978. Charlie Giordano: piano.

"Night Flight" (Genya Ravan), 1981. Denice & Genya: background vocals; Connie Taylor: guitars; Walter Libero: bass; Owen Swenson: violins (overdubbed 2001).

"Carry Me Carrie" (Shel Silverstein), 1978. Martin Luther King Choir: chorus; Charlie Giordano: piano; Bobby Chen: drums; Conrad Taylor: guitar; Richard Fliegler: guitar; Paul Opalach: bass.

"Reconsider" (Joe Droukas/Peter Salomon), 2001. Engineered and mixed by Jerry Plotkin and Al Varner; Dennis Dibrizzi: piano; Jamie Bannon: guitar; Peter Scance: bass; Bobby Chen: drums; Jerry Plotkin: organ; Joe Droukas: duet vocals.

"Take Me for a Little While" (Trade Martin), 2001. Engineered and mixed by Jerry Plotkin and Al Varner; Dennis Dibrizzi: piano; Jamie Bannon: guitar; Peter Scance: bass; Bobby Chen: drums; Jerry Plotkin: organ.

PRODUCTION CREDITS

1974: Linda Bennett, singles, independent recording.
1975: Cryer and Ford, *Cryer and Ford*, RCA Records.
1976: Rosie, *Better Late Than Never*, RCA.
1978: Genya Ravan, *Urban Desire*, 20th Century-Fox Records.
1978: Dead Boys, *Young, Loud and Snotty*, Sire Records.
1978: The Cryers, *The Cryers*, Mercury.
1979: Genya Ravan, *... And I Mean It!*, 20th Century-Fox Records.
1980: Miamis, singles, independent recordings.
1981: El Futuro, *Rikers Island*, Polish Records.
1981: Mr. Lucky, *Do You Feel Lucky?*, Polish Records.
1981: Metromen, *Metromen*, Polish Records.
1981: Manster, *In the Basement*, Polish Records.
1982: Ronnie Spector, *Siren*, Polish Records.
1982: Tiny Tim, "They're Coming to Take Me Away, Ha-Haaa!," independent recording.
1983: Joy Rider, *Real to Reel*, Polygram (Germany).
1984: The Shirts, *The Shirts*, CBGB Records.
1985: Sylvia Bullet, *Sylvia Bullet*, J&A Productions.

1985: Lizzy Borden and the Axes, *Never Found Guilty*, independent recording.

1986: Tom Elias, singles, J&A Productions.

1987: Crumbsuckers, *Beast on my Back*, (re-mix), Combat.

1994: Bring Back Joel, independent recording.

1993: Last Crack, *Sinister Funkhouse*, Roadrunner Records.

1995: CeLange, *New Day Comin'*, 11th Street Records.

1996: Avis Davis, independent recording.

1997: The Wives, *The Wives*, CBGB Records.

1998: Susan Blue, *Studio One*, independent recording.

1998: Dripping Goss, *Blue Collar, Black Future*, CBGB Records.

1998: Certain General, *Signals from the Source*, CBGB Records.

INDEX

Note: Page numbers in italics indicate photographs

A

ABC Dunhill Records, 173, 174, 177

Ace Trucking Company, 142

Aerosmith, 158

Ali, Muhammad, 163

Allman, Gregg, 155

Allman Brothers, 155

And I Mean It!, 215, 224–226, 229, 241, 273

Angel of the Odd, 269

Animals, 93, 94, 96–97, 98, 109, 111, 112

Annie Golden and the Shirts, 198

Ascher, Ken, 193

Atlanta Pop Festival, 149–150

Atlantic Records, 63

Avory, Mike, 113

"Aye, Co'Lorado," 214

B

Babbitt, Bob, 188, 193

"Baby Baby Where Did Our Love Go?", 90

Baccus, Barbara, 160, 161, 162, 163, 164, 166, 167, 184

"Back Home Again," 45

"Back in My Arms Again," *213*, 219

Bailey, David, 90

Baldry, Long John, *117*, 274

Barber, Adrian, 84–87

Barcelona, Frank, 99

Batman, 220

Bators, Stiv, 201–202, 203, 204, 207

Beast, 220–221, 223

Beck, Jeff, 95, 105, *106*, 106

"Beck's Bolero," 95

Bell, Madeline, 102, 119

"Be My Baby," 233, 234

Be My Baby (R. Spector), 235, 236

Benatar, Pat, 220

Bendel, Marsha, 52–53, 56

Bergamo, John, 183

Berlin, Cy and Eileen, 239, 240

Berniker, Mike, 192, 194–195

Bernstein, Sid, 138–139, 142, 159, 192

Better Late Than Never, 195

Betts, Dickey, 155

Betty Ford, 270

Bishop, Joey, 167

Bitter End, 139, 141, 147

"Black Sheep Boy," 141

Blackwell, Chris, 119–120

Blitz, Johnny, 203, 205

Blondie, 248

Blood, Sweat and Tears, 132, 139, 150

Blue, 270

Blue Collar, Black Future, 272

293

Bowie, David, 153, 210, 224

Brando, Marlon, 153

"Breadline," 178

Brecker Brothers, 130, 137–138

Bregman, Martin, 210

"Brief Replies," 147, 157–158

Brief Replies, 154

Briggs, Lillian, 38–39

Bring Back Joel, 270

Brubeck, Dan, 250, 251

Burdon, Eric, 93, 94, 97, 99, *121*

Burt, Michael, 260, 264, 266, 267

C

Canned Heat, 150

"Can't You Hear My Heart Beat?", 98–99, 108–109, 112

Carnegie Hall concert, 152–153

"Carry Me Carrie," 37

Carson, Johnny, 164–166, *165*, 167

CBGB Records, 271, 272

CBGBs, 197, 201–203, 204, 271

CBS Records, 160–162, 166–167, 168, 173

Central Park concert, 151–152

Chambers Brothers, 146, 155

Chandler, Chas, 99

Chantels, 17, 38

Charles, Ray, 71, 99, 105–106, 110, 130

Checker, Chubby, 63, *64*, 66

Chen, Bobby, 210, 212, 220, 224, 273

Cher, 162, 172

Chess Janus, 177, 178

Chrome, Cheetah, *203*, 204, 207, 230, 235

Clapton, Eric, 122, 176–177

Clarke, Alan, 109

Clayton-Thomas, David, 150

Clearmountain, Bob, 188, 205, 206–207

Cliff, Jimmy, 161

Clive: Inside the Record Business (Davis), 167

Colby, Paul, 138

Coleman, Bess, 119, 120

Coleman, Ornette, 164

"Come and Get Your Love," 175

Construction #1, 141, 157

Cook, Peter, 98

Cooper, Harvey, 212, *218*, 219, 224, 225, 226

Coral Records, 42, 46

Cracker Club, The, 191

Creedence Clearwater Revival, 150

Crewe, Bob, 122

Cryer, Gretchen, 192–194

Cryer & Ford, 192–194

INDEX

D

Davies, Dave, 113

Davies, Ray, 113, 114

Davis, Avis, 270

Davis, Clive, 160–161, 162, 166–167, 168, 173, 219

Davis, Miles, 139, 148

Davis, Spencer, 119

Dead Boys, 201–204, *202*, 205–207, 235

Decca Records, 45, 119

Dee, Joey, 84, 86

Delaney & Bonnie, 176

Delet, Jerry, 210, *218*, 226

DeMerle, Les, 129–131, 137

Dennis (husband), 252–253, 258, 259, 260

Derek and the Dominos, 177

Diablos, 17

Diamond, Godfrey, 188

"Disappointed Bride," 119–120

Dixon, Luther (Barney Williams), 61–62

Draper, Guy, 157

Dr. Hook and the Medicine Show, 37

Drifters, The, 38

Dripping Goss, 272

Droukas, Joe, 209, 224, 273

Duke, George, 183

Dunbar, Aynsley, 183

E

Eagles, 240

Electric Circus, 146

Electric Lady Studios, 205

El Futuro, 230, 238, 242

Elliott, Robert, 109

Ellison, Lorraine, 157

Ertegun, Ahmet, 63, 89

Escorts, The, 40–42, *44*, 45, *46*, 46, 47, 48, 51

E Street Band, 236

Evans, Robert, 216

"Everyone Knows You Were Caught with the Meat in Your Mouth," 202

"Eye of the Needle," 141, 146–147

F

Faithfull, Marianne, 112

Fallon, Larry, 161

Fame, Georgie, 119

Farlowe, Chris, 147, 148

Fats Domino, 38

Fenton, John, 116–118, 120–121, 167

Fields, Billy, 133–135, 136, 138, 159

Fillmore East, 142–145

"First Time I Met the Blues, The," 106

Fitzpatrick, Robert, 168–169, 177

Fliegler, Richie, 212, 214

"Flying," 162

"Fly Me to the Moon," 274

Foley, Ellen, 224

Ford, Nancy, 192–194

For Fans Only, 273–274

Foster, Frank, 130

Four Seasons, The, 61

Francis, Andy, 230

Francis, Connie, 41

G

Gadd, Steve, 162

Gash, Gyda, 230

Gatchell, John, 186–187

Gaye, Marvin, 45, 46–47

Genya Ravan, 161–162

Giordano, Charlie, 210, *211*, 212, 220

Glancy, Ken, 192, 194

Glazer, Joe, 80

"God Only Knows, He's Gone," 17

"Going Back," 121–122

Goldberg, Harvey, 188–189, 191, 195, 225

Golden, Annie, 198–199

Goldie and the Gingerbreads, *69*, *88*

  at Air Force bases, 70–71

  break-up of, 115, 116

    British tour, 95–99, 102–109, *103, 104, 106, 107*, 111–114
  in car accident, 76–77

  costumes, 89, 104–105

  formation of, 49, 52–63, *53*

  German tours, 63–67, 99–102

  junkie groupies, 84–89

  male reactions to all-female band, 74–75

  mob connection, 77–81, 84

  at Mods and Rockers Ball, 89–91

  new members, 68, 70, 71–74

  in Paris, 109–110

  pregnancy, 81–84

  reunion of, 122–129, *123*

  talk of New York City, 89

  at Wagon Wheel, 85, 92–94

"Goldie and the Gingerbreads, Yeah," 94

Goldie Zelkowitz, 181, 183

Goss, Brian and Tommy, 272

Grand Funk Railroad, 150

Greenberg, Florence, 61, 62

Greenberg, Stanley, 61

Greif, George, 172–174, 175, 176

Guy, Buddy, 105–106

H

Handman, Wynn, 167

"Hang on to a Dream," 141

Hanson, Lars, *211*, 220, 239–240

Hardin, Tim, 141–142

Harrison, George, 98

Harry, Debbie, 248

Havens, Richie, 142

Headliner Lounge, 79, 80, 81–83

"Headlines," 122

Hearts, The, 41, 119

Hektoen, Mike, 208–209, 210, 212, *218*, 219, 225, 226

Heller, Trudy, 48, 56–57

Hendrix, Jimi, 123, 146, 205

"Here Today, Gone Tomorrow," 235

Herman's Hermits, 95, 96, 98–99

"Hey Joe," 123

Highsmith, Luther (Uncle Louie), 23–24, 28–29

"Hi-Ho Silver Lining," 95

Hoff, Louis, 138

"Hold On, I'm Comin'," 94

Hollies, 108, 109

Holzer, Baby Jane, 89–90, 91

Horowitz, Tom, 18

"House in Central Park," 151–152

"House of the Rising Sun, The," 93

Hunter, Elin, 270

Hunter, Ian, 224–225

I

Ian, Janis, 142
"I Can't Stand It," 93

"If I Were a Carpenter," 141

India, Jack, 22–23, 26

Island Records, 119, 120

Isley Brothers, 54

Ivil, Annie, 94, 98

"I Want You to Be My Baby," 38–39

J

Jacobs, Karen DeLayne, 215–216

Jagger, Mick, 106–108, *107*, 111–112, 113–114, 121

Jamerson, James, 188

James, Brian, 207

James, Etta, 23, 178–179

Jeffries, Mike, 93–95, 96, 97, 98–99, 101, 102, 104

Jerome, Henry, 45

Jimmy James and the Vagabonds, 118

Jimmy Miller Productions, 173–177

Jobete Music Publishing, 194

Joel, Billy, 236

Jones, Brian, 107, 108

Jones, Paul, 112, 118

Jones, Thad, 120–130

Joplin, Janis, 139, 147–148, 150–151, 155, 166, 173, 223

"Junkman," 224

K

Kandy–Kolored Tangerine–Flake Streamline Baby, The (Wolfe), 90

King, B. B., 122, 123

King, Carole, 121, 122

Kinks, 108, 112, 113

Kirson, Doc, 86, 245, 248, 255, 259–260, 261, 269, 274

Knee, Frankie, 86

Knee, Steven, 270, 273

"Knock on Wood," 126

Kool and the Gang, 188, 189

Kooper, Al, 132

Kramer, Carole, 264

Kristal, Hilly, *202*, 197–198, 201–203, *202*, 205, 206, 207, 230, 260, 271, 272

L

LaLane, Norma, 129

Lane, Mickey, 48–49

Lasley, David, 194, 195

Lawford, Peter, 171–172

Lawrence, Trevor, 178

Layla and Other Assorted Love Songs, 177

Led Zeppelin, 150

Lee, Brenda, 72

Lee, Will, 193

Lennon, John, 193

Levin, Tony, 162

Levinsky, Mr., 18–19

Lewis, Margo, 58–61, 65, 67, 70, 71, 77, 81, 85, 92, 103, 109–110, 115, 122–123, 124, 129, 267

Liebman, David, 148

Linda Potatoes, 271–272

Lindstrom, Pia, 240

Little Big Horn, 153

"Little Boy," 85–86

"Lonely Nights," 22, 41–42

Lords of the New Church, 207

Louis, Mel, 129–130

"Love Me," 156

M

McCracken, Hugh, 193

MacDonald, Carol, 63, 71–74, 77, 86, 103, *124*, 124–126, 140

McGowan, Cathy, 102

McVie, Terry, 111

Magnum, Jeff, 206

Malone, Tom, 148

Manfred Mann, 112, 113, 118

Manster, 197, 201, 230, 238

Maranno, Lana, 194

Martin, Trade, 273

Massi, Nick, 61

May, Lilly, 248–249, 251, 252

INDEX

May, Tony, 157

Meat Loaf, 191

Media Productions, 209–210

Media Sound Studios, 208, 209

Meisterman, Richard, 138

Mekler, Gabriel, 178, 191

Melanie, 142

Messina, Jay, 158

Metromen, 238

Miamis, 201

Mickie Most and the Playboys, 95

Midem Music Expo, 238–239

Miguel, Jose, 120

Miller, Jimmy, 176, 177

Miller (Jimmy) Productions, 173–177

"Misty Roses," 141

Mods and Rockers Ball, 89–91

Moody Blues, 96, 117

Moody, James, 162

"Moody's Mood for Love," 112, 162

Moondance, 157

Moonglows, 17

Moore, Dudley, 98

Moran, Mike, 195

"Morning Much Better," 154, 157

Morotta, Rick, 193

Morrison, Van, 98, 155, 157, 161, 223, 224–225

Most, Mickie, 94, 95, 98–99

Most Brothers, 95

Mr. Lucky, 238, 242

Muni, Scott, 152

Murray, Charles Shaar, 196

N

National Academy of Recording Arts & Sciences (NARAS), 239–240

Newton, Wayne, 130

"Night Time Is The Right Time," 99

Nilsson, Harry, 98, 193

"No Next Time," 158–159

Nossov, Donny, 212, 220

O

Odetta, 142

O'Grady, Carol, 52, 63

Olatunji, 162

Oldham, Andrew Loog, 114, 121–122

Otterstein, Jurgen, 100

Owens, Charles, 183

P

Panabianco, Ginger, 49, 50, 51, 52, 54–55, 57, 59, 60, 61, 62, 66–67, 74, 77, 81, 84, 103, 107, 109, 115, 123, 124, 128, 260, 267

Pappalardi, Felix, 207

Parisi, Dennis, 138

Paul, Steve, 147

Peculiar Friends, 158–159

People, 192

Peppermint Lounge, 71, 80, 85

Perry, Richard, 40, 42–44, *43*, *44*, 45, 46, 47, 48, 49, 51, 161, 172, 173

Peterman, Nancy, 68, 70, 81–84

Phillips, John, 191–192

Phonogram Records, 226

Pinder, Mike, 117

Pink Floyd, 150, 153

Pisters, Katherine, 261, 263, 264, 267

Pitney, Lynn, 194

Planer, Susan, 210

"Polar Bear Rug," 136

Polish Records, 229–231, 232, 236, 237, 238, 242, 248

Polydor Records, 139, 153, 160

Powder Ridge Festival, 155

Pratt, Dean, 148

Pretty Things, 112

Price, Alan, *121*

Price, Jim, 173–175, 176, 191

Purdie, Bernard, 45

Q

Quaife, Peter, 112, 113

R

Radin, Roy, 211–212, 215–216, 226

Radner, Gilda, 191

Ragovoy, Jerry, 157

Raim, Walter, 141, 153

Ramone, Joey, 235

Randall, Tony, 165, 167, 191

Rare Earth, 155

Rascals, 75, 159

"Rattle Snake Shake," 274

Ray, Hal, 159, 163, 166

RCA, 192, 193, 194, 226–227, 231

"Reason to Believe," 141

"Reconsider," 273

Redbone, 175

"Red Top," 112

Reed, Lou, 195, 214–215, 239, *240*

Relf, Keith, 123

Rhinoceros, 152

Richards, Keith, 108

Richards, Mandy, 56–57

Ripped, 271

Riviera, Jake, 230

Rix, Leon, 137

Roberts, Dawn, 260, 261, 262, 264, 267

Roberts, John, 209, 210, 215

Robinson, Dave, 230

INDEX

Rolling Stones, 90–91, 96, 102, 105, 106–108, 111–112, 114, 121, 173

"Roll Me Through the Rushes," 194

Ronettes, 233

Ronson, Mick, 224, 225

Rosenberg, Joel, 209, 210, 215

Rosie, 194–195

Roundtree, Richard, 166

Russell, Leon, 176

Ryder, Joy, 270

S

"Sailor Boy," 89

Satten, Steve, 147

Saturn Records, 269

Saville, Jimmy, 98

"Say Goodbye to Hollywood," 236

Scepter Records, 61

Schefrin, Aram, 135–138, 140–141, 142–143, 143, 147, 149, 153, 154–157, 158, 159, 161, 162

Schefrin, Ettie, 137, 154, 156

Schlacter, Marvin, 177–178

Schoenbaum, Jerry, 139–140, 153, 158, 160

Segal, Bernie, 263

Sellers, Peter, 120–121, 167

"Shadowboxing in the Rain," 212

Shady Lady, 168

"Shake A Hand," 23

Sha Na Na, 145

Shatzberg, Jerry, 89–90, 91

Sheridan, Tony, 66–67

Shirts, 198

"Shootin' the Breeze," 158

Shrimpton, Chrissie, 107, 112

Shrimpton, Jean, 90

Shuggie Q, 58, 63

Shy, Meike, 271

Silva, Jay, 138

Silverstein, Shel, 36–37

Simon, Stephen, 153

"Sincerely," 17

Siren, 232, 237, 238, 239, 242

"Skinny Vinnie," 61

Sly & the Family Stone, 150, 155, 160, 162

Smith, Jimmy, 60

Snow, Phoebe, 193

Solomon, Harry and Sheila, 12, 14

"Something's Got a Hold on Me," 274

"Somewhere," 43, 45, 46

"Song for You, A," 176

"Sonic Reducer," 205–206

Soul Sisters, 93

Spector, Phil, 122, 232–234, 237

Spector, Ronnie, 229, 231–239, *232*

Spiders from Mars, 210

Springfield, Dusty, 102, 119, 122

Springsteen, Bruce, 225

Stagmore, Larry, 133

Starlighter Lounge, 84

Starr, Ringo, 98

"Stay With Me," 157

Steele, Alison, 152, *211*, 211, *218*, 229

Stein, Chris, 248

Steppenwolf, 142, 145

Steve Miller Band, 145

Steve Paul's Scene, 147–148

Stewart, Rod, 141–142

Stiff Records, 230

Stiles, Danny, 17

Stilettoes, 248

"Stormy Monday Blues," 155

Streisand, Barbra, 192

"Stupid Cupid," 41

"Submarine Race Watching," 45

Summer, Donna, 223–224

"Sunny Gets Blue," 130

Sutton, Annie, 159

Swenson, Owen and Lucy, 248, 249, 273–274

"Sylvia's Mother," 37

T

Taj Mahal, 142

Takas, Bill, 130, 137

"Take Me for a Little While," 273

Talmy, Shel, 113, 114

Taylor, Conrad, 210, 212, 220

Taylor, Elizabeth, 171–172

Ten Wheel Drive, 130, *140*

   albums, 141, 154, 157, 158–159

   at Atlanta Pop Festival, 149–150

   at Bitter End, 139

   at Carnegie Hall, 152–153

   Central Park concert, 151–152

   fans, 158

   at Fillmore East, 142–143, *144*, 145

   formation of, 134–138

   horn section, 147, 148–149

   jamming with, 148

   management, 138–140, 159

   relationship with Aram, 154–157

Them, 112

They Love Me, They Love Me Not, 175–177

"They're Coming to Take Me Away, Ha–Haaa!," 216–217

Thompson, Howard, 119–120

Thorne, Mike, 198, 210

"Tightrope," 141, 148, 223

INDEX

"Time," 17

"Time is Money," 183

Tiny Tim, 72, 216–217

Tommy, 153

Tonight Show, 164–167, *165*, 216

Tony Williams Lifetime, 146

Torres, Liz, 187

Traffic, 161

Tregunna, Dave, 207

Trudy Heller's, 47–48, 56–57

Tuff Darts, 201

Turner, Tina, 236

"Turn on Your Love Lights," 162

20th Century–Fox Records, 212, 217, 224, 225–226, 229

TWM Management, 210, 226

"Two Steps from the Blues," 274

U

Ungano's, 77, 78–79

Urban Desire, 142, 212, 214–215, 217, *218*, 219, 225, 226, 273

Urban Desire tour, *220*, 220–221, *221*, *222*, 223–224

V

Valentine, Hilton, 93, 94, 97, 112, *121*

Valli, Franie, 61

Varner, Al, 188

Vegas, Lolly, 175

Vreeland, Diana, 90

W

Wagon Wheel, 79, 80, 85, 92–94, 95, 129

Waldron, Vince, 235

Wall, The, 153

Warhol, Andy, 90

Washington, Baby, 17, 22, 54, 119

Watts, Charlie, 108

We Have Come for Your Children, 207

Weiss, Chuck, 157

Wells, Mary, 38, 85

Wharton, Alex, 95

"What'd I Say," 71, 110

"What Now, My Love?", 130

"When You Got Trouble," 175

Whiskey a GoGo, 155, 223

Whitlock, Bobby, 176–177

Who, 112, 113, 153

"Why Am I So Easy to Leave Behind," 159

Wickham, Vicki, 102–103, 115

Williams, Paul, 193

Willwerth, James, 167

"Wind," 17

Winwood, Steve, 119

"Wired," 229

Wives, 271

Wolfe, Tom, 90

Wyman, Bill, 108

Y

Yardbirds, 96, 105

"You Know You Make Me Wanna Shout!," 54

Young, Loud and Snotty, 205–207

"You Really Got Me," 113

Z

Zacherle, 216

Zagarino, Joe, 174, 175, 176

Zager, Jane, 137, 140

Zager, Mike, 135–138, 140–141, 142, 143, 149, 153, 155–156, 158, 159, 161, 162, 193

Zappa, Frank, *182*, 182–183

Zelkowitz, Yadja (mother), 2, 8–10, 11, 12, *13*, 13–15, 16–20, 24–25, 26–27, 55, 87, 97, 110–111, 120, 124, 125, 131, 152–153, 180–181, 228, 255, 258, 265, 269, 274–275

Zelkowitz, Helen (sister), 9, *13*, 15–16, 17, 22–23, 26, 86, 179, 180, 181, 245, 248, 255, 258, 259, 260, 261, 264, 266, 267, 269, 274

Zelkowitz, Nathan (father), 9, 11, *13*, 15, 20, 23, 24–25, 26–27, 28, 86, 87, 152, 179–181

Zero, Jimmy, 203